Strategic IT Governance 2.0

Weinzimer provides industry case studies of companies that have implemented multiple components of The Strategic IT Governance 2.0 model. These companies successfully leveraged collaboration between technology and the business to deliver technology projects that provide the best customer value, improve cost efficiencies, and create a governance culture across business areas. In his book, you will learn valuable lessons to implement an innovative governance model for your company.

**– Ashley Pettit, CIO, and Senior Vice President,
Enterprise Technology, State Farm**

In **Strategic IT Governance 2.0**, *Phil provides a number of exciting case studies of how CIOs are leveraging technology to innovate and create value. They are following Phil's model, building strategic and tactical relationships within the business to drive technology growth strategies, collaborating with partners to improve customer service and increase value with process optimization and best practice metrics. Each of these companies offers a slightly different take on the multiple components of the Strategic IT Governance 2.0 model; however, these organizations' collective and individual success indicates the strength of the components.*

**– Dawn Kirchner-King, Vice President and Chief Information Officer,
Armstrong World Industries**

Today's business environment is more complicated, creating additional challenges for the successful execution of strategic enterprise projects. Unless an organization revisits its governance model, strategic projects are at risk of negatively impacting business success. So, how do companies succeed in overcoming these obstacles to improve project success? **Strategic IT Governance 2.0: How CIOs Succeed at Digital Innovation** explains how IT executives can take the lead and successfully drive digital transformation initiatives and associated projects. The book presents the Strategic IT Governance 2.0 model that focuses on project alignment, process reinvention, and leadership excellence. It is filled with case studies of the model's implementation, giving practical insight into how organizations have successfully executed digital transformation.

At the very heart of *Strategic IT Governance 2.0* is the notion that there must be a fundamental balance and partnership between the business and IT teams. After nearly 40 years of working to deliver value through strategic IT, I've really only learned one thing for certain; When business and IT leaders are linked together in a bond of trust and joint goals, the job is pretty easy, and great things will happen.

Rob Carter, Executive Vice President-FedEx Information Services and CIO & Co-president, FedEx Services

Reading Phil Weinzimer's new book "Strategic IT Governance 2.0" is like taking a masters class from the top CIOs in the world. He has created an engaging and informative walk through the strategic imperative of governance driving business and IT alignment to maximize returns for people, processes, and technology. As IT continues to dominate strategic business portfolios, the timing of Phil's book could not be better, and his emphasis on relationships and collaboration is particularly insightful.

Tom Murphy, Senior VP of IT & University CIO-University of Pennsylvania

As a CIO, I've had the advantage of learning from Phil, and several of the CIOs he profiled in his last book. His frameworks and tools have been invaluable to my teams and me over the last several years! As we collectively move into the metaverse, web3, and beyond the world, I do not doubt that Phil's thinking on governance will become increasingly important. I encourage you to dig in and dig deep to avoid costly or disastrous leaps into the future tech for your company and take out of this the confidence to move forward with authority.

Walt Carter, Chief Digital Officer & CIO, Homestar Financial Corp.

Strategic IT Governance is an essential read for today's CIO and business leaders. Phil masterfully shares the experiences of several leaders and brings together the fundamental concepts of business value, leadership excellence, IT efficiency, and project/process excellence. This book is an excellent resource for IT and business leaders as it lays out a roadmap for collaboration and partnership or leveraging technology as a part of the enterprise strategy. Phil... you have done it again...great book.

Margaret Brisbane, CIO-Dade County Miami Florida

Phil Weinzimer's Strategic IT Governance 2.0 is a playbook that defines a methodology, tools, and techniques, and numerous case studies for any organization that's looking to drive customer value by getting the most out of their technology investments.

Christopher G. Burger, Founder & Managing Director of Transform

Weinzimer reinforces the need for company executives to recognize IT Governance as a major challenge for success in Digital Transformation initiatives. Strategic IT Governance 2.0 provides great case study examples of CIOs and IT/Business teams working together that utilized the Strategic IT Governance 2.0 framework, methodology, and tools, to succeed at digital transformation initiatives.

Tony Salvaggio, CEO, CAI, Inc.

Strategic IT Governance 2.0
How CIOs Succeed at Digital Innovation

Philip Weinzimer

CRC Press
Taylor & Francis Group
Boca Raton London New York

CRC Press is an imprint of the
Taylor & Francis Group, an **informa** business

AN AUERBACH BOOK

First edition published 2023
by CRC Press
6000 Broken Sound Parkway NW, Suite 300, Boca Raton, FL 33487-2742

and by CRC Press
4 Park Square, Milton Park, Abingdon, Oxon, OX14 4RN

CRC Press is an imprint of Taylor & Francis Group, LLC

© 2023 Taylor & Francis Group, LLC

Library of Congress Cataloging-in-Publication Data
Names: Weinzimer, Philip, author.
Title: Strategic IT governance 2.0 : how CIOs succeed at digital innovation / Philip Weinzimer.
Description: First edition. | Boca Raton : CRC Press, 2023. | Includes bibliographical references and index.
Identifiers: LCCN 2022018436 (print) | LCCN 2022018437 (ebook) | ISBN 9781032329611 (hardback) | ISBN 9780367342869 (paperback) | ISBN 9781003317531 (ebook)
Subjects: LCSH: Information technology--Management--Case studies. | Strategic planning--Case studies. | Chief information officers.
Classification: LCC HD30.2 .W4517 2023 (print) | LCC HD30.2 (ebook) | DDC 658.4/038--dc23/eng/20220810
LC record available at https://lccn.loc.gov/2022018436
LC ebook record available at https://lccn.loc.gov/2022018437

ISBN: 978-1-032-32961-1 (hbk)
ISBN: 978-0-367-34286-9 (pbk)
ISBN: 978-1-003-31753-1 (ebk)

DOI: 10.1201/9781003317531

Typeset in Garamond
by SPi Technologies India Pvt Ltd (Straive)

To my loving wife, Lynn, who has been by my side since High School, nurturing my every whim and sharing a life filled with endless love, adventurous travels, and appreciating the value of patience.

Contents

Foreword: Ashley Pettit

I had an opportunity to present our State Farm® IT Transformation initiative to IT executives at a conference in Las Vegas a few years ago. After my presentation, Phil Weinzimer introduced himself and asked to interview me because my presentation aligned with the theme of his upcoming book.

During our conversation, I shared four key components of our State Farm IT Transformation:

- **Strategic Alignment** to an outcome-oriented and integrated technology and business plan
- **Delivery Speed** for right solutions through viable products and delivery automation
- **Cost Efficiency** of IT assets through rationalization, modernization, and transparency
- **Operating Model** oriented on functional priorities to improve operational effectiveness

Phil provided more information about his Strategic IT Governance 2.0 model that includes six key competencies including: Executive Sponsorship, Business/IT Partnership, Strategic Alignment, Collaboration, Process Optimization and Best Practices/Metrics. As Phil provided more information on each of these competencies, the parallels were clear between our two models.

My IT career has enabled me to focus on transforming how technology impacts business success at State Farm. The goal has always been to improve customer experiences, adapt our products and services to the ever-changing markets, optimize costs, and operate as efficiently as possible. I hoped by sharing our transformation story, readers of Phil's book will gain critical tips, tools, and techniques to navigate their own journey and provide business benefits for their companies.

The Strategic IT Governance 2.0 model includes success factors of collaboration, process optimization, and Best Practice Metrics that focus on IT Efficiency and Project/Process Excellence. Collaboration and Process Optimization are critical in any enterprise transformation initiative. We fundamentally changed how technology solutions are built and delivered by forming integrated IT and business teams within our "One Team" theme. Integral in every IT Transformation is teamwork and process improvement. To build collaboration and process improvement across the enterprise, we implemented several techniques:

- We leveraged our Finance department to broker a process between IT and our business partners, helping to define the business outcomes and the steps needed to get there.
- We held monthly joint meetings with technical and business teams to discuss project status.
- We formed a cross-discipline leadership team comprising key stakeholders – business partners, finance, and technology – to develop a new IT Investment Decision Model.
- And we created a two-day workshop where business and IT employees identified key objectives and business results as a foundation for developing a collaborative working relationship. This created a collective culture of collaboration and optimized our processes across State Farm.

The sixth competency in The Strategic IT Governance 2.0 model is Best Practice Metrics. To achieve and sustain improvement over time requires constant attention. At State Farm, our focus was to ensure a balanced set of metrics to track our progress, build momentum towards bold goals, and identify any unintended consequences along the way. Additionally, we used visible metrics to build confidence in our plan as it provides visibility into the value delivered through IT investment. Scorecards now support collaboration through monthly discussions and reports in business review meetings. These help maintain alignment with the highest-level enterprise priorities and the overall transformation of IT. The scorecards help individual product teams identify features and prioritize work to help deliver the intended business outcomes. Each department scorecard reflects and measures alignment with the transformation goals. These transformation goals connect to an overall transformation scorecard used by senior executives to evaluate the overall success.

Our success focused on Strategic Alignment, Delivery Speed, Cost Efficiency, and an Operating Model. Each of the four elements enabled us to fundamentally change how technology solutions are built and delivered. Our digital and technology transformation has allowed business areas and IT to align better with the organization's business goals, translating to better customer experiences.

Business and IT are now aligned to one mission: to enable our associates to personalize the customer experience in a seamless, efficient way. Our success results from great people working together in teams to provide our customers with great products and services. Today, our teams have a keen sense of the marketplace, understand how customer expectations have changed, and know why relationships, supported by technology, are still as imperative today as they were when we were founded a hundred years ago.

Weinzimer provides industry case studies of companies that have implemented multiple components of The Strategic IT Governance 2.0 model. These companies successfully leveraged collaboration between technology and the business to deliver technology projects that provide the best customer value, improve cost efficiencies, and create a governance culture across business areas. In his book, you will learn valuable lessons to implement an innovative governance model for your company.

If your organization wants to improve the maturity of your company's governance competencies, Strategic IT Governance 2.0 is a must-read. It will guide you to dramatically improve project performance and drive business success through project alignment, process reinvention, and leadership excellence.

Ashley Pettit
CIO, and Senior Vice President
Enterprise Technology
State Farm

Foreword: Dawn Kirchner-King

In today's ever-changing business world, the lines between Information Technology and business continue to be blurred. The business is powered and empowered by technology. To succeed, a plan and a governance model is imperative. More importantly, the Chief Technology leader for any given organization must work to be a part of the business and a part of the transformation. That integrates company strategy with the real world, easy-to-understand, and implement tactical playbooks. It is no longer good enough to be a trusted partner or to provide secure access to your company's ERP. Reliable technology and platform services are table stakes in any modern organization and ordinary in many legacy companies.

If you, as a Chief Technology leader, are not prepared to lead business transformation, there are plenty of consulting firms knocking on the CEO's email inbox and selling their snake oil in online forums. Your C-Suite colleagues are looking for ways to grow faster and improve profits to invest in new ideas, create innovation pipelines, and build digital forums. If you are not prepared and leading the way, they will do it without you.

In *Strategic IT Governance 2.0*, Phil provides a number of exciting case studies of how CIOs are leveraging technology to innovate and create value. They are following Phil's model, building strategic and tactical relationships within the business to drive technology growth strategies, collaborating with partners to improve customer service and increase value with process optimization and best practice metrics. Each of these companies offers a slightly different take on the multiple components of the Strategic IT Governance 2.0 model; however, these organizations' collective and individual success indicates the strength of the components.

At Armstrong, our leadership team has embraced technology as an enabler of our business strategy, both in driving growth and in improving our capacity and efficiency. We aligned our frontline leaders and engaged them in our digital initiatives governance, ensuring that each initiative ties back to our strategy and the outcome metrics provide a tangible return on investment. Our stakeholders define the project success criteria and have direct responsibility for identifying and mitigating project risks. The roles of IT and stakeholders are defined and are communicated clearly.

Our governance structure continues to contribute to our digital project success and is evidenced in the strategic and financial outcomes Armstrong is achieving. Therefore, it's not surprising that our structure is so closely aligned with the best practices Phil covers in the *Strategic IT Governance 2.0* model.

In this book, you will learn valuable lessons you can apply to improve business outcomes and drive value for your company. Chief Technology leaders who focus on business strategy and create measurable value will succeed. Reading this book will elevate your thinking and help you focus on optimizations to the business's value. If you are a CIO who wants to improve your organization's performance and help your company grow profitably, *Strategic IT Governance 2.0* should be at the top of your reading list. It will help you improve project innovation and performance, drive business engagement, and guide you to a remarkable change in how Information Technology is perceived within your organization.

Dawn Kirchner-King
Vice President and Chief Information Officer
Armstrong World Industries

Acknowledgments

You would think that writing my third book would be easier than my first two books. Well, in some ways, it was. But in others, it wasn't. There are endless hours of researching various topics to support the book's premise. And, of course, deciding who to interview, scheduling the interviews, transcribing the interview notes, scheduling follow-up calls, and then, of course, writing the chapters. And let us not forget editing the chapters; a never-ending process. But I must say, the experience was educational and enriching as I developed new insights into the subject of IT Governance. And of course, there is the added benefit of making new friends and expanding my professional network.

As many writers have told me, focusing while writing is critical. And I've followed this rule for each of my three books. The only problem is that one loses sense of time. As was the case in my last book, The Strategic CIO, my family bore the brunt of my countless hours in my office researching, talking on the phone, or typing away on my laptop. My wife, Lynn, would always remind me to drink and eat, to the point that she would bring up a tray of drink and food during these focused periods. It got to the point that we would always joke about this. So I thank my beloved soul mate for taking good care of me during the writing of this and my previous two books.

I want to thank Ashley Pettit, CIO and Senior Vice President of Enterprise Technology, for State Farm, and Dawn Kirchner-King, CIO of Armstrong World Industries, for writing the forewords. I met Pettit at a CIO event and was very impressed with her insights on how CIOs must focus on business outcomes and partner with business unit peers. I met King at a CIO event that I spoke at several years ago. We discussed CIO challenges after the event, and we've continued our discussions over the years, sharing insights on the role of the CIO.

I've also included chapters of State Farm and Armstrong World Industries as each company has reinvented its governance competencies that align with the Strategic IT Governance 2.0 model.

Pettit from State Farm engaged some of her staff in interviews with me as they shared how they participated in transforming the governance competencies. Pettit and King both also agreed to my interviewing them for my book. I discovered that each had transformed the governance processes of their respective IT organizations and transformed how technology improves operating performance.

Pettit engaged six transformation team members to speak with me and share how their organizations participated in the transformation. I want to thank Randy McBeath, Brett Weber, Jeff Bertrand, Ritesh Saraf, Mahesh Chandrappa, and Chris Lay for sharing their insights on the State Farm transformation initiative. To speed up the interview process, I worked with Angie Harrier, State Farm Public Affairs Senior Specialist, at State Farm to coordinate the interviews. Her relentless efforts and follow-up are greatly appreciated.

King from Armstrong World Industries invited me to the corporate offices to interview her. At that meeting, King shared information on the governance transformation program. We followed up that meeting with many Zoom video calls to continue the interview. As it turned out, King and her team shared a lot of information, and I've included the Armstrong story in Chapters 4–6. I want to thank David Sauder, Brent Lewis, John Brabazon, and Craig Nadig for sharing their perspectives on the transformation process. I'm sure you will be amazed at what King and her team accomplished.

I heard from many readers regarding the value of case studies in my last book, *The Strategic CIO*, that they found the case studies most valuable. As a result, I've included ten case studies in this book. This would not be possible without the efforts of the CIOs, IT Executives, and Business Executives, who shared their insights, experiences, successes, and lessons learned. I wish to thank them. Listed below are these individuals in alphabetical order. I thank each with my sincerest appreciation.

- Ron Arnold – former Sr. VP & Chief Strategy Officer, Just Born, Founder Ironclad Management Consulting
- Lisa Bobo – former CIO, the City of Rochester, and founder of Bolder IT Strategies, LLC
- Ross Born – CEO, Just Born, retired
- Ed Broczkowski – Vice President, Strategy Realization Office at Just Born, Inc.
- Rachel Hayden – former CIO Just Born, and currently Sr. EVP & CIO, ScanSource
- Dean Johnson – former COO, Georgia Enterprise Technology Services, State of Georgia, and currently Senior Executive Government Advisor, Ensono
- Erica Keller – COO, Georgia Enterprise Technology Services, State of Georgia
- Valeriy Kutsyy – CEO, Miratech Group
- Tony Lombardi – former CIO, The Andersons
- Bruce Leidal – CIO-Carestream
- Alexander Maximenko – Director of the Application Development Services, Miratech Group
- -Alex Petit – Chief Technology Officer for the State of Colorado

- Poonam Soans – State of New Jersey Chief Data Officer & Director of Application Development at the State of New Jersey
- Teresa Reilly – Director Enterprise Portfolio Management Office at Georgia Technology Authority
- Markus Waser – Founder, Markus Waser Academy AG
- Mel Weinzimer – former Deputy Program Manager, Raytheon

During the research phase, I spoke with over 80 CIOs and IT Executives. Choosing the case studies for this book was challenging, as I found many compelling examples from these executives. Following, in alphabetical order, are a select group who shared their wisdom and experience, which appear in various chapters of the book.

Chris Burger, Founder and Managing Director at Transform; Walt Carter, Chief Digital Officer and CIO-Homestar; Lee Crump, former CIO-Rollins, and Founder and Managing Partner at The Crump Group;

Richard Douglas, CEO Markets (Hong Kong) at Saxon Bank; Larry Frey, CIO at Beazer Homes

Todd Kimbriel, CIO, State of Texas; Financial; Michael Sullivan- VP and CIO-Southern Company Gas;

Mark Perry, Founder of BOT International; Michael Sullivan, VP and CIO at Southern Company Gas;

Brain Watson, author of *Confessions of a Successful CIO*; and Principal at CIO Clarity Advisors

I also want to thank John Wyzalek, Senior Book Acquisition Editor, Taylor & Francis Group, who shepherded me through this book and my last book offering his wisdom and guidance. I truly appreciate his help.

I also thank Charles Anderson, Director of Governance at Computer Aid, Inc. & VP Operations CAI Medical Solutions He worked with me in developing the four phases of The Strategic IT Governance 2.0 model that appears in Chapters 3 and 18. We worked through various iterations until we got it right. Thanks, Charles, for your patience and insights.

Finally, I'd like to thank Richard Wood, Publisher, CAI Media Group at CAI, Inc, for creating the book cover. Wood also designed the book cover for my previous book, The Strategic CIO. His talents are endless, and all who work with him admire his dedication to perfection.

I apologize if I missed acknowledging anyone, and I thank all who made this book possible.

I'm always appreciative to hear from my readers. I encourage you to share your thoughts with me as you embark on your journey of improving the maturity of your Strategic IT Governance 2.0 competencies.

Philip Weinzimer
Email: pweinzimer@gmail.com
Twitter: @pweinzimer

About the Author

Philip Weinzimer is an accomplished consultant, author, thought leader, and international speaker focusing on helping organizations implement change management initiatives that improve operational performance.

Mr. Weinzimer uses creative and innovative coaching techniques through workshops, focusing on organizational change to enhance new skills, knowledge, and teamwork.

Mr. Weinzimer's consulting experience at BMC Software, Sapient, Xerox, Unisys, ITM, CAI, and Strategere Consulting includes building team effectiveness through organizational change initiatives. As a Managing Principal, he sold professional services and managed multiple engagement teams in the US and Europe.

Weinzimer's management experience at ITT, AEL Labs, and Arrow International includes executive positions in the defense, communications, pharmaceuticals, and manufacturing industries focused on vendor management, logistics, operations, and finance.

Mr. Weinzimer has authored three books that focus on helping personnel *collaborate, coordinate, and communicate* as they work in teams to implement company strategies that improve operational efficiency, corporate profitability, and shareholder wealth. Each book shares methodologies, tools, techniques, and a variety of case studies that organizations can utilize to assist their teams in improving team performance and achieving enterprise goals and objectives.

His most recent book, **Strategic IT Governance 2.0**, (October 2022) describes a new model that comprises six key competencies that teams across the business enterprise utilize to improve digital innovation success by embracing leadership excellence, process optimization, and project governance.

His second book, **The Strategic CIO**, focuses on how teams across the enterprise work in concert to leverage information and technology using a four-phase methodology to create new customer value, improve operational processes, and increase profit margins on company products and services.

Weinzimer's first book, **Getting It Right**, shares a 3-P strategy to assist organizations Prepare personnel to work together as a team, Perceive customer needs, and Provide new products and services that create sustainable and profitable value

Mr. Weinzimer regularly speaks on Organizational Change and IT Strategy in the US, Europe, and South America. He has written columns for CIO.com and AITS.org on *Transforming IT for Business Success* and articles for CIO magazine, co-authored a case study for Harvard Business School (HBS), and was corporate faculty at Harrisburg University of Science and Technology in the Master's Project Management Program.

Weinzimer interviewed CIOs, IT/ business executives on Leveraging Information and Technology for Competitive Advantage, and hosted a video series, *The Strategic CIO*, interviewing business executives on the strategic use of information and technology and how teams successfully work together to create improved customer value and operational profitability.

Mr. Weinzimer holds a BA and MBA in finance from Adelphi University with postgraduate studies in international finance and computer science at New York University. He resides in Allentown, PA, with his wife, Lynn.

Introduction

As a CIO, CEO, CFO, or CxO, your company is most probably leveraging technology at a greater pace than ever before. Why are you doing this? Because you and your colleagues realize that leveraging technology in strategic enterprise digital transformation initiatives as part of your business strategy will enhance customer value, improve operational processes, and, in some cases, reinvent your business models to improve your competitive position. To accomplish these goals, your company most probably initiated strategic projects that, if successful, resulted in increased revenues, improved margins, and enhanced shareholder wealth. If this is the case in your company, I congratulate you on a job well done. Unfortunately, many companies are in the minority, and strategic initiatives fail to achieve their stated objectives. Why? The answer is in years of statistics that reflect project failures due to lack of executive sponsorship, poor participation by business personnel, inadequate metrics, and a host of other issues. These issues appear year after year in research that analyzes why projects fail. *(Chapter 1 – Introduction provides numerous statistics in further chapters to reinforce project failure rates.)* These issues fall under the umbrella of an inadequate governance model that does not provide the necessary oversight in roles, processes, and metrics to succeed in strategic and tactical projects.

Today's business environment is more complicated, creating additional challenges for the successful execution of strategic enterprise projects. Here's why. Technology is more complex, management continuously challenges IT budgets, and strategic projects impact a broader portion of your value chain than ever before. Unless you revisit your governance model, your strategic projects are at risk of negatively impacting business success. So, how do companies succeed in overcoming these obstacles to improve project success? The answer is for IT executives to take the lead and successfully drive digital transformation initiatives and its associated projects project using an enterprise Strategic IT Governance 2.0 model that focuses on project alignment, process reinvention, and leadership excellence.

To help you navigate through the book, I'd like to provide you with a brief overview of the Strategic IT Governance 2.0 Framework (see Figure 1.1) with a

DOI: 10.1201/9781003317531-1

1

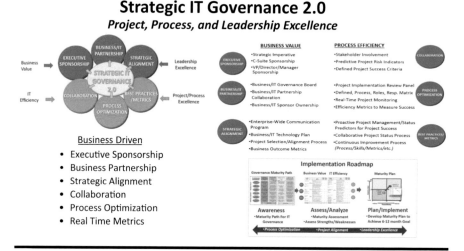

Figure 1.1   Strategic IT Governance 2.0.

brief explanation. To further help you navigate this book, I am providing you with a summary of each chapter that will enable you to determine which chapters to focus on as part of your reading plan.

Strategic IT Governance 2.0 Framework

As shown in Figure 1.1, this framework addresses an enterprise approach to governing strategic projects.

It includes the six competencies of the Strategic IT Governance 2.0 model, the six characteristics of a proactive governance competency, a set of best practices for each of the six competencies, and an implementation path for your organization to improve the maturity of your governance competency.

Each framework area is discussed in more detail in Chapter 3: Strategic IT Governance 2.0: An Introduction; Chapter 18 – How to Assess the Maturity of Your Company's Strategic IT Governance Competencies, and Chapter 19 – How to Analyze, Plan, and Implement Strategic IT Governance 2.0 Competencies in Your Company. Following is a summary of each of the framework components.

■ The Strategic IT Governance 2.0 model comprises three competencies (*Executive Sponsorship*, *Business Partnership*, and *Strategic Alignment*) that focus on Business Value and are heavily influenced by the C-suite and business unit executives. The remaining three competencies (*Collaboration*, *Process Optimization*, *Best Practice Metrics*), which the IT organization heavily influences, focus on Process Efficiency in project execution.

- ■ The six business-driven characteristics that are representative of an organization that proactively approaches governance.
- ■ The best practices are representative of best-in-class processes for each of the six Strategic IT Governance 2.0 competencies.
- ■ The Implementation Path provides a three-step approach to improve your organization's Strategic IT Governance 2.0 maturity.
  - Create awareness in your organization of the four-phase maturity path for improving your governance competency.
  - An Assessment to measure the current maturity of your organization's Strategic IT Governance 2.0 competency.
  - A three-step implementation path to improve the maturity of your Strategic IT Governance competencies.

The book encompasses the following.

Chapter 2 provides an overview of the changing competitive landscape and why companies are revisiting their business strategies and leveraging technologies in new and innovative ways, driving the need to improve the maturity of their IT governance competencies for both transformational and tactical projects. Chapter 3 provides an overwrite of the Strategic IT Governance 2.0 model.

Chapters 5–18 contain 11 case studies of companies in different industries who have improved the maturity of their governance competencies to achieve their goal of improving business outcomes, increasing revenue, and enhancing shareholder wealth. These case studies are an excellent way for you to learn and apply how companies navigate the challenges of potential project failures within your organizations by implementing components of the Strategic IT Governance 2.0 methodology and achieving the goals of their strategic enterprise projects.

Chapters 18 and 19 provide you with an assessment process to determine the maturity of your governance process and a framework for implementing your maturity plan using a case study of a midsized manufacturing company. The Assessment process will help you to assess, analyze, prioritize, and develop a plan to improve the maturity of your Strategic IT Governance 2.0 competencies. The implementation framework will assist you in executing maturity initiatives that will enable you to successfully executive your strategic and tactical projects.

To further assist you in navigating this book, I include a summary for each chapter below. My goal is to provide you with some golden nuggets you can utilize within your company to improve project performance and overcome the historical failure rates other companies have experienced. As companies leverage technology as part of their business strategies, it is now time to improve the maturity of your Strategic IT Governance competencies to finally create a track record of successfully implementing strategic and tactical projects.

Good luck with your journey. Fasten your seat belts and enjoy the ride, and you learn how IT executives drive project success through project alignment, process reinvention, and leadership excellence.

Chapter	Title	Description
Book Foreword 1		Ashley Pettit – CIO and Senior Vice President of Enterprise Technology – State Farm
Book Foreword 2		Dawn Kirschner-King – Vice-President and Chief Information Officer-Armstrong World Industries
1	Introduction	This chapter provides an overview of the book and answers the following questions. a) Why are companies leveraging technology as part of their enterprise strategy? b) Why are immature and inadequate governance processes driving enterprise strategic project failures? c) What are the components of a Strategic IT Governance 2.0 Framework? A high-level overview. d) Why do case studies of companies in different industries provide value in helping you better understand the business value of implementing a Strategic IT Governance maturity initiative to improve your company's business performance? e) How will chapter summaries help you navigate your book reading strategy?
2	The Changing Landscape: The Case for Change	This chapter answers the following questions. a) What are the root causes of continuous project failure rates year after year? b) Why are immature governance competencies the driving force in causing project failures? c) What are the characteristics of the reactive Project Governance 1.0 model and a proactive Project d) What is the Governance 2.0. model, its components, and the value it provides to improve business performance? e) What are the three Business Value Competencies and the three Process Efficiency competencies? f) How to describe each of the six competencies and brief examples of how companies use them to improve business performance?

Chapter	Title	Description
3	Strategic IT Governance 2.0: An Overview	This chapter provides an overview of the Strategic IT 2.0 methodology, its framework, and the best-in-class practices for each of the six competencies. This introduction provides a basic understanding of the methodology. To support the model's validity, subsequent chapters provide case studies of companies in different industries that embraced and implemented components of the methodology.
4,5,6	Armstrong World Industries	Armstrong World Industries embarked on a digital transformation strategy to improve the value of its products and services by leveraging technology in new and innovative ways. To succeed, the CIO and her IT and business team reinvented their governance processes. How they accomplished this and examples of the processes and tools they used are explored in depth in these three chapters.
7	How State Farm Transformed its Governance Process to Improve Business Success	When your company is 42nd on the Fortune 500 list, you cannot sit on your laurels. Maintaining this position and moving up to a higher ranking requires strong leadership, innovative thinking, and operational culture that thrives on challenge and change. The CIO and CDO teamed together to implement an IT Transformation focusing on project alignment, process optimization, and leadership excellence, all components of a Strategic IT Governance 2.0 model.
8	How the State of Georgia Implemented a Governance Solution Saving Millions of Dollars Each Year	The State of Georgia is one of the fastest-growing states in the United States. And as you can imagine, the State requires a technology organization that is visionary, innovative, and agile in anticipating the technology needs of its 100 plus State agencies that provide a myriad of services to its private and business citizens. The COO transformed an insourced infrastructure services model to an outsource infrastructure model with a services governance process for managing the technology and associated infrastructure

Chapter	Title	Description
		that position the State of Georgia to continue its rapid growth. This case study takes you through the process of how the COO and his team developed the new governance model, how it operates, and its alignment with the Strategic IT Governance 2.0 model.
9	How the CIO of an Agriculture Conglomerate Reinvented Its Governance Competency to Improve Project Success	The Andersons is a multibillion-dollar conglomerate that provides grain, ethanol, plant nutrient, and rail service across North America and Canada. The new CIO recognized that the existing project governance processes were outdated, inefficient, and impacting the company's operational performance. With years of experience under his belt, the new CIO reorganized the IT organization, reinvented the governance processes for strategic projects, and created a governance culture that improved the company's operational performance. This case study takes you through the step-by-step process of creating a new governance process that aligns with the Strategic IT Governance 2.0 model.
10	How the State of New Jersey Applied an Innovative Governance Model to Crete a Transparency Website to Track COVID-19 Cares Act Funding	During the COVID-19 pandemic, the federal government's CARES Act provided funds for states to utilize emergency programs. The state of New Jersey's governor issued an Executive Order to provide transparency for how these funds would be used and challenge the IT organization to create a website in 90 days to accomplish this goal. To achieve this aggressive goal, the Director of IT Applications and Development and her team collaborated with other State Agencies to develop a governance model to achieve the ambitious 90-day goal. This case study takes you through the process, challenges, and the alignment of the governance model utilized to the Strategic IT Governance 2.0 model.

Chapter	Title	Description
11	How a Raytheon Team Collaborated with Stakeholders to Improve Project Success	The Federal Aviation Authority (FAA) embarked on an ambitious multiyear, 1 billion dollar program to modernize the aging equipment air traffic controllers utilize in 331 airports across the United States. Raytheon Company (now known as Raytheon Technologies) received the award. During the first few years of the program, everything was supposedly progressing on schedule. One of the project's milestones was to conduct a user meeting with a team of air traffic controllers to view and evaluate the Raytheon engineers' prototype design. Unfortunately, the FAA did not involve the air traffic controllers in the early design reviews. When they were allowed to review the design, thousands of hours had been expended and a totally new design was required. A new Deputy Program Manager was assigned to evaluate the program and engage the Air Traffic Controllers as a collaborative partner. This case study describes the step-by-step approach to get the project on track using a collaborative model that aligns with the Strategic IT Governance 2.0 methodology.
12	How a Candy Confectionery Mastered a New Governance Model to Improve Business Performance	If you are a candy enthusiast, you must be familiar with Mike and Ike fruit-flavored candy, or Hot Tamales, the very popular, spicy, cinnamon-flavored chewy candies, or Peeps, the three-dimensional marshmallow shaped like chicks and bunnies that are very popular at Easter. Candy making is as much an art as a skill. Most companies succeed in developing a strategy but fall short in executing these strategies into tangible business outcomes. Just Born is a 100-year-old company with a great history in candy making. But it needed to dramatically improve its governance processes around strategic and tactical projects. The Sr. Vice President and Chief Strategy Officer created the Strategy Realization Office (SRO)

Chapter	Title	Description
		that revamped the governance processes around strategic projects to accomplish this goal. The goal was to ensure that projects were strategically aligned and successfully implemented to achieve the company's goals and objectives. This case study takes you through the entire development and implementation process of the SRO and its alignment to the Strategic IT Governance 2.0 model.
13	How the CIO at Carestream Reinvented Its Strategic IT Governance Competency to Improve Project Success	Carestream is an innovator in the health care industry, providing medical imaging systems to customers throughout the world. The newly appointed CIO created an entirely organizational operating model and project governance model that dramatically improved project performance and aligns with the Strategic IT Governance 2.0 model. This case study provides a step-by-step walk-through of the new model he developed, how he reorganized IT, the processes and tools used as part of this transformation initiative, and its alignment to the Strategic IT Governance 2.0 model.
14	How Miratech Implementing a Governance Methodology to Rescue a Failing Project	The Western European Principality of Liechtenstein needed a significant redesign of their tax revenue process and supporting application. After difficulties with a vendor, they partnered with the Miratech Group to rescue the project. Miratech did indeed rescue the 80,000 person-hour project by delivering on time and under budget. The Miratech Governance process utilizes their Agile Portfolio System™ Methodology that aligns closely with the collaboration, process optimization, and best practice metrics competencies of the Strategic IT Governance 2.0 model. This case study takes you through the project's history, the Miratech Agile Portfolio System methodology, processes, and tools to redesign the tax revenue process and successfully support the application project.

Chapter	Title	Description
15	How the State of Georgia Implemented a Governance Solution Saving Millions of Dollars Each Year	The State of Georgia has over 100 State agencies that design, develop, and implement hundreds of projects each year that impact citizens' and business services. This case study provides the background, development, and implementation of a Governance solution that saved millions of dollars in project costs each year. The methodology used provides details on the background, planning, and execution of this transformation project that aligns with the Strategic IT Governance 2.0 model.
16	How the Rochester, NY, CIO Improved Citizen Services with an Innovative Strategic Governance Process	Anyone involved in City Government understands the immense challenges in providing services to its citizens. There are numerous budgetary constraints, infrastructure issues, and economic redevelopment challenges to improve the quality of life for its citizens. Lisa Bobo was CIO for the City of Rochester in Upstate New from 2012 to 2019. During her tenure, she took on a multiyear initiative to improve the services for Rochester citizens by developing a governance process on how city agencies could leverage technology in new and innovative ways. Bobo shares her insights and experiences on this transformational initiative that improved the collaboration, business processes, and strategic alignment across city agencies to improve citizen and business services.
17	A State CIO Shares Insights on the Importance of Strategic IT Governance	Dr. Alex Pettit joined the Colorado Office of Information Technology (OIT) as Chief Technology Officer in January 2020. As the Chief Technology Officer, Alex is responsible for keeping systems operating, information flowing, applications advancing, and technology transforming. He guides enhancements of the world-class IT infrastructure, the use of cloud services, and the applications of modern technologies, such as blockchain and Artificial Intelligence (A.I.). Pettit shares his insights on the importance of

Chapter	Title	Description
		Strategic IT Governance and shares examples of why he views governance as an absolute necessity in private or public sector. Before joining the State of Colorado, Alex served as the Chief Information Officer for Oregon and Oklahoma and most recently served as the Chief Architect for the Oregon Secretary of State. As a state CIO, Dr. Pettit was responsible for information and telecommunication systems for all state agencies for both Oklahoma and Oregon.
18	How to Assess the Maturity of Your Company's Strategic IT Governance Competencies	This chapter uses a case study of a CIO and Directors who attended a series of workshops to assess the maturity of their organization's Strategic IT Governance 2.0 competencies. This case study will help you to learn how to utilize a best-in-class assessment tool and process and gain an understanding of the four phases of maturity for evolving to your organization's strategic IT Governance 2.0 model.
19	How to Analyze, Plan, and Implement Strategic IT Governance 2.0 Competencies in Your Company	This chapter uses a case study for an organization that utilized a series of workshops to develop a three-step Implementation Path to improve its Strategic IT Governance 2.0 maturity. Create awareness in their organization of the four-phase maturity path for improving its governance competency. Use Assessment to measure the current maturity of their organization's Strategic IT Governance 2.0 competency. Develop a plan to achieve their Strategic IT Governance 2.0 maturity goal.
20	Final Thoughts	This chapter provides the reader with a summary of the key concepts and graphics as a means to review key points and use them as a checklist in revisiting your company's Strategic IT Governance 2.0 competencies and improve its project governance maturity to improve business performance.

Chapter 2

The Changing Landscape: The Case for Change

It is Sunday evening, and John, the recently hired CIO for a manufacturer of industrial metal cabinets for companies in the United States and Europe, is preparing for a busy week. On Tuesday, Bill will attend his first Executive C-Suite meeting. The CEO mentioned to Bill during one of their earlier interviews that the company was planning on some significant digital transformation initiatives and the executive team was concerned that the IT organization is not performing well when it comes to implementing strategic initiatives. The CEO further expressed his concern that the performance of the current IT organization was impacting company performance. The current CIO was technically competent. However, milestone dates on strategic projects were falling behind, and there were numerous quality glitches. More importantly, the IT department did not have a good working relationship with business unit management. The CEO was looking for a strategic CIO to successfully implement strategic digital transformation initiatives and improve the delivery of its associated projects. More importantly, he wanted the new CIO to develop a more collaborative relationship with business units. This would be critical in successfully planning for and implementing the strategic digital initiatives. During the previous three weeks, Bill met with the Business Unit VPs to hear their concerns about the IT organization. He shared his background and success in building successful IT organizations. His message was clear. He was eager to work with each VP to improve the business value IT provides business units and the company by leveraging technology in new and innovative ways.

DOI: 10.1201/9781003317531-2

Does this scenario sound familiar? Probably so. I've heard this many times from CIO clients and the ones I've interviewed for my books. And statistics prove this out. Digital transformation initiatives comprise many projects that need to be executed successfully. Project failures cost the U.S. economy billions of dollars and threaten the existence of companies. And 50% of projects over $1 million have a higher failure rate than projects below $350,000. If you don't think these statistics scare you, hear this one. Most projects fail due to communication breakdowns and a lack of senior management involvement (see Figure 2.1[1]).

A *Forbes* article states that IT organizations keep failing at projects over and over again. Here are some more statistics.[2]

- *Only 58% of organizations fully understand the value of project management.*
- *IT projects are notoriously difficult to manage. A survey published in* HBR *found that the average IT project overran its budget by 27%.*
- *One in six IT projects turns into a "black swan" with a cost overrun of 200% and a schedule overrun of 70%.*
- *For instance, Kmart's massive $1.2B failed IT modernization project was a big contributor to its bankruptcy.*
- *A PWC study of over 10,640 projects found that a tiny, tiny portion of companies – 2.5% – completed 100% of their projects successfully. The rest either failed to meet some of their original targets or missed the original budget or deadlines.*
- *Failed IT projects alone cost the United States $50–150B in lost revenue and productivity.*

And let's not forget the State of Rhode Island, where a $110 million strategic digital transformation project cost nearly three times as budgeted initially.[3]

I provide these statistics to reinforce the persistent problem of failed projects. It's not just the execution phase; it's more complicated than that. Organizations

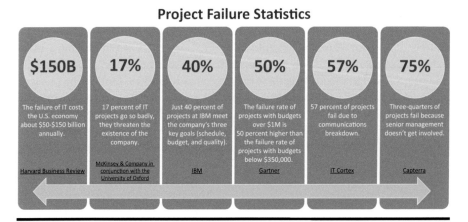

Figure 2.1   Project failure statistics.

identify technology projects in two ways. Business units and IT identify projects to improve business performance, and IT also identifies projects to improve technology infrastructure. Projects identified by business units involve a process that occurs before the project execution phase. Business units and IT identify potential projects to improve business performance: define requirements; develop a business case; determine strategic alignment; prioritize project portfolio; gather IT estimates on resources, timeline, and technology risk; obtain approval; etc. Why do I bring this up? Well, most business unit organizations believe that the cause of failed projects is due to IT execution issues. While this may be the case, it's not the fundamental cause for failed projects.

To better understand the issue of failed strategic projects, MIT partnered with Capgemini to conduct a study with over 1,300 worldwide executives. Guess what was on the list? These executives identified the lack of a mature Governance Competency as one of the significant obstacles in successfully executing Digital Transformation efforts that leverage technology as a strategic asset.[4,5]

As you can see from Figure 2.2, companies focus on three main areas to leverage technology to improve business performance.

■ Improve the customer experience by better understanding its customers, improving top-line growth, and leveraging customer touchpoints to deliver enhanced customer value.
■ Optimize operational processes through improved digitization, enable improved efficiencies of workers, and improve performance management.
■ Develop new business models by incorporating digital modified businesses, developing new digital businesses, and creating a more globalized presence through digital technology.

The MIT Center for ⇒ Digital Business   **Digital Transformation Study**   Capgemini Consulting

- 3-Year Study
- 1500 IT/Business Executives
- Increase of Transformation Projects Focus on 3 Key Areas

Customer Experience	**Operational Processes**	**Business Models**
• Understanding Customer • Top Line Growth • Customer Touch Points	• Process Digitization • Worker Enablement • Performance Management	• Digitally Modified Businesses • New Digital Businesses • Digital Globalization

.... Identified MISSING or IMMATURE GOVERNANCE COMPETENCY as a Major Obstacles to Success

Figure 2.2   MIT/Capgemini consulting digital transformation study.

Suppose you are a CIO, C-suite executive, or Board Member. Your company has probably undertaken digital transformation initiatives as part of an enterprise strategy to improve its competitive position. These initiatives aim to innovate value by executing a series of programs and associated projects to enhance the customer experience, optimize value-chain processes, and even reinvent business models by leveraging technology strategically. Sounds promising? Well, hopefully, your results have been successful. But this is not the case with many others. It's not all a bed of roses. According to a Harvey Nash global CIO research study, 41% of companies surveyed have an enterprise digital strategy, and only 18% of companies rate their use of digital technology as "very effective."[6]

A KPMG global study supports the Capgemini and Harvey Nashresearch study. The study found that one in three CEOs feel their organizations failed to achieve the value from digital transformation initiatives.[7]

A McKinsey research article further reinforces the above. It identified how companies are embarking on five initiatives to improve the customer experience, optimize processes, and develop new business models as CEOs are rethinking their business strategy due to the COVID-19 Pandemic. And these priorities all involve leveraging technology in new and innovative ways.[8]

- Center Strategy on Sustainability: Many companies rethink how they produce goods and services while "exacting minimal damage to the environment."
- Transform in the cloud: Companies now recognize the value of moving into the cloud as "it is beginning to bring real results in innovation and productivity." To succeed at this, people need to be cloud-literate in understanding the capabilities of cloud technology.
- Cultivate Your Talent: The human element is a critical success factor for every business. "The organization of the future will need to be more flexible, less hierarchical, and more diverse."
- Press The need for Speed: It's all about improving the speed of business. "The pace of change is speeding up, and the landscape of business is more fluid than ever." Speed is more than just increasing the pace, and it's about designing the business processes to operate more efficiently and intelligently.
- Operate with Purpose: Business leaders need to rethink their purpose. How will we operate in the future? How do we adapt to new ways of working? How do we embrace digitization and reinvent our supply chains? Leaders need to recognize that people want meaning in their lives and work. To put it another way, leaders need to step back, take a breath, and consider a broader perspective.

So. Net..net. There will be a dramatic increase in technology projects. And your organization needs to be prepared to effectively and efficiently manage the project lifecycle process and improve project success.

I'm sure you're wondering why I keep providing survey statistics that reinforce project failure issues. I'm doing this to let you know that these statistics keep occurring repeatedly, and companies are not solving the problem. The MIT-Capgemini study (see Figure 2.2) identifies the lack of an adequate governance competency as one of the significant obstacles in successfully implementing projects. As a CIO, C-suite executive, or board member, I'm sure you don't want to be the next statistical reference. Your business is at tremendous risk if you continue to embark on digital transformation initiatives without an effective governance process.

Listen to what two executives have to say on why governance is a strategic imperative

■ Brett Weber is the Enterprise Technology Executive at State Farm and focuses on risk and compliance. Weber understands the strategic value of IT Governance. "Governance is critical for IT to partner with business units to implement technology effectively in supporting the business goals and objectives of our business. If you don't have a governance framework, proper metric, you are guessing about doing the right thing."[9]

■ Charles S. Anderson is director, Governance and Project Office at CAI, Inc. He has his certification as a PMP and looks at governance from a different perspective. "It is essential that all approved projects provide business value to the organization. The Project Governance process ensures that the proposed business value has merit and is monitored throughout the project life cycle. Project Governance ensures that each project meets the business goals and technical standards of a proposed project before approval and monitors the project until close to ensure those goals and standards are met and maintained."[10]

One of the significant failures of current governance processes that manage the project lifecycle is that they are designed as *reactive* processes. I've spoken to hundreds of CIOs, and they all agree. Most say they find that IT drives most of the project governance processes. Getting executive buy-in is always a challenge. Business units view their roles and associated responsibilities as separate from the IT organization and have a "they vs. us" *culture*. Projects identified by the business may not align with the business strategy. And the list goes on. I view these characteristics as part of a Governance 1.0 culture. Figure 2.3 summarizes a list of the seven primary characteristics.

What businesses require is a "proactive" governance project competency that is more strategic. A proactive governance competency includes the following characteristics. It must be driven by the business, embraced by the executive team, promote a business/IT partnership, align selected projects to business strategy, enabled by a business/IT collaborative culture, include real-time and not historical metrics, and optimize project lifecycle processes. Figure 2.4 shows the evolution of the characteristics of a Governance 1.0 JT Project compared to what is needed in, what I call, a Governance 2.0 model.

Governance 1.0

- IT Driven
- Lack of Executive Buy-In
- Conflicting Responsibilities
- Misaligned Projects
- They vs Us
- Lack of Process
- Historical Metrics

Figure 2.3   Governance 1.0.

The Evolution of Strategic Governance

Governance 1.0		**Governance 2.0**
• IT Driven		• Business Driven
• Lack of Executive Buy-In		• Executive Sponsorship
• Conflicting Responsibilities	Reactive Proactive	• Business Partnership
• Misaligned Projects		• Strategic Alignment
• They vs Us		• Collaboration
• Lack of Process		• Process Optimization
• Historical Metrics	➡	• Real Time Metrics

Figure 2.4   The evolution of strategic IT governance.

The move to a more *proactive* Governance 2.0 model has never been more critical than now. Why? Because companies are focusing on technology initiatives at a greater pace than ever before. Just listen to what Rich Lesser, Chief Executive of the Boston Consulting Group at the time of this writing, says about today's changing economy.

> The COVID-19 Pandemic had a dramatic change on business strategy. Companies realize that things have changed in a permanent sense: the way consumers and workers live their lives. Digital, which was already on the acceleration path before the COVID-19 pandemic, just jumped to a different curve. And people are looking for more flexibility and different models of collaboration.[11]

Lesser is correct. An example to support his premise is the insurance industry. A McKinsey article discusses how leveraging digital technology will fundamentally change how insurers connect with customers and the products and services they provide.[12]

The auto insurance industry will leverage technology in new and innovative ways. To reduce risk around facilities, insurers will use satellites, drones, and real-time data sets to provide visibility, leading to greater accuracy. Automation will dramatically improve the speed of claims processing for natural catastrophes. Insurance products will seamlessly adjust coverage based on the evolving needs of customers. These are just three examples of how the insurance industry will leverage technology.

Five technological trends will have the most pronounced impact on insurance as these will materially change insurance products and the core functions that support them.

- <u>Applied AI</u>: Insurance carriers will leverage Automated Intelligence to reengineer their core processes to be more predictive, creating a <u>"human in the loop"</u> model that increases productivity and creates high-quality customer touchpoints.
- <u>Distributed Infrastructure</u>: Cloud technology, enabled with 5G technology, will act as a hub connecting the technology ecosystem among customers, distributors, healthcare providers, carriers, and reinsurers.
- <u>Future of Connectivity</u>: Insurers will rely on IoT devices to reshape life, health, property, and commercial lines products. In-car tracking devices monitor customer driving habits, recording vehicle speed, mileage, total driving time to determine the policyholder's car insurance premium.
- <u>Next-Level Automation</u>: Leveraging technology to automate processes and use digital twin capability will provide a "predict and prevent capability" to reduce potential claims and improve factory efficiency.
- <u>Trust Architecture</u>: Insurers will leverage blockchain technology to provide a more safe and consistent manner as customers share more information. A zero-trust security approach creates a resilient network that protects against cyber intrusions.

There is no doubt that there will be a dramatic increase in strategic projects by almost every company. And guess what, if you are one of these companies and you still have a "reactive" governance process in place, you are in big trouble. You should begin to think about transforming your current *reactive* governance process into a more *proactive* model. Better yet, you need to assess your current governance process to determine its maturity level and potential risk to projects and then develop a maturity plan to improve your governance competencies. Figure 2.5 represents the Strategic IT Governance 2.0 framework to accomplish this. The following chapter provides more detail on the model.

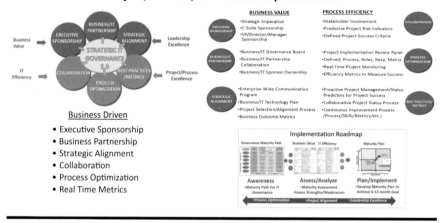

Figure 2.5   Strategic IT Governance 2.0 framework.

Citings

1. http://blog.mavenlink.com/21-shocking-project-management-statistics-that-explain-why-projects-continue-to-fail
2. https://www.forbes.com/sites/steveandriole/2020/12/01/why-no-one-can-manage-projects-especially-technology-projects/?sh=50ed9d0b2da2)
3. https://www.govtech.com/computing/Rhode-Islands-Biggest-Ever-IT-Project-Goes-Live.html
4. https://www.capgemini.com/consulting/service/digital-transformation/
5. https://youtu.be/zUmVJcC6Xhk
6. https://assets.kpmg/content/dam/kpmg/xx/pdf/2017/07/harvey-nash-kpmg-cio-survey-2017.pdf
7. https://assets.kpmg.com/content/dam/kpmg/pdf/2016/05/global-transformation-study-2016.pdf
8. https://www.mckinsey.com/business-functions/strategy-and-corporate-finance/our-insights/what-matters-most-five-priorities-for-ceos-in-the-next-normal?cid=other-eml-ttn-mip-mck&hdpid=a5d107b7-71ca-474f-b0d4-c8fbb4d7a548&hctky=1570524&hlkid=4aec43871c2b4e878fecdade4991871a
9. Brett Weber/Phil Weinzimer interview June 7, 2020.
10. Charles Anderson/Phil Weinzimer interview August 15, 2020.
11. https://www.nytimes.com/2021/09/24/business/corner-office-rich-lesser-bcg.html
12. https://www.mckinsey.com/industries/financial-services/our-insights/how-top-tech-trends-will-transform-insurance

Chapter 3

Strategic IT Governance 2.0: An Overview

The previous chapter cited several statistics that reflect companies' challenges in successfully implementing strategic and tactical projects. I ended the chapter by stating that companies need to assess, analyze, plan, and implement a maturity program to improve their governance competencies. There are three reasons I believe this is a strategic imperative for every company.

- Statistics continue to reflect the failure of projects year after year.
- The MIT/Sloan study referenced in the previous chapter found that transformation projects fail due to a lack of or immature governance competencies.
- A McKinsey study of senior technology leaders and business executives sought to determine how CEOs and board members can support their technology leaders better. The study identified the following key best practices CEOs and boards can take to provide CIOs with the needed support to leverage technology to improve business performance.[1]

These best practices align with the Strategic IT Governance 2.0 model competencies (in parenthesis at the end of each study best practices).

DOI: 10.1201/9781003317531-3

- Ensure long-term support in understanding the business value of technologies *(Executive Support)*
- Align priorities to match strategic objectives. *(Strategic Alignment)*
- Make business a magnet for tech talent *(Collaboration)*
- Understand tech implications *(Process Optimization. Metrics)*
- Build up tech literacy *(IT/Business Partnership)*

I firmly believe the Strategic IT Governance 2.0 model is a strategic imperative for companies to investigate and employ for the previously stated reasons.

This chapter provides an overview of The Strategic IT Governance 2.0 model that accomplishes that objective. Subsequent chapters provide ten case studies of how companies implemented the model, interviews with two CIOs and their insights of Governance, and chapters on how to assess, analyze, plan, and implement the Strategic IT Governance 2.0 methodology within your organization.

To begin your journey in better understanding the Strategic IT Governance 2.0 framework, let's start with a basic knowledge of the model. Figure 3.1 is the framework for the model.

There are four levels of maturity in the Strategic IT Governance 2.0 model. Each of the four maturity paths in Figure 3.2 reflects the characteristics exhibited in each of the six Strategic IT Governance 2.0 competencies. You will note that I have also identified the Maturity Level (from 1 to 10) for each of the four paths. Additionally, I have identified the potential percentage improvement in project performance for each of the four levels. This maturity model is discussed in more

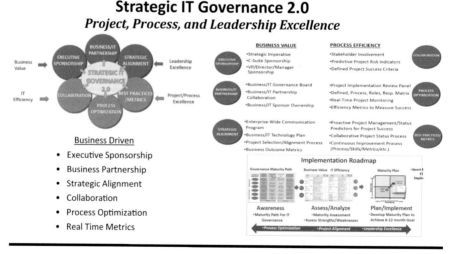

Figure 3.1   Strategic IT Governance 2.0 framework.

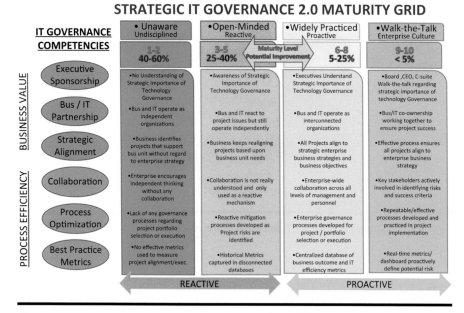

Figure 3.2   Strategic IT Governance 2.0 maturity grid.

detail in Chapter 18 – How to Assess the Maturity of Your Company's Strategic IT Governance Competencies.

I've spoken on the subject of Strategic IT Governance at many IT executive events and met with IT executives who shared their insights, challenges, and opportunities in overcoming the challenge of an increasing portfolio of strategic and complex projects. They all agree that the number of digital transformation initiatives is increasing rapidly, the technology component is more complex, and its impact cuts across the entire enterprise value chain. These three factors compound the overall risk of executing these initiatives successfully. So, what should you do?

When CIOs ask me my thoughts on effective Governance for strategic programs and associated projects, I share the importance of two fundamental principles that comprise strategic IT governance.

■ Business Value: The goal of every digital program and its associated projects is to enable your company to achieve its strategic goals and objectives. To accomplish this requires executive leadership to walk the talk by supporting a collaborative strategic IT governance culture across the entire business enterprise.

Figure 3.3   Strategic IT Governance 2.0 competencies.

- IT Efficiency: A governance methodology must encompass a focus on process excellence that embodies proactive risk mitigation, enterprise collaboration, process optimization, and a set of best practice metrics that enable the efficient execution of strategic projects that achieves the desired business outcomes.

These two principles are fundamental to any governance methodology you embrace within your company to improve project success. In the following graphic, I capture these two basic principles and the accompanying six competencies (See Figure 3.3).

Strategic IT Governance 2.0 – A High-Level Overview

The following section provides a high-level overview of the Strategic IT Governance 2.0 methodology. As I mentioned earlier, my research includes interviews with over 80 CIOs and IT executives, and clients to uncover their issues, challenges, and opportunities regarding how they govern their digital transformation and other strategic programs and associated projects. Each has incorporated elements of this model and shared their journey. Richard Douglas, the COO of Saxon Bank in Denmark, talks about the value of the Strategic IT Governance 2.0 model.

> The Strategic IT Governance 2.0 model provides a mechanism to strengthen and enforce tight alignment between IT and their respective stakeholders and commercial counterparts. This model contains all of the elements required to achieve a collaborative environment and to enable the Strategic CIO to execute and deliver on strategic outcomes critical to business success.[2]

Why have I named this a 2.0 version of strategic IT governance? The answer is simple. No longer can any business enterprise succeed with bifurcated models that segregate the business from the technology organization. Today, we need a newer model that is all about succeeding at digital as more and more companies recognize that, at their core, technology underpins every product, service, and supporting business process across the entire virtual value chain. And as such, you cannot effectively implement any new product or service without business and technology personnel working together as a collaborative team.

Strategic IT Governance 2.0 embraces six key competencies. Three of the six competencies – *Executive Sponsorship, Business/IT Partnership, and Strategic Alignment* – support the Business Value principle through Leadership Excellence. The remaining three – *Collaboration, Process Optimization*, and *Best Practice Metrics* – support the IT Efficiency principle through Project/Process Excellence discipline.

Each of these six competencies forms a component of the Strategic IT Governance 2.0 methodology. Following is a brief description of each of the competencies to the overarching principles of Business Value or IT Efficiency.

Business Value Competencies

Executive Sponsorship and Business and IT Partnership

Executive Sponsorship and Business and IT Partnership are an absolute necessity for effective governance and a key competency that the entire executive hierarchy must embrace. Three best practices that exhibit *Executive Sponsorship* are recognizing that governance is a strategic imperative, sponsorship by the C-suite, and VPs, Directors, and Managers embracing this methodology.

Today, a Business/IT Partnership is a core necessity as business and technology personnel work together to develop new products, services, and support business processes. Three best practices that exhibit Business/IT Partnership are establishing a business/IT governance Board, ensuring a collaborative business/IT partnership, and establishing a business owner sponsorship for key programs and projects.

The Fulton County School system is an excellent example of how a CIO obtained Executive developed a Governance Model by getting Executive Sponsorship and a Business/IT Partnership. First, here are some statistics on the immense size of the school district. The district is the fourth largest school system in Georgia, with 10,900 employees, 6,900 teachers, and certified personnel. The school district encompasses 108 schools, 19 middle schools, 19 high schools, and 10 start-up charter organizations.[3]

Serena Sacks, the CIO at Fulton County School Systems (FCS) from 2014 to 2020, is a transformational IT leader with over 30 years at IBM, Walt Disney World, Wyndham, Florida Virtual School. Sacks is currently U.S. Customer Success Leader at Microsoft. In her role, she empowers organizations, students, and teachers to achieve more through Microsoft platforms and solutions.

Sacks's success has not gone unnoticed. The Women of IT, a professional association for women in the technology industry, awarded Sacks the Woman-of-the-Year award in 2019.[4]

Sacks is passionate about leveraging technology to transform education through personalized learning. She is certified in Enterprise IT Governance and realizes the power of collaboration. When Sacks arrived at FCS, IT had some challenges. The website had some challenges, and SAP had limited success. In addition, each business unit was siloes from the other business units. There was a lot to fix. Sacks initiated a District Technology Governance Council (DTGC) to develop a partnership between the key stakeholders and the IT organization to rectify these challenges. Her goal was to bring together the key stakeholders in a partnership to "ensure that IT creates value for the district, in alignment with its strategic objectives, while managing IT-related risks.[5]

The Council acts as an Executive Steering Committee. The Solutions Architecture and Application Governance Committee (SAAG) and the Information Technology Governance Subcommittee (ITGS) support the Council. The SAAG ensures "… the technology solutions align to Strategic Objectives and IT architecture. The Architecture team verifies the solution complies with all security, regulatory, and legal requirements and confirms relevancy and efficacy to technology solutions selected." The ITGS "endorses and prioritizes resources, manages issues and mitigates risk, defines and verifies the design of the solution, and assesses, analyzes, organizes, and prepares information to support the DTG Council."[Ibid]

The scope of the Council focuses on five key areas: Strategic Alignment, Value Delivery, Performance Measurement, Resource Management, and Risk Management.

The key stakeholders include Chief Academic Officer (Academics), Chief Communication Officer (Communications), Chief of Staff (Executive Management), CIO, PMO, Enterprise Applications (Technology), Chief Talent Officer (Human Resources, Chief Operations Officer (Operations), Chief Financial Officer (Finance).

Figure 3.4 reflects the cover page and table of contents of the DTGC. As you can see, it's pretty detailed.[6]

How has the DTGC improved leveraging technology and improving learning at the FCS? Judge yourself. Following are comments from some of the DTCS Board Members who shared their positive experiences.[5]

Chief Talent Officer: "We used to work in a silo, and the Council has allowed us to break through the silo. We now partner with IT work to work collaboratively and leverage our interdependencies to be more efficient."

Chief Academic officer-deputy superintendent: "The value it brought to me is the collective wisdom. We now understand the potential land mines in projects, and this group brings perspective to navigate those land mines that are also collaborative and collective. We want success for all projects, and this creates a powerful team environment."

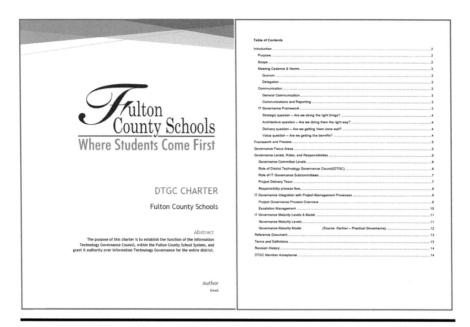

Figure 3.4   Fulton County Digital Council charter – cover page and table of contents.

Chief Communication Officer: "The Council has improved the governance function. Including PMO as a member provides us full input on projects that help us make strategic decisions, and we also have a much better handle of prioritizing and sequencing projects."

Chief Operations Officer: "Over time, this committee has gotten mature about pain points and minimized pain points and get to the north star. Being able to say NO and come together as a team, as a lot of value."

Emily Bell: Enterprise application: "This team helped focus on the students, parents, and teachers, and has helped us provide a Student information System (system of records of discipline, grades, and attendance) that improves transparency."

Chief Financial Officer: "Governance has helped us get on the same page and use the same language. Previously each of us worked within silos. Now we are collaborative, partner together regularly, and more importantly, understand each other better and operate more efficiently."

Strategic Alignment

Strategic alignment consists of best practices that ensure the selection/executive of projects aligns with the business's strategic goals. The four best practices that exhibit *strategic alignment* are establishing an enterprise communication program, creating a single business/technology plan, developing and practicing a process to select and align projects based upon the strategic value, and identifying business outcome metrics as key-value indicators of project execution.

Every company has a different method of prioritizing projects to ensure strategic alignment. McKinney says that many companies are now conducting a "…more regular, objective, rules-based prioritization of their projects, along with a subjective assessment based upon strategic goals."[7]

Prioritizing projects on a more regular basis provides significant benefits. Companies can increase spending for growth projects, reduce costs, improve margins, and reduce business complexity. A high-tech company redirected 20 percent of its development budget to new areas of innovation and growth. Cutting costs enables a chemicals company to reduce the number of development projects by 40 percent. And a food and beverage company forecasted a 15 percent increase in profits based upon focusing efforts on high-profitability projects.

In the public sector, many cities are prioritizing projects using different methods. Following are examples of how a few cities strategically align projects around transportation initiatives. Each of these cities followed some basic principles:[8]

- The prioritization process needs to be collaborative.
- Traffic congestion is a big issue, and sequencing projects need to be based on data to build project selection legitimacy.
- Setting broad goals first helps to insulate projects from politics.
- Most importantly, each city recognized that data drives good decision-making and that quantitative data is better than qualitative data.

   Atlanta: The City of Atlanta and MARTA, the transportation agency, signed an agreement to establish and guide the process of selecting projects to fund. The agreement established a technical and stakeholder advisory committee that included a complete list of potential projects. It also established a programming process and Joint Prioritization Leadership Group to coordinate across agencies.

   L.A. Metro: At the County level, staff used performance metrics to rank projects based upon mobility, economy, accessibility, safety, sustainability,

   Charlotte: Evaluated projects based upon the long-term need for congestion relief, capital cost, long-term land-use opportunity, jobs, and housing within half a mile of transit stations.

   Denver: The annual process identifies projects according to three main categories; compliance, renewal, and enhancement. There are multiple reviews with each department, the finance organization, and by an investment review panel. Final approval by the board is required for the advancement of the project to the implementation phase.

IT Efficiency Competencies

Collaboration

Collaboration enables the proactive participation of key business and technology personnel to actively work together to focus on achieving the business goals and objectives of the company. Three best practices that exhibit collaboration are the involvement of key stakeholders in the project management process, identifying predictive project risk indicators, and defining project success criteria.

Here is an example of a successful collaboration initiative. In 2019 Johnson & Johnson's leadership team identified an enterprise strategy to "…enable and empower a global workforce to help patients, doctors and nurses, mothers and fathers, and all those who use Johnson& Johnson products and services." To accomplish this required a collaboration initiative that focused on an operating model that empowers teams. Business and technology leaders were aware that "…the IT organization needs to be more empowered, responsive and agile." To accomplish this, a cross-functional team identified critical points of friction across workflows. For example, numerous handoffs took time; multiple technology teams required coordination. The cross-functional team developed a set of concrete principles that defined the accountabilities, boundaries, and flexibility. Three principles described the tactics of this initiative.[9]

- *Work as one high-performing team*: Business and IT personnel worked together on technology-enabled offerings.
- *Focus on employee outcomes:* The teams would demonstrate how their products and services would value the business.
- *Empower the front line:* Working teams had predefined boundaries but were free to achieve goals that still met the overall project objective.

Before the 2019 transformation, the Corporate Business Technology Team (CBT) successfully met regulatory and financial requirements but not the needs of the business. In six weeks, the company established a product team that built and successfully delivered a global tracking software. This initiative resulted in a 20 percent reduction in the need for "coordination resources" and a 25 percent reduction in fewer non-value-added meetings. An added benefit was "… the ability for Johnson and Johnson to react quickly to the COVID-19 Pandemic. This new software-enabled employees to self-report when they were sick, so they could quickly get help and care when needed."[Ibid] "The new IT collaboration between IT and the business created partnership, trust, and joint ownership that enables Johnson and Johnson to build new and innovative products for its customers.

Tom Weck is CIO of Corporate Technology and summarizes the key lessons learned from this initiative.[10]

Empower teams by providing boundaries but let them decide how to accomplish it.

- Make sure the business and IT have shared goals focused on business impact.
- Provide educations for business leaders to understand the power of technology and what it can accomplish.

Process Optimization

Process optimization across all the project execution activities is critical to achieving project success and enabling proactive risk mitigation. The four best practices that exhibit *process optimization* are implementing a project implementation review panel and defining the process, roles, and responsibility matrix for all personnel involved in the project management execution activities.

A great example of process optimization is the reengineering of the Field Service process at Rollins, Inc., the Atlanta-based $2 billion pesticide conglomerate company. You may recognize one of its most popular brands, Orkin, the 115-year-old company that is the largest pesticide company in the United States.

In 2015, Lee Crump, CIO and Group Vice President of Rollins, approached the executive committee to inform them that the current Field Service process to engage with customers is outdated and inefficient.

> We'll lose customers if we don't improve it. *Our customers want to engage with us as they do with Amazon. We need to be more creative. Our current technology, customer engagement processes, and supporting technology are outdated, and we need to do something about it. We are no longer working to outperform our competitors in the pest Industry. Our customers' expectations have evolved far beyond that, and their demands are now being set by companies such as Amazon and Uber and UPS.*[11]

Crump was able to convince the executive committee to approve the reengineering of the Field Service processes. He organized a cross-functional team that included IT, business, sales, and technicians, revamped the processes, updated the technology, and dramatically improved customer satisfaction, saving over a million dollars a year.[12]

Crump is a seasoned IT executive with over 45 years of IT experience and has a long track record of successfully delivering major systems implementations and reengineering many IT and business processes in his career. Before his role at Rollins, Crump spent ten years as the CIO of the largest and most profitable ServiceMaster subsidiary in Memphis, TN. In 2012 Crump was named Georgia CIO of the Year (Global Division) by the GeorgiaCIO Association. He is a member of American Mensa, the GeorgiaCIO Association, the Project Management Institute (PMI), the

Technology Association of Georgia (TAG), the Association of Telecommunications Professionals (ATP), and the Society of Information Managers (SIM).

The technology used to support the Field Service technicians dated to the 1990s with outdated green screens and manual paper-based processes. Crump recognized that the "…field technicians are the face of Orkin to the customer, and we knew we need to equip our frontline employees better to deliver the kind of experience our customers have come to expect."[12]

Crump explains one of the antiquated processes "Every branch had an old impact-line printer, and once a week the service manager would print out three-part service tickets for each technician and hand them out."

> It was up to the technicians to manage their routes and schedules, and they were required to take notes on each job using the service ticket, which caused many problems – you have everything from the handwriting that is hard to read to lost tickets. Once a week, the service manager would print out three-part service tickets for each technician and hand them out. To make matters worse, someone in the back office had to take each of those tickets and organize all of the information to put into the system before we could invoice the customer.[ibid]

The 22-month program to shift to a Customer-Centric Field Service Solution dramatically improved customer service while reducing costs. Following are some of the process improvements:

- Involvement of Field Personnel as part of the Reengineering team
- Using Agile Development to create new software
- Enterprise-wide communication program focusing on status and upcoming milestones
- Piloted new process and rolled out carefully across all field locations
- Field personnel at each location trained the entire staff on process and technology
- Equipped each filed technician with an iOS-compatible Brother PicketJet mobile printer when customers wanted a printed receipt

The implementation of a new Field Service process enabled company-wide visibility across the sales, service, dispatch, call center, and management functions. A portal enables customers to access all the information they need, and there are no paper tickets. A cloud-based scheduling and routing system eliminates the need for technicians to schedule their customer visits. And customers can use the Same-Day Scheduling feature of the new system. An added benefit of the new process is improved cash flow as customers can pay by credit card on-site using iPhones or on-file credit cards.

Crump summarizes the success of the reengineered process:

> This modernization of our processes and technology enables us to pro-
> vide a level of service our customers have come to expect. Continuing
> to understand and meet those expectations is the only way to deliver on
> our mission of being the best service company in the world.[11]

Best Practice Metrics

Best practice metrics is all about proactively identifying critical metrics that can
anticipate potential project risk areas. The four best practices that exhibit *best practice metrics* are: practicing proactive project management/status activities that focus
on current as well as the potential areas of project risk; identifying and reviewing the
critical predictors of project success against current project status; being proactive,
incorporating a collaborative project status process on all programs/projects; and
identification of the efficiency metrics that measure project execution success.

Metrics matter. Imagine driving a car without a dashboard of dials that indicate
your speed, amount of gas, or radiator water temperature. Or think about the next
time you fly in an airplane; imagine if the pilot had no dashboard dials. Better yet,
remember the days without GPS?

Metrics define progress, quality, financials, and other necessary data. Without
these critical metrics, project managers face uncertainty in projected true project
status. When developing metrics for your project, you can follow these five simple
guidelines.[13]

1. Metrics require planning and analysis.
2. Metrics answer questions that identify issues, obstacles, and risks (opportunities and threats).
3. Metrics provide information that, once acted on, will change the project either
   positively or negatively.
4. Metrics tell a story about the initiative's progress or lack thereof.
5. Metrics can be lagging or predictive learning and tell the story of how well you
   have done or what the prediction is for the future

The Strategic IT Governance 2.0 model identifies two distinct metrics: business
outcome and IT efficiency metrics. Business outcome metrics measure the business
impact of a project on your business. Here is an example. Suppose your company
has a series of project initiatives to improve supply chains, modernize your websites
to enhance customer engagement, or innovate customer services to promote brand
and product stickiness. You would measure the success of these initiatives through
a series of metrics; inventory reduction dollars, customer retention rate, or revenue
increase. On the execution side, metrics measure the progress of the project. The
primary metrics used in project execution are quality, cost, and timeline. But there

Figure 3.5 Project management metrics cheat sheet.

are other metrics that one can use to measure project status that answers the following key questions.[14]

- Where are we going?
- Where should we be?
- Where are we?
- Why are we here?

To answer these questions, you can develop forecasting or predictive metrics. Forecasting metrics will help you predict project cost and duration outcomes to understand current progress and performance. Diagnostic metrics help you identify progress and performance issues to inform corrective actions.

Adobe Workfront is the project management platform that "keeps teams and enterprise running efficiently, even in the face of unpredictable challenges." It provides a cheat sheet for project managers that identify ten key predictive and forecasting metrics project managers should utilize in managing the project (Figure 3.5).[15]

Summary

Companies recognize that embracing technology as a core strategy to improve competitive advantage is necessary for today's digital age. As a CIO, C-suite executive, and, yes, even a member of the boards of directors, you need to recognize that the emerging trend of incorporating Strategic IT Governance 2.0 competencies within your company will dramatically improve the success of your digital transformation initiatives.

Now that I have provided a high-level overview of the Strategic IT Governance 2.0 competency model, let me share more detail in the following chapters as I provide you with 11 case studies of companies that have implemented Strategic IT Governance 2.0 competency components and two chapters on how to assess, analyze, and plan to improve your current Strategic IT competencies as well as implementing your plan to achieve a Strategic IT Governance 2.0 within your company.

Citings

1. https://www.mckinsey.com/business-functions/mckinsey-digital/our-insights/what-cios-need-from-their-ceos-and-boards-to-make-it-digital-ready
2. Richard Douglas/Phil Weinzimer book interview – January 14, 2020.
3. https://www.fultonschools.org/aboutus
4. https://patch.com/georgia/sandysprings/fulton-schools-chief-information-officer-wins-international-award
5. Phil Weinzimer/Serena Sacks/Fulton County District Council Board interview October 30, 2019.
6. Phil Weinzimer/Serena Sacks interview September 15, 2019; Fulton County District Technology Council Charter.
7. https://www.mckinsey.com/business-functions/operations/our-insights/matching-the-right-projects-with-the-right-resources
8. https://www.apta.com/wp-content/uploads/Group3_Project-Prioritization-.pdf
9. how-johnson-and-johnson-transformed-its-corporate-business-technology-operating-model.pdf (mckinsey.com) https://www.mckinsey.com/business-functions/mckinsey-digital/our-insights/a-new-it-operating-model-to-better-serve-employees
10. https://www.mckinsey.com/business-functions/mckinsey-digital/our-insights/a-new-it-operating-model-to-better-serve-employees
11. Phil Weinzimer/Lee Crump interview June 17, 2019.
12. https://www.fieldtechnologiesonline.com/doc/orkin-embraces-the-field-service-evolution-0001
13. https://www.pmworld360.com/blog/2021/03/24/why-project-metrics-matter/
14. https://www.nwccc.org/wp-content/uploads/2017/04/Metrics-that-Matter-Ali-Mostafavi.pdf
15. https://www.workfront.com

Chapter 4

Digital Transformation Governance Model at Armstrong World Industries: Introduction

---

A few years ago, Armstrong World Industries (AWI) embarked on a digital transformation strategy to improve the value of the products and services it provides to its customers by leveraging technology in new and innovative ways. To accomplish this, AWI created a digital governance model, methodology, tools, and best practices that align closely with the Strategic IT Governance 2.0 model's six components.

Chapters 5 and 6 provide an overview of the transformation governance model at AWI. They also provide additional details on the digital transformation strategy, the digital governance model for digital acceleration, and the six components of its governance model, and its alignment with the Strategic IT Governance model.

Chapter 5 reviews three of the six components of the AWI governance model: How executive sponsorship is a crucial ingredient to the success of its digital strategy. How business unit leaders and personnel partner with IT personnel in executing its strategy. And the importance of strategically aligning digital transformation projects with AWI business goals and objectives.

DOI: 10.1201/9781003317531-4

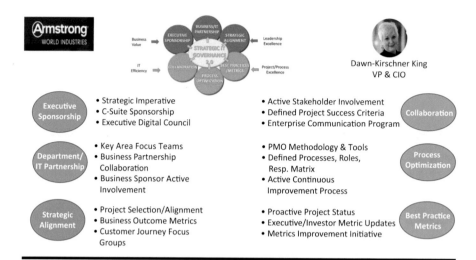

Figure 4.1   Armstrong World Industries digital governance model – best practices.

Chapter 6 explores how AWI developed a collaborative culture across the organization and how the IT Project Management Office (PMO) developed a project life-cycle methodology, tools, associated techniques, and best practice metrics to manage and communicate digital transformation projects status.

Earlier chapters provide you with an overview of the Strategic IT Governance 2.0 model and the best practices associated with each of the six underlying competencies. Figure 4.1 uses the same model but identifies the Armstrong World Industries best practices for each of the six underlying competencies. The subsequent two chapters explore each of the six competencies and how AWI leverages technology to implement its digital acceleration initiative.

Before we delve into the AWI governance model's details, I thought it would be instructive to provide you with some background of AWI and how it developed its current digital strategy.

Armstrong World Industries has a historical legacy of customer innovation dating back to 1860 when Thomas Armstrong started the cork-cutting company in Pittsburgh, Pennsylvania. Armstrong was an innovator. He was among the first to challenge the basic business principle *–let the buyer beware –* leaving the customer responsible for checking the quality of products. Armstrong felt that his company needed to stand behind its products and provide customers the confidence in Armstrong products. Thus, the phrase *Let the buyers have faith* was born. To further embrace this slogan, Armstrong stamped each cork with the name Armstrong and included a written guarantee in each burlap sack of cork shipped from his factory. As buyers grew more confident in Armstrong corks, sales skyrocketed, and by the mid-1890s, Armstrong was the world's largest cork company.[1]

By 1909 Armstrong found new uses of its cork, from shoe insoles to acoustic insulation. By 1909 the company manufactured and sold linoleum, the beginning of a robust portfolio of products that would emerge from its humble beginnings. One of the core principles at Armstrong was "…to stick to its core business and core value and be willing to adapt and innovate to meet customer demand and market conditions."[ibid]

Fast-forward to April 2016, when Armstrong World Industries separated from Armstrong Flooring, Inc. to focus its assets and resources in the design and manufacture of innovative commercial and residential ceilings, wall, and suspension system solutions. Today, Armstrong has a market cap of $4.5B with over 2,800 employees and a manufacturing network of fifteen facilities plus six facilities dedicated to its WAVE joint venture.[2]

AWI's (https://www.armstrongceilings.com) success is all about innovation and transformation, recognizing that customer needs and market demands drive its business strategy. As executives realized how consumerization drives companies to change their business strategy, business models, and operational processes, AWI executives saw the writing on the wall. They needed to adapt and continue the innovation model started by their founder, Thomas Armstrong. The current AWI executive team includes Victor Grizzle (President and CEO), Brian MacNeal (Senior Vice President and CFO), Ellen Romano (Senior Vice President, Human Resources), Mark Hershey (Senior Vice President, Americas), Jill Crager (Senior Vice President, Sales Operations), Charles Chiappone (Senior Vice President, Ceilings and Wall Solutions), and Dawn Kirchner-King (Vice President and Chief Information Officer). This executive team recognized that the customer landscape is changing and that digital transformation is necessary to drive business success. The goal of the AWI digital strategy, as articulated by Grizzle, is

> To grow the core and expand into adjacencies by using digital technology in all parts of the company. It is imperative to ground our digitalization work primarily in the needs and experiences of our customers. This is where and how we will become more capable and competitive.[3,4]

Read on to find out how Armstrong World Industries implemented a governance model with a set of best practices that improved its products and services for its customers. I'm sure you will find the AWI journey exciting and valuable in learning how your organization can implement a governance model to improve your digital transformation initiative.

Citings

1. https://www.armstrongflooring.com/corporate/en-us/about/heritage.html
2. https://www.armstrongworldindustries.com/en-us/about-us.html
3. Armstrong World Industries internal corporate announcement October 25, 2019.
4. Dawn Kirchner-King/Phil Weinzimer interview, December 20, 2019.

Chapter 5

How Armstrong World Industries Focus on Executive Sponsorship, Business/IT Partnership, and Strategic Alignment in Governing Digital Acceleration Initiatives Improved Business Performance

The Armstrong Work Industries (AWI) Digital Transformation governance model includes six components that align with the Strategic IT Governance 2.0 model. This chapter will explore why AWI decided to embark on a digital acceleration strategy and how it utilized the first three – executive sponsorship, business/IT partnership, and strategic alignment – as the foundation to its digital acceleration program.

DOI: 10.1201/9781003317531-5

The next chapter will explore how AWI leveraged collaboration, process optimization, and best practices/metrics to successfully implement the digital acceleration programs and projects.

Leveraging the IT Organization

To help enable the AWI digital strategy, the IT organization would need to be a critical component in developing the technology strategy and implementing the operational technology components. Dawn Kirchner-King is Vice-President and Chief Information Officer. Kirchner-King understands how leveraging technology strategically can drive innovation leading to successful business outcomes that improve AWI's competitive position in the ceiling and wall solutions industry. Kirchner-King says,

> by digitalizing our business, we advance our goal of helping our customers get more value from AWI products and services. Additionally, it improves our productivity in how we develop and deliver our products and services, adding speed, reducing costs, and improving quality. (Figure 5.1).[1]

Kirchner-King considers herself an influential business executive striving to leverage technology in driving organizational growth, performance, profitability, and protection of business assets. Her focus is driving transformative change by orchestrating transformative business strategy through data-driven decisions. A core principle that drives Kirchner-King's pursuit of leveraging technology for competitive advantage is to create customer value, operational success, and shareholder value. These goals enabled her to successfully leverage her technical, administrative, leadership, and team-building skills at AWI. Kirchner-King is successful because building and

Figure 5.1 Dawn Kirchner-King.

leveraging relationships with her business peers to drive successful business outcomes collaboratively is a core component of executive leadership.

Since arriving at AWI in 2016, Kirchner-King succeeded in developing and implementing several strategic initiatives. Kirchner-King successfully executed the tax-free spin-off of the $1.2 billion Armstrong Flooring subsidiary and realigned the operational budget-due to the spin-off without impacting any services reduction. Kirchner-King has also led cross-functional initiatives in the due diligence and integration of eight acquisitions. Recognizing project governance as a necessary discipline, Kirchner-King has implemented a new project management governance methodology to engage business leaders in achieving revenue results, cost savings, and return on invested capital. In 2019, Kirchner-King and her team executed the divestiture of Armstrong European and Asian Operations by providing Transitional Services to Knauf, turning IT into a profit center for the company.

The Inspire CIO organization recognized Kirchner-King as an industry leader and in 2020, she received an ORBIE award. Inspire CIO is an organization devoted to building professional relationships with colleagues facing similar challenges. The ORBIE honors chief information officers who have demonstrated excellence in leadership and management effectiveness, the business value created by technology innovation, and engagement in industry and community endeavors.[2]

Digital Transformation/Strategic IT Governance at Armstrong World Industries

Grizzle, AWI's CEO, articulated in his digital strategy: "it is imperative to ground our digitalization work primarily in the needs and experiences of our customers."[3] An AWI Customer Digital Usage Trends Study supports Grizzle's strategy and reflects how digital customer interaction has grown exponentially.

Figure 5.2 summarizes the study. Following are the three main findings.

- Self-service activity increased by more than 20 percent over two years.
- Active digital customers increased significantly over four years.
- Digital orders grew to 71 percent, an all-time high.

As a result, the team embraced a digital strategy that focuses on innovative ways to embrace the customer, improve manufacturing efficiencies, and improve personnel productivity. Technology has been a crucial component. Since these three areas embrace the AWI value chain and cut across organizational boundaries, the AWI executive team recognized that a new strategic digital governance model was required to enable success. The AWI digital governance model embraces process optimization, project alignment, and leadership excellence, the key core principles of a Strategic IT Governance 2.0 methodology. More details of AWI's digital governance model and how it aligns the Strategic IT Governance 2.0 follow.

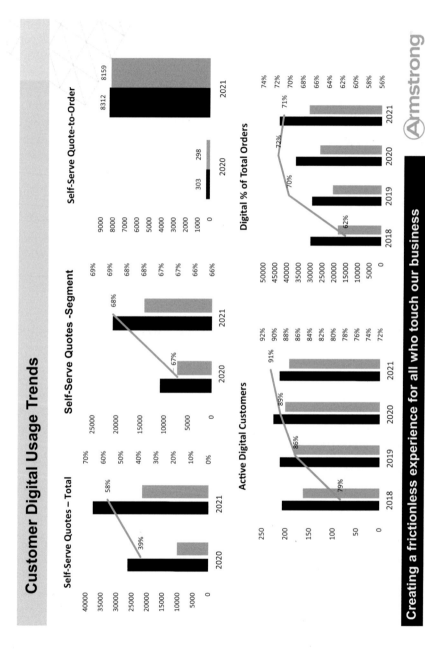

Figure 5.2 Customer digital usage trends.

Executive Sponsorship

As described previously, AWI executives recognized that the customer landscape is changing and that a digital transformation strategy was necessary to drive future business success. The goal is to advance the AWI business strategy through digital technology across all parts of the business. The executives accomplished this by developing the *Governance Model for Digital Acceleration*, as shown in Figure 5.3. This governance model incorporates executive sponsorship of the digital strategy and a business and IT partnership that embraces personnel from across the organization at various management levels to collaborate to achieve AWI's digital strategy. Let's explore the model in more detail, in terms of structure, membership, and responsibilities.

Governance Model for Digital Acceleration

AWI executives recognize that strategy needs to be executed by operational personnel.

The governance model includes two distinct levels to accomplish this. The first layer provides for executive-level sponsorship for the digital strategy. The second layer comprises an operating layer where business and IT personnel work collaboratively to execute the digital strategy.

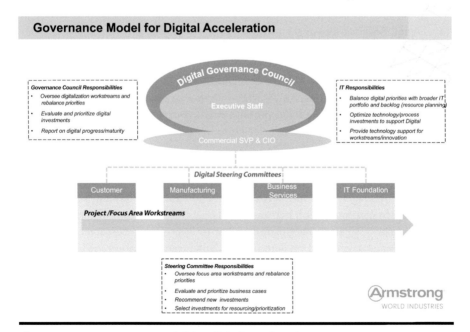

Figure 5.3   Governance model for digital acceleration.

The executive-level consists of the C-Suite and other senior executives. The operational level, known as Digital Steering Committees, consists of senior and middle managers from both business and IT organizations. These teams focus on the Customer, Manufacturing and Supply Chain, Business Services, and the IT Foundation, which are considered the digital acceleration strategy's four focus areas.

- Digital Customer focuses on improving the customer experience and driving speed for the customer.
- Digital Manufacturing integrates technology using predictive controls in manufacturing and maintenance, automates the warehouse, and provides visibility and control into each supply chain component.
- The Digital Business Services leverages data analytics and state of the art Enterprise Resource Planning (ERP) Tools, Human Resources Information Systems (HRIS) to improve employee experience and productivity.
- IT Foundational Services provide the solid foundation and infrastructure for collaboration, productivity, and security across the organization based on the Armstrong 5A principles: Anytime, Anywhere, Any Device, Always On, Always Available.

Digital Council Members

The Digital Council members include the CEO, CFO, the Chief Information Officer, and all SVPs, and direct report to the CEO.

Kirchner-King shares how the CEO viewed the importance of his digital strategy; "it is imperative to ground our digitalization work primarily in the needs and experiences of our customers. This is where and how we will become a more capable and competitive."[2] One way to accomplish this is to appoint a leader to the Digital Governance Council who has extensive customer experience. The CEO selected Jill Crager, SVP Sales Operations, to lead AWI's Digital Governance. Crager is a 20-year AWI veteran holding various positions that span all areas of the business. Her previous roles included Vice President of National Accounts and Customer and Sales Operations, Manager, Customer Focus Center and Inside Sales, and IT Customer Service. When combined with her undergrad degree in Computer Science, her customer focus at AWI perfectly positioned her to leverage her customer knowledge and technology background on commercial digital transformation initiatives.

As shown in Figure 5.3, the governance model includes Digital (Focus Area) Steering Committees. These committees include business and IT vice-presidents, managers, directors, and subject matter experts with expertise in each focus area. These Digital Steering Committees are also known as Digital Councils.

The Governance Council represents both C-Suite and business executives that enable the digital strategy to be operationalized. The model accurately represents executive sponsorship that spans both executive and operational management. The model also defines specific responsibilities for its members. These details follow.

Governance Council Key Responsibilities

The Enterprise Governance model defines a set of key responsibilities for the Digital Governance Council, IT Organization, and the Digital (Focus Area) Steering Committees.

Provide oversight of digital initiatives and rebalance priorities based on current and changing market conditions and the strategic direction of AWI.

- Evaluate and prioritize digital investments.
- Provide communication and direction to AWI organizations on digital initiatives progress and digital maturity.

IT Organization

Since technology is a key enabler of any digital strategy, the Digital Governance Council identifies the following three primary technology responsibilities.

- Ensure the balance of digital priorities with the broader IT portfolio.
- Optimize technology investments to support digital initiatives.
- Provide technology and project management support for digital advancement within the workstreams. For example, supporting projects for quality or out-of-date equipment which don't have a high return on investment (ROI), but have significant business impact.

Digital (Focus Area) Steering Committees

The Digital Steering Committees provide guidance and operational oversight for each area's programs/projects.

- Oversee focus area workstreams and rebalance priorities.
- Cultivate, prepare, and review program/project business case.
- Evaluate and prioritize programs/projects.
- Provide technology support for workstreams/innovations.

Also, the Steering Committees are responsible for executing the enterprise digital strategy for each of the key areas (Customer, Manufacturing, Business Services, and IT Foundational) with an emphasis on leveraging technology to drive key business outcomes.

The Enterprise Digital Governance model provides the framework, structure, and executive sponsorship for the digital enterprise strategy. With the governance model in place, the next challenge is to drive a collaborative partnership across the various business units and IT to translate the AWI digital strategy into successful operational programs and projects that achieve the AWI business goals.

Business/IT Partnership

"It's important for IT to be a PART of the Business, not merely a partner to the business. Only then can we achieve truly collaborative innovation."[3] – *Dawn Kirchner-King.*

Many organizations that embark on digital transformation include an executive council or steering committee as an excellent first step in establishing executive sponsorship. But talking-the-walk is different than walking-the-talk. The successful implementation of an enterprise digital strategy requires business and IT personnel to work collaboratively. Remember the old days when business units identify a project request and, figuratively, hurl *the project request over the wall to the IT organization to* execute, *waiting for IT to communicate to the business unit. OK, the project is complete.* This just does not work in today's environment where technology plays an ever-important role in business strategy and process. Today business executives recognize that a partnership between the business and IT is required to achieve business strategy successfully. Craig Nadig, Director of Customer Solutions and Business Transformation, works with business personnel to interact with customers regularly to gain insight into their needs. "We work closely with our business unit peers to build trust and develop strategic relationships between IT and the business to improve customer value. June 20, 2019."[4]

AWI is one of these businesses that recognize that a close working relationship between business and IT personnel. AWI accomplishes this by personnel from business units and IT personnel working together in various digital transformation activities. Maintaining Digital Steering Committees, project implementation processes, and including business stakeholders as part of the project team are three key examples of how business and IT personnel partner. Each of these digital transformation activities requires business and IT personnel to not only work together but have joint responsibility in ensuring the digital initiatives are identified and executed successfully. How these two groups work together is explored throughout the rest of the chapter.

As mentioned previously, the Digital Governance Model includes an operational layer that provides for individual Digital Steering Committees for each of four initiatives (customer, manufacturing, business services, and foundation). The teams include personnel from both business units and IT that work collaboratively in executing the digital strategy. Each of the three focus areas teams has their own Digital Steering Committee. For example, the Digital Customer Council includes a business and IT leader who shares responsibility and accountability for ensuring the focus area initiatives and projects are successful. The council also includes subject matter experts (SME) from both the business and IT side to provide the depth of skill required to ensure that its programs and projects are successful. For strategic programs and projects, a separate steering committee is established to provide tactical oversight and guidance. All strategic programs are sponsored by a business leader, governed by a business and IT committee, and led by an IT project manager.

Nadig, a longtime AWI employee, really understands how AWI operates. He has worked in manufacturing, supply chain, logistics, finance, and the IT organization, and has always been customer-focused. *During the past few years, improving the customer experience is a new focus.*[6] Nadig was part of a team that evolved the *customer experience* focus into the three major digital focus areas that drive the AWI digital transformation program. "Once we identified these three major digital focus areas, it was easy to align each of the projects and programs to one of the three. We thought this was the best way to develop the organization's appropriate organizational communication about the projects and programs that improve the customer experience" (Customer, Manufacturing, Business Services).[ibid] The fourth digital focus area, IT Foundation, underpins the entire process and provides the foundation necessary to deliver digital transformation.

The three digital focus areas provide a central framework to improve the customer experience. To ensure that each is successful, a separate working committee for each focus area develops the projects and programs and acts as a steering committee. The SVP of Sales Operations, Jill Crager, reports to the CEO, and Craig leads the Digital Customer Steering Committee. Other committee members include vice presidents from the Sales Organization, Directors from Customer Service, Finance, Product Management, Pricing, and Human Resources.

One of the techniques used by Kirchner-King's organization is the *Gemba Walk*, a process where teams of IT and business personnel get together for a short interactive session.[5] Toyota's process team owners originated the Gemba Walk concept as a means for teams to meet and share project status and learn from each other. At AWI, the objective is to share information about key projects, critical tasks, and milestones, and learn from each other to improve execution processes. "We use it as a collaboration space," says Kirchner-King; "we have daily stand-up Gemba walks. For example, at a recent Gemba Walk, we talked about the service desk for 10 minutes, then we moved into business delivery areas, talked about open items, next actions, etc." adds Kirchner-King.[4] During the pandemic, while employees were working from home, these Gembas have been conducted virtually via Microsoft Teams meetings.

Strategic Alignment

The Customer, Manufacturing, and Business Services initiatives form the basis for strategic digital programs and projects. AWI executives understand that any of these digital programs and associated projects must align with one or more of these digital business initiatives. CEO Vic Grizzle stated that "It is imperative to ground our digitalization work primarily in the needs and experiences of our customers. This is where and how we will become more capable and competitive."[3] AWI accomplishes this using *Customer Journey Maps*. These maps capture positive, negative, or neutral experiences identifying potential new programs and projects. The Customer Journey Map summarizes customer feedback on market trends – customer desires, wants, needs. This information is valuable because, as Kirchner-King describes,

> …Customer Journey Maps identify what we describe as 'Moments that Matter', which are the most critical steps on the customer journey. Get them wrong, and you lose customers. Get them right, and our customers become lifelong advocates. We use the Customer Journey Map process to understand our customers wants and needs. It helps us identify why the customer wants to do business with us, improve our products and services, and leverage technology to drive customer value.[6]

AWI prepares Customer Journey Maps for various customer types. For example, there are Journey Maps for distributors, contractors, and even architecture and design customers; these customer types represent opportunities to create value by improving AWI products and services. Figure 5.4 is an example of one type of customer journey map reflecting feedback from distributor purchases.

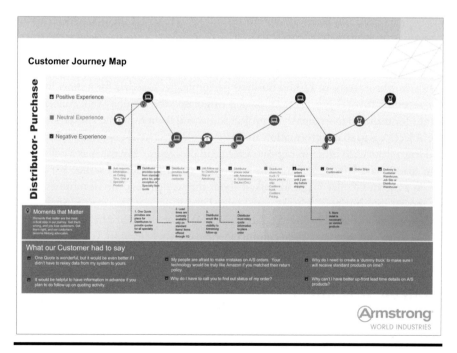

Figure 5.4   Customer journey map-distributor purchases.

Craig Nadig works diligently to understand customers better. "It's all about improving the customer experience. Nadig recognizes that improving customer service in not an internal discussion. "Our discussions are not internal. We always talk directly to customers."[4] Nadig talks about one exciting project.

> We asked ourselves the following questions. How do we improve our relationship with contractors? How can we make their job easier? As a result of a lengthy discussion, we agree that we could digitize the design process to help them visualize the ceilings during their design process. Developing this type of software will make their job easier and is a win-win for us. Our CEO was very interested in this effort and wanted our committee to speed up our efforts. He has challenged us to move more quickly and even asked if we needed more funds to speed up the project. The Customer Journey map is an outcome of our committee work.[ibid]

Nadig and his Focus Area teammates talk to customers regularly:

> We do a lot of preparation for our meetings. During some sessions, we review projects, status updates and prepare for our customer meetings. During a recent week, we had four calls with customers and contractors. We recognize that we cannot improve the customer experience if we do not include the voice of the customer as part of our committee process.[ibid]

The Customer Journey Maps provide potential opportunities for digital projects that will result in innovative new products, processes, and services for customers. Project ideas also emanate from both business and IT organizations. Let's explore how a project idea becomes an official project of the digital transformation initiative.

How an Idea Becomes a Project–Business Relationship Manager Assignments

The Business Relationship Manager role (BRM) is an integral part of the project ideation process. BRMs from the IT organization work closely with business personnel to capture potential project requests and provide project documentation to the appropriate Focus Council. This joint responsibility offers a further example of how AWI integrates business and IT personnel into its day-to-day processes.

IT personnel have multiple roles. Kirchner-King believes that all IT personnel who interface with the business have a BRM responsibility. As a result, Kirchner-King assigns the role of BRM to numerous IT personnel. Figure 5.5 reflects the business areas within AWI and their corresponding BRM role by area. The business teams are segmented by areas of responsibility; for example, operations/

BRM Coverage

Area	Strategic BRM	Business Stakeholder - Executive	Operating brm	Business Stakeholder - Key	Service Delivery Manager	Service Delivery Architect	Key Stakeholders
Go-To-Market / Customer							
Sales -Core Comml / WAVE							
Marketing							
Digital Marketing							
Sales - Arch Specialties							
Sales – Retail/Natl Accts							
Marketing – Residential							
Customer Focus Center							
Transportation							
Price Management							
Architectural Specialties							
AS GTM / Customer							
Operations							
New Business Development							
Sustainability							
Operations/Manufactg/Tech							
Quality / Business Sppt (BOS)							
Supply Chain							
Procurement							
Trade Compliance							
Technology / NPD / AS Ops							
Innovation							
Capital / Engineering							
New Product Development							
Facilities Apps							
Facilities – Conf Rm Tech							

Armstrong WORLD INDUSTRIES

Figure 5.5 BRM coverage assignments.

manufacturing is segmented by quality/engineering, supply chain, procurement and trade compliance.

Strategic BRMs are assigned at the focus area level and aligned to an executive within the business. Operating BRMs are assigned at the segmented level and aligned with a key business stakeholder. Figure 5.5 shows the basics of this alignment along with the alignment of IT Service Delivery Manager and IT Service Delivery Architects.

For example, the first column includes five business areas: Go-To-Market/Customer, Architectural Specialties, New Business Development, Operations/Manufacturing/Technology, and Technology/New Product Development/Architectural Specialties Operations. The vertical columns reflect names of BRMs assigned to these business areas as well seven organization areas the BRMs are assigned to. For example, BRMs have multiple assignments. For example, a BRM may be aligned to both Market Customer and New Business Development areas within his/her primary role as an IT Service Delivery Manager.

The BRM role is an integral part of the business and IT partnership in identifying technology initiatives and partnering with business sponsors and business projects. An example of this is the project request process explained in more detail in the next section.

How an Idea Becomes a Project – the Process

Most businesses have a process for identifying projects. Some only capture a project idea without a level of justification for aligning the project idea with corporate strategy. We all are familiar with what is known as black-box projects, those supported by business unit executives to promote their goals but may not align with the enterprise strategy. Then there are companies at the other end of the spectrum where project alignment is an integral part of the process.

At Armstrong, the Digital Steering Committees gather requirements and cultivate projects. The BRM and the PMO teams work with Digital Steering Committees to complete a cost/benefit analysis and resource planning to recommend the Digital Governance Council on prioritization and approvals. "We review the scorecard, resources, compliance impact, and other issues and make appropriate recommendations to the executive steering committee."[7]

The scorecard AWI uses to evaluate the value of a project is included in Figure 5.6. This is an example of one of the tools used to help prioritize projects; however, it does not represent a final decision on prioritization for strategic initiatives and continues to be refined over time.

The Digital Steering Committee, the PMO, BRM, the IT Service Delivery Manager, and an IT Architect assess the project based on its financial impact, business unit strategic fit, and probability of success. Each of these categories is assigned

Prioritization Scorecard

Financial Impact				
Scale	**Low**	**Medium**	**High**	**Score**
Guideline	Measureable benefits: CIA: NPV < 100K and/or Payback > 2 yrs Un-measureable benefits: Productivity: <= 1000 hrs Audit - Green Gov/Legal - Control Deficiency: <= 1M HW/SW End of Life: >2 years	Measureable benefits: CIA: NPV > 100K and/or Payback 1 > x < 2 yrs Un-measureable benefits: Productivity: 1000 hrs > x < 3000 hrs Audit - Yellow Gov/Legal - Significant Deficiency: 1M < x > 5M HW/SW End of Life: 1-2 years	Measureable benefits: CIA: NPV > 100K and/or Payback < 1 years Un-measureable benefits: Productivity: >= 3000 hrs Audit - Red Gov/Legal - Material Weakness: >= 5M HW/SW End of Life: 0-1 year	
Score	1	2	3	0.00

Business Unit or AI^{2}S Impact				
Scale	**Low**	**Medium**	**High**	**Score**
Guideline	Project not directly tied to Business Unit strategic or operation plans	Project important to compliment Business Unit strategic or operation plans	Project vital to deliver significant Business Unit strategic or operation plans	
Score	1	2	3	0

Probability of Success				
Scale	**Low**	**Medium**	**High**	**Score**
Guideline	Poorly defined process; no clear/weak process owner	Strong Process owner defined, process is evolving	Strong Process owner and well-defined process	
Score	1	2	3	0

SCORE			
Section	**Assessment**	**Weight**	**Component Score**
Financial Impact	0.00	40%	0.00
Business Unit Impact	0.00	30%	0
Prob of Success	0.00	30%	0
SubTotal	*** load Assessment in ServiceNOW***		**0.00**

Armstrong
WORLD INDUSTRIES

Figure 5.6 Prioritization scorecard.

a score of 1 (low impact), 2(medium impact), or 3 (high impact). The scores are summarized, and a total score is calculated and used to help prioritize resources.

Financial Impact: For this category, the metrics are both objective and subjective. The objective metrics that correspond to a low, medium, or high score include Cash in Advance (CIA), and Net Present Value. The subjective metrics include Productivity, Audit, Gov't/Legal, and Hardware/Software end of life.

Business Unit or IT's Impact: A low score equates to projects not directly tied to a business unit's strategic or operational plan. A medium score corresponds to projects that are important components to a business unite strategic or operational plan. A high score corresponds to projects vital to delivering the significant business unit strategic or operational plan.

Probability of Success. A low score equates to projects with a poorly defined process or no clear or weak process owner. A medium score corresponds to projects where a process owner is identified, and the associated process is evolving. A high score corresponds to projects with a strong process owner as well as a well-defined process.

How an idea becomes a project comprises five distinct process phases; Idea Review, Project Cultivation, Prioritization and Approval, Resource Planning, and Project Initiation as depicted in Figure 5.7. Following is a description of each phase.

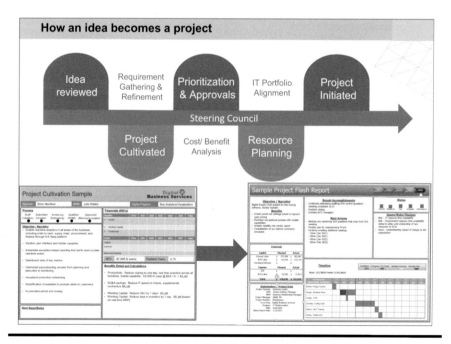

Figure 5.7   How an idea becomes a project.

Project Idea Reviewed and Cultivated

1. Project Ideas are identified and reviewed by the appropriate Digital Steering Committee. If approved, the project idea moves to the project cultivation phase, where business and financial data justification documentation is prepared.
2. In the lower left-hand corner of Figure 5.7, the sample project idea contains the business and financial justification. Please notice that a business sponsor and the BRM prepared the documentation. This particular business case identifies the need for an intuitive user interface and mobile capability using real-time analytics in various business processes that support a new technology platform (e.g. order to cash, supply chain, procurement). Once approved by the Digital Steering Committee, the IT organization prepares a more detailed business case summary and project charter.

Prioritization, Approval, and Resource Planning

3. After approval by the Digital Steering Committee, the IT organization prepares a Project Charter and a Project Appropriation Request (AR) that includes both capital and expense details and scores the project against other competing projects.
4. The IT PMO, BRMs, and Service Delivery Managers (SDMs) meet monthly, first, to review project intake against the existing portfolio, and second, to make recommendations to provide options to the Digital Governance Committee.
5. The approved Project Authorization Request (AR) is circulated through Business and IT authority approvals depending on the size of the project.
6. The Digital Governance Council makes the final decision on the alignment of priorities with the company strategy. They also resolve resource constraints and conflicts by realigning priorities or approving additional resources.

Project Initiation

7. Once approved, the IT department initiates the project, sets the schedule, and prepares the project Flash report, a one-page status report used to report on progress throughout the project's life. See the lower right side of Figure 5.7 for an example.

A Balanced Approach to Strategic Alignment

When I use the terms "strategic alignment" in this book, I refer to a process that ensures that programs and associated projects support the enterprise business strategy. The strategic alignment process at AWI provides a balance to ensure that projects

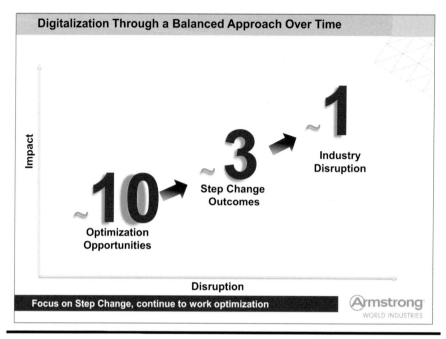

Figure 5.8   Strategic alignment – a balanced approach over time.

align with strategic goals. Figure 5.8 is known within AWI as the 10-3-1 digitalization approach that leverages technology to improve business outcomes through digitalization. The AWI project portfolio consists of approximately 175 projects annually that leverage technology and involves the IT organization. These projects are categorized into ten key program/project *Optimization Opportunities*. The Digital Governance Council also identified *three* key initiatives with *Step Change Outcomes* to drive growth and is still looking for a true industry disruptor.

Kirchner-King describes the importance of strategically aligning projects to business goals and objectives.

> We have approximately ten key initiatives that are aligned and enabled to the Armstrong strategy. These initiatives include multiple projects/programs and may span several months or even years. The entire portfolio of projects is aligned within these initiatives. We optimize our resources to focus on business outcomes that achieve our strategic goals through these initiatives.[8]

Kirchner-King provides an example of a 10-3-1 initiative.

> An example is the Digital Customer initiative. The goal is to leverage technology in integrating the customer in our value chain process.

Kirchner-King talks about how AWI wants to change the construction industry. We want to advance the industry by leveraging technology to improve the entire construction project interaction between the architects, designers, engineers, distributors, contractors, and facility managers. If we can provide value to our customers by improving how they interact with us, we can not only change the industry but also improve Armstrong's growth in the process.[ibid]

Kirchner-King provides another example. We are building an information model for architects and designers at architectural firms so that it is easy for them to include and specify Armstrong products in their designs. "Information from our Customer Journey mapping process identified that when we provide the necessary product information to architects & designers that help them specify Armstrong products, we win the job 7 out of 10 times."[ibid]

Aligning projects to the business strategy can produce significant benefits for your company. It can improve project success rates when project teams recognize that the project aligns with a business strategy and can deliver business value. The project team provides a magnetic focus when they know the project has significant business value. Also, strategically aligning projects to business strategy eliminates wasteful projects that tie up resources, assets, and company finances.

Chapter Summary

This chapter detailed AWI's digital transformation of its governance competencies relating to Executive Sponsorship, Business Unit/IT Partnership, and Strategic Alignment – the first three competencies of the Strategic IT Governance 2.0 model. The next chapter details the transformation relating to Collaboration, Process Optimization, and Best Practice Metrics, the remaining three Strategic IT Governance 2.0 competencies.

Citings

1. Dawn Kirchner-King/Phil Weinzimer interview, December 20, 2019.
2. https://www.prweb.com/releases/phillycio_announces_recipients_of_2020_cio_of_the_year_orbie_awards/prweb17462446.htm
3. Dawn Kirchner-King/Phil Weinzimer interview, December 25, 2019.
4. Craig Nadig/Phil Weinzimer interview. June 16, 2020.
5. https://kanbanzone.com/2020/the-gemba-walk-identify-improvements-at-the-place-where-value-is-created
6. Dawn Kirchner-King/Phil Weinzimer interview, February 12, 2020.
7. Dawn Kirchner-King/Phil Weinzimer interview, February 13, 2020.
8. Dawn Kirchner-King/Phil Weinzimer interview, March 2, 2020.

Chapter 6

How Armstrong World Industries Focus on Collaboration, Process Optimization, and Best Practice Metrics to Implement Digital Transformation Projects

In the previous chapter, we focused on how AWI utilizes executive sponsorship, business/IT partnership, and strategic alignment to identify the key strategic initiatives and associated programs and projects to pursue their goal of digital acceleration. However, projects need to be successfully executed and implemented to succeed at AWIs digital acceleration strategy.

This chapter explores how AWI leverages collaboration, process optimization, and best practice metrics to accomplish this.

DOI: 10.1201/9781003317531-6

Collaboration

A core component of any successful governance methodology is collaboration. Creating a collaborative environment where groups of people work together to produce a defined outcome is more than just issuing an edict or directive for personnel to work together. For collaboration to produce effective results, the participants must actively agree on the desired outcome and process for achieving the desired results and work together.

Business and IT partnerships within AWI are a common practice, as seen in the examples provided. Many organizations view the Information Technology organization as more of a cost center than a value-added business partner. At AWI, the information technology organization is recognized as an equal partner with Sales, Manufacturing, Finance, and Human Resources. Business Relationship Managers work with business partners to identify new project ideas. Business sponsors are an integral part of how an idea becomes a project process. The IT Business Relationship Manager works together to identify and process project requests to the Digital Steering Committees for approval.

Collaboration within AWI is not a task but rather an embedded behavior by all personnel within the company. This is a direct result of the digital enterprise strategy of leveraging technology to improve competitive performance and translate this strategy into tangible actions where personnel across the organization, regardless of organization title, work together in a collaborative environment to achieve the company's business goals objectives.

Every digital initiative program/project involves business and IT personnel. AWI recognizes that digital initiatives will succeed only if business and IT personnel work collaboratively. Earlier, AWI accomplished this through the Digital Governance Council that is referenced in AWI's Governance Model for Digital Acceleration (see Chapter 5, Figure 5.2). The Digital Governance Council's core members include executives, business and functional subject matter experts, and the commercial leader. The extended team consists of separate digital steering committees from the four digital initiatives AWI executives recognized. A collaborative network of business and IT personnel was required for their digital acceleration strategy to succeed.

David Sauder, Manager-IT Portfolio Management, believes collaboration is a key success factor in the digital transformation initiative.

> During our monthly strategy meetings, project managers report of the status of their projects. Attending these meetings is the business sponsor, business relationship manager, and business stakeholders. We involve them and engage stakeholders during the project planning process. For example, all stakeholders have to agree with the requirements during the design phase. It's a collaborative effort during the entire project.[1]

In the previous chapter, I identified how AWI exploits the strategic IT Governance 2.0 model's first three competencies through executive sponsorships, business/IT partnerships, and strategic alignment of projects. We explored how AWI collaborates with customers as well as within the executive and tactical teams. More details on each and how AWI personnel collaborate and work in teams to achieve business outcomes jointly follow.

> Collaborating with Customers: AWI commissioned a study to examine digital usage trends. Also, focus groups of specific customer types discussed their wants, needs, and desires through an interactive process. Collaborating with customers is an essential tool for determining what customers want, exploring their needs, and determining opportunities to identify new ways to create customer value.
>
> Collaboration within Executive and Tactical Councils: The Digital Governance Model integrates business and IT personnel as part of the Digital Governance Council and the Digital Steering Committees. AWI executives realized that was the only way to achieve the digital acceleration strategy and change personnel's culture and behaviors.

Process Optimization

Process optimization is a critical component of a Strategic IT Governance 2.0 model. Improving governance processes results in improved efficiencies in executing governance activities. These processes define the activities that support the governance process and enable personnel to follow a defined set of activities from project identification through deployment and project value realization. Several approaches to optimizing governance processes eliminate redundant activities, streamline workflows, and improve communications.

AWI team supports the project lifecycle, and many examples are shared. The best way to share these examples is to categorize the governance processes AWI optimized into the following three distinct categories; Project Methodology, Tools, and Techniques, Project Administration Structure, and Project Execution.

Project Methodology, Tools, and Techniques

Kirchner-King and her team developed a robust project management methodology and associated processes. Following is an overview of the project methodology framework and some underlying processes supporting the methodology.

The AWI methodology, 5th Dimension™, is very robust and instructive. It includes five phases of project management; define, design, develop, deliver, and

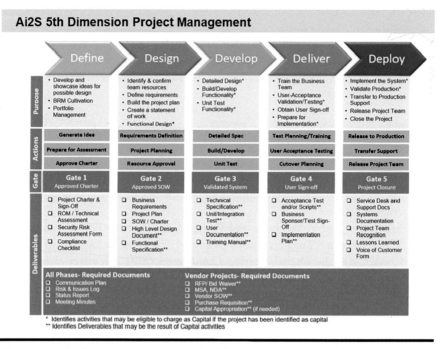

Figure 6.1 Project management methodology.

deploy (see Figure 6.1). Each phase includes a purpose, key actions, associated phase gate, and key deliverables. Please note the list of documents required for each project. These include a communication plan, risk and issues log, status reports, and meeting minutes. If a vendor is involved, the required documents include a Request for Proposal, Bid Waiver, Master Services Agreement or Non-Disclosure Agreement, Statement of Work or a Letter of Engagement, purchase requisition, and capital appropriation if required.

Similar to many software developments and project life cycles, AWI's 5th Dimension, has phases and stage gates for requirements: Definition (Define), Project Design (Design), Programming and Development Tasks (Develop), User Acceptance and Implementation (Deliver). The big difference in Armstrong's methodology is the Deploy phase. Kirchner-King says, "The Deploy phase is the differentiation and follows the project past go-live and through hyper-care. This allows us to close a project and truly realize project benefits before moving onto the next objective."[2]

Many PMOs provide a multi-phase methodology as an excellent first step. The challenge is always whether program managers provide the necessary follow-through in implementing each phase.

Roles and Responsibilities

One of the challenges in any enterprise initiative is identifying personnel's activities, responsibilities, and accountabilities. The process to overcome this challenge is to create a matrix that identifies the roles and responsibilities of personnel involved in the initiative.[3] The most common matrix used is named a RACI chart, where each letter represents a defined personnel function (**R**esponsible, **A**ccountable, **C**onsulted, **I**nformed). Figure 6.2 is the RACI chart that AWI uses, and following is a description for each role. Below is a commonly used definition for each of these roles.

- **Responsible:** People or stakeholders who do the work. They must complete the task or objective or make the decision. Several people can be jointly *Responsible*.
- **Accountable:** Person or stakeholder who is the "owner" of the work. He or she must sign off or approve when the task, objective, or decision is complete. This person must make sure that responsibilities are assigned in the matrix for all related activities. Success requires that there is only one person *Accountable*, which means that "the buck stops there."

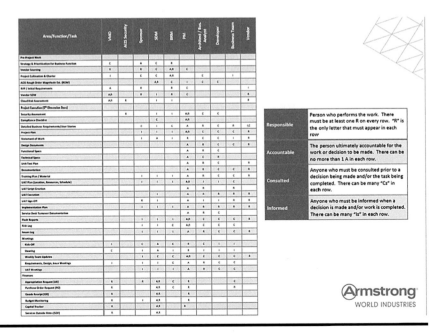

Figure 6.2   RACI diagram.

■ **Consulted:** People or stakeholders who need to give input before the work can be done and signed-off on. These people are "in the loop" and active participants.
■ **Informed:** People or stakeholders who need to be kept "in the picture." They need updates on progress or decisions, but they do not need to be formally consulted or contribute directly to the task or decision.

The AWI RACI Diagram defines all of the area, functions, and tasks and the associated RACI responsibility.

Project Administration Structure

Communication Plan

The AWI communication plan identifies the categories of project stakeholders and the communication opportunity, frequency, and media used for the communication. Figure 6.3 provides information for each type and is a valuable tool for project managers.

The communication plan template identifies the stakeholder types that need communication. More details on the communication types follow.

Stakeholder	Opportunity	Frequency	Media
Customers	Sales/Marketing per usual	Ongoing	Multiple
	Digitalization Launch(es)	Bi-Annual	Per usual
	Newsletters	TBD	Article/Infographic
	Salesperson talking points	Monthly	PowerPoint/WORD
	VOC/Focus Groups	TBD	TBD
Employees	All-Employee Meetings	Quarterly	PowerPoint
	LookUp Articles	Monthly +	LookUP
	Posters/Awareness	Quarterly	Posters/tent cards, etc.
	Direct Emails	Monthly +	Email
	Staff meeting talking points	Monthly +	PowerPoint/WORD
	CEO communication	Quarterly	Email
	Dashboards/Metrics	Real-time	Multiple/PowerPoint
	VOC Surveys	TBD	Survey Monkey & Other
	Focus Groups	TBD	TBD
Committees	Monthly/quarterly meetings	As needed	PowerPoint/WORD
	Dashboards/Metrics	Real-time	Multiple/PowerPoint
Board	BOD Meeting	Quarterly	BOD Meeting Presentation
Multiple	10-30 second talk tracks	As needed	WORD/Email
Investors	Investor Day	Annual	Meeting with IR Team
	IR Team Touchpoints	Quarterly	PowerPoint

Alignment of messaging, media and frequency in progress

Ⓐrmstrong
WORLD INDUSTRIES

Figure 6.3   Communication plan.

Customers are an important stakeholder in the communication plan, and there are many opportunities to provide valuable information on technology initiatives that impact them. Digital media, newsletters, focus groups, and other voice-of-the-customer interactions provide a unique opportunity to communicate regularly. Communicating to customers about how AWI provides improved customer value promotes the AWI brand and reflects its key strategy of innovating ways to provide new and improved products and services.

Employees require various touchpoints in terms of the target audience for communication, communication frequency, and media type. Projects impact how AWI operates on a day-to-day basis, and it is imperative that personnel understand the business value of projects and how these projects impact their daily activities and improve business performance.

Committees exist in every company and provide an opportunity for communicating projects that impact their activities. Committees usually meet weekly, monthly, quarterly, semi-annually, or even annually and each of these events provides an opportunity to communicate the status of digital initiatives.

Investors only need to be communicated on an annual or quarterly basis through presentations at annual meetings or quarterly newsletters. Providing communication to investors provides insight into how AWI is leveraging technology to improve its competitive position and improve shareholder value. All Communication to Investors is done through collaboration with the Investor Relationship team at AWI.

The AWI Communication Plan provides a standard template and process for project communication and enables a collaborative process that includes all project stakeholders, regardless of organization. Remember, technology projects impact the entire enterprise, and AWI projects integrate key stakeholders into the project management process. Kirchner-King's goal is to provide "...a transparent process, so all stakeholders are aware of project status and avoid the chasm that sometimes occurs between business units and the IT organization."[3]

Team Documentation

One of the many challenges for a project team is storing project documentation. To ensure consistency and ease of accessing project information.

Kirchner-King's team developed a standard file folder structure to store all project documents to ensure consistency and ease of availability. This enables anyone on the project team, PMO, or personnel to access project documents consistently.

The folder structure is simple. It consists of team folders based upon the organization and subfolders for each sponsoring organization based upon specific project topics. Figure 6.4 reflects a Teams Site folder structure.

As you can see, the Team Folders comprise the sponsoring project organization (Customer Experience, Supply Chain, Manufacturing, Finance, HR/Payroll,

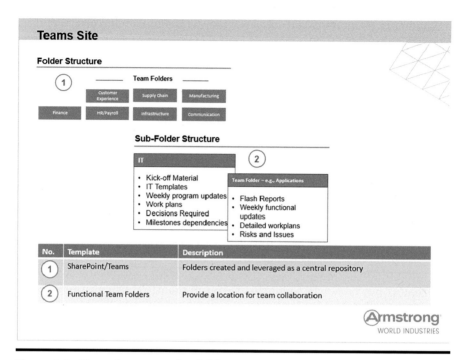

Figure 6.4   Team documentation folder structure.

Infrastructure, and Communication). And for each sponsoring organization, a sub-folder structure exists for specific IT project topics, e.g., kick-off materials, IT Templates work plans, and project information, such as flash reports, weekly updates, work plans, risks, and issues.

Organizing a file folder structure for project documentation provides the uniformity, consistency, and transparency necessary for easy access of project information. This structure helps personnel on the project team gain quick access to needed project data and provides project status to personnel across the organization.

Project Execution

The AWI Project Management methodology requires specific documentation for every project. These include a risk and issues log, status reports, and meeting minutes. To aid program managers (PMs) in accomplishing this, Kirchner-King's PMO team developed templates that PMs can utilize. Following are template examples.

Status Reports/Flash Reports

Project Managers are responsible for preparing a status report and reporting on progress for every project. Figure 6.5 is an example of the status report that AWI uses.

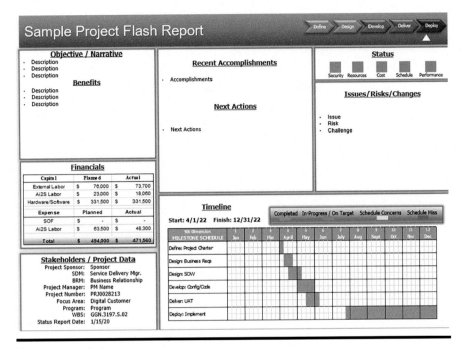

Figure 6.5 Flash report.

The one-page update includes background and expected benefits, project financials, recent accomplishments, next steps, unmitigated risks and issues, and a brief project timeline.

Issue Log and Dashboard Updates

Project Managers are responsible for preparing a risk and issue log for every project. Figure 6.6 is an example of an issue log and dashboard update.

Pertinent issue data is captured, such as the functional team's issues and dependencies, the owners, required actions, and potential impact on the business. The issue log also identifies the risk types and resolution action items.

The dashboard identifies a risk profile in a 2 × 2 matrix that provides a risk profile represented using a bar chart that reflects the number of issues categorized by low, moderate, high, very high, and extreme. An additional bar chart categorizes the potential pre-mitigation impact for each risk as insignificant, minor, moderate, major, severe, or catastrophic. The bar chart also associates the probability of the risk impact occurring based upon extremely rare, rare, unlikely, possible, likely, almost certain.

The issue log and risk profile dashboard provides the type of information needed by program managers, the PMO, steering committee, and Digital Steering

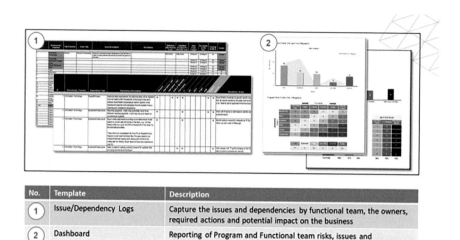

No.	Template	Description
1	Issue/Dependency Logs	Capture the issues and dependencies by functional team, the owners, required actions and potential impact on the business
2	Dashboard	Reporting of Program and Functional team risks, issues and dependency profiles, including outstanding items and key items for resolution

Figure 6.6   Issue log and dashboard updates.

Committee to assess the potential risk associated with projects. It also reflects the project teams' oversight in identifying and assessing potential project risk.

Project Steering Committee

In addition to the Digital Steering Committee oversight, a project steering committee may be established if the project is of significant value or has significant strategic impact. The Digital Steering Committee, the PMO, BRM, the IT Service Delivery Manager, and an IT Architect assess the project's need for a project steering committee based on its financial impact, business unit strategic fit, and probability of success. Each of these categories is assigned a score of 1 (low impact), 2 (medium impact), or 3 (high impact). The scores are summarized, and a total score is calculated and entered in the AWI ServiceNow application that stores project data (see Figure 5.5 from the previous chapter).

Supplier Management

As technology becomes a more complex digital transformation initiative, companies rely upon suppliers to provide the technology and consultant services. AWI relies on suppliers to provide technology and consulting services. Brent Lewis is responsible for Supplier/Vendor Management

> We try to choose strategic suppliers as part of an ongoing relationship. It's not always easy to find the right partner. Our goal is to develop a strategic partnership, where the supplier truly understands our issues and how their capabilities can provide value to AWI.[4]

Historically, AWI utilized suppliers to provide technology hardware and software. Lewis describes why the need for strategic suppliers at AWI. "Now, as software applications are more complex, we need to rely on suppliers, who have deep competencies in these complex technologies, that will enable AWI to meet its strategic digital goals."[ibid.]

Supplier/Vendor Classification

AWI categorizes suppliers/vendors into one of four categories: Strategic, Emerging, Tactical, and Legacy, as described by the quadrant in Figure 6.7.

AWI uses the following guidelines for classifying suppliers/vendors. The team also uses the classifications to determine the schedule of quality business reviews with suppliers/vendors.

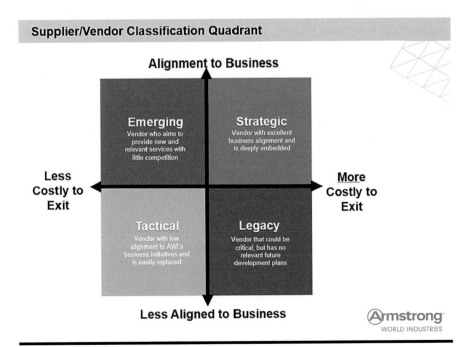

Figure 6.7   Vendor classification.

Emerging Supplier/Vendor

Vendors classified as Emerging normally provide a service or solution that is new to the marketplace where the market competition is minimal. They should be looking to drive innovative solutions into AWI's business initiatives that will give our organization a competitive advantage through early adoption.

When trying to classify an Emerging vendor, ask the following questions:

- Are the products and services provided by the vendor new to the marketplace?
- Are the vendors' products and services able to drive innovation and align with our future business model?
- Benchmark the vendor. (This type of research can be completed with Gartner and other research firms.) What level of competition does this vendor have in the marketplace?
- Do we foresee a long-term relationship developing from this engagement?

Conduct Quarterly Quality Business Review

Strategic Supplier/Vendor

Vendors classified as Strategic normally provide a service or solution that is in excellent alignment to our business requirements and has a deeply embedded set of services (large-scale asset lifecycle, enterprise software, etc.). They are commonly identified by the size of AWI's investment with them.

When trying to classify a Strategic vendor ask the following questions:

- Does the vendor have a deep understanding of our business requirements?
- Are the products and services provided by the vendor mission critical to the business?
- What level of spend does this vendor represent to our business?
- How difficult would it be to exit the relationship and shift to an alternative supplier?
- Does the vendor understand our future business model and is willing to innovate and promote our business goals?

Conduct Quarterly or Semi-Annual Quality Business Review

Tactical Supplier/Vendor

Vendors classified as Tactical normally have low alignment to AWI's business initiatives, are a commodity provider, and represent a low spend relationship or provide services or goods in a market that is saturated with competitors.

When trying to classify a Tactical vendor ask the following questions:

- Are the vendors' products and services readily available from others in the marketplace?
- Does the vendor mission-critical provide the products and services to AWI's business initiatives?
- What level of spending does this vendor represent to our business?
- How difficult would it be to exit the relationship and shift to an alternative supplier?
- Is it possible for this vendor to shift into an Emerging vendor role based on their products and services supplied?

Conduct Annual Quality Business Review if spend is in excess of $50k.

Legacy Supplier/Vendor

As technology has advanced, we find the vendor's drive and commitment to continue developing the relationship and business model is waning. Vendors classified as Legacy may vary from deeply embedded in business-critical legacy systems to smaller components. This is commonly found in legacy software systems that are targeted for replacement. When trying to classify a Legacy vendor, ask the following questions:

- Are the vendors' products and services a part of the company's five-year future business model?
- Does the vendor understand our future business model and is willing to innovate and promote our business goals?
- How difficult would it be to exit the relationship and shift to an alternative supplier?
- Does an exit strategy already exist for this vendor's product or services?

Conduct Annual Quality Business Review.

Supplier/Vendor Scorecard

As vendors become a more integral part of the project delivery team, the team realized a need for a process to assess four critical vendor capabilities; strategic fit, performance, risk, and relationship. To accomplish this, the team uses a Vendor Scorecard to assess these key areas.

As you can see from Figure 6.8 the Vendor Scorecard includes four categories (Strategic Fit, Performance, Risk, Relationship). Each of the four categories represents 25 percent of the total rating. And each category includes specific criteria, a

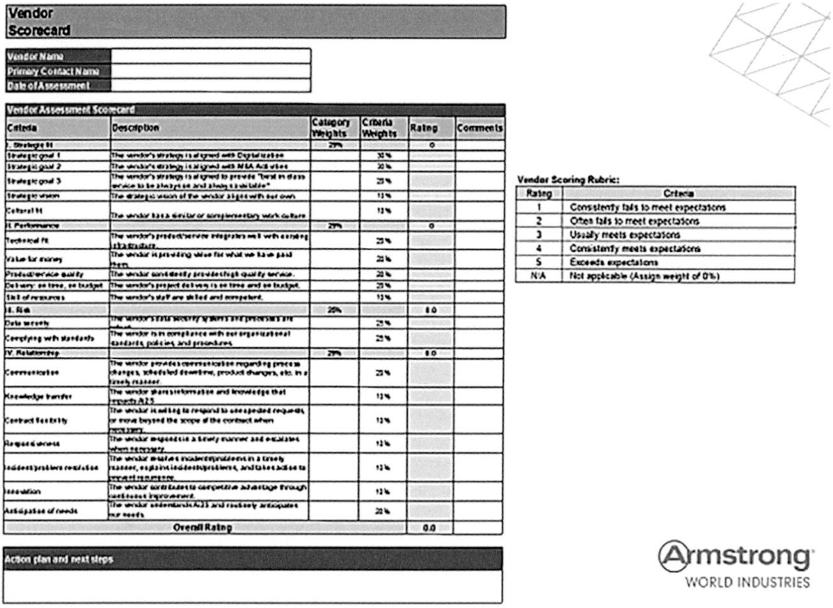

Figure 6.8 Supplier/vendor scorecard.

description, and an assigned criteria weight percentage. From a process perspective, Lewis's goal focuses on the "…top 20 percent of suppliers which is also aligned with our strategic vendors."[ibid.] This is identified by spend with a given supplier. Note that AWI spend distribution follows the Pareto principle, where 80% of IT spend is attributable to 20% of the total suppliers.

The Supplier/Vendor Scorecard is completed by business and IT stakeholders and reviewed at least annually with each supplier. The Quality Business Review attendees include supplier representatives and from AWI- the Service Delivery Manager (SDM), the Director of the Office of the CIO, Lewis, and other critical stakeholders that utilize the supplier's services.

The Supplier Scorecard assessment and supplier QBRs are helpful. Lewis describes why.

> Most people do not like confrontations. The Supplier Scorecard process enables us to *share the assessment findings with each supplier, and have an open and productive dialogue to identify the improvement areas for both AWI and the supplier that result in optimal value.*[ibid]

Seisan, one of AWIs strategic suppliers, is a local consulting company headquartered in Lancaster, Pennsylvania. John Brabazon is Sr. Manager, Customer Solutions at

AWI and has held roles in AWI as a Project Manager and Digital Experience Team Leader. Brabazon manages the relationship with Seisan. Brabazon describes the relationship as follows.

> We started our relationship with Seisan about 2012 when we decided to look for local resources to replace some offshore resources. We were looking for a company that we could develop a long-term strategic relationship. We recognized that offshore supplier rates were less expensive than onshore suppliers, but we needed to focus on quality and overall responsiveness to our business needs. We built a pretty good business case that a local partner would work better for us and Seisan proved to be a valuable partner. They met all their estimates, and the quality of work far exceeded that of our offshore partner.[5]

The relationship started with some Web design work that proved to be excellent. AWI followed up with additional technology projects that supported Seisan's vision statement; "we believe in the power of technology to add massive value to your business."[ibid]

"Seisan has become a true strategic partner. They help us by providing developers, supporting our break-fix activities, and providing programmers for our digital project work. They are integrated into our business as they understand our business strategy, our operational tactics and support our needs regularly."

Meeting Cadence

Meetings should have a purpose. David Sauder, Sr. Manager, IT Portfolio Management, talks about the weekly project review meetings. "Every Wednesday, we have a project review meeting attended by the project managers, business sponsors, business relationship managers, and other key stakeholders. We hold the session for 45 minutes and focus on five to 10 projects each week. This provides us enough time for the project manager and business sponsor to provide a fairly detailed review and status of each project."[1]

Craig Nadig, who co-leads the Customer Digital Steering Committee, talks about the importance of their team meetings. "We make sure that the committee meetings are very focused. We do a lot of meeting preparation. We try and schedule meetings every six to eight weeks. One of our initiatives is to explore how we can improve the way customers request design services. Following are some of the questions we want to answer."[6]

> *How do we digitize the ceiling design process so we can more effectively engage with customers?*
> *How do we develop a stronger relationship with our customers?*
> *How do we engage with become a strategic partner with our customers?*

How can we improve our relationships with contractors?
How can we shorten the sales cycle?

Kirchner-King believes that "meetings facilitate timely communication and resolution of issues, dependencies, and decisions."[2] The PMO team developed a sample Meeting Cadence schedule to establish regular, meaningful progress, as shown in Figure 6.9. This cadence reflects the need for both strategic and tactical meetings.

This cadence reflects the need for both strategic and tactical meetings. From a strategic perspective, the Digital Governance Council meets monthly to set strategy and prioritization. The Digital Steering Committees meet every 6–8 weeks to cultivate new projects and review progress against in-flight projects. Capital Planning is completed monthly with the Chief Information Officer, the Project Management Office (PMO) Leader, Service Delivery Managers (SDM), and Business Relationship Managers (BRM). At a more tactical level, the PMO, BRMs, and SDMs meet monthly to discuss project prioritization. At this meeting, BRMs communicate the background and strategy for project intake and help to make recommendations for prioritization of resources. A week later in the month, the PMO lead and the SDMs meet to review resource plans, address constraints, and assign project managers. The project review meeting is held weekly and allows all projects across the IT portfolio of projects to be reviewed by the collective team at least once monthly.

PMO Monthly Meeting Cadence

		Week 1	Week 2	Week 3	Week 4
STRATEGIC	**Digital Governance Committee** *Strategy Alignment*			Executive Staff	
	Digital Steering Committees *Cultivation of Projects*				Business Leaders BRM *Every 6-8 weeks*
	Capital Planning *Alignment of Capital Spend*	CIO PMO Lead SDMs/BRMs			
TACTICAL	**Portfolio Review** *Project Intake/ Priortization*		PMO BRMs SDMs		
	Resource Planning *Alignment of Resources/ IT Planning*			PMO Lead SDMs	
	Project Review Meetings	PMO BRMs SDMs	PMO BRMs SDMs	PMO BRMs SDMs	PMO BRMs SDMs

(A)rmstrong WORLD INDUSTRIES

Figure 6.9 Meeting cadence.

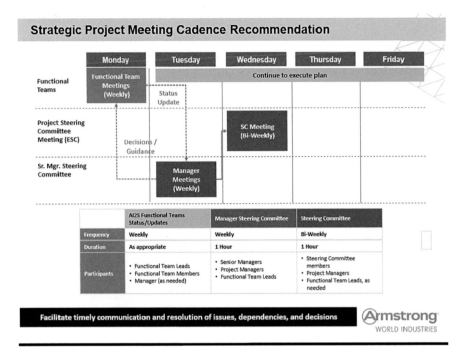

Figure 6.10   Strategic project meeting cadence.

The PMO team developed a recommended meeting cadence for large projects, as shown in Figure 6.10.

The meeting cadence guidelines provide a structure for the various meetings required on a large program initiative. The meeting cadence template identifies the suggested duration of the meetings as well as the participants. For example, Functional Teams meet weekly on Mondays, Steering Committee meets biweekly on Wednesdays, and the Manager Steering Committee meets weekly on Tuesdays.

As mentioned previously, the PMO provides the structure, practices, tools, and methodologies used by the personnel involved in executing and managing projects. The meeting cadence template provides a framework for the various key meetings that maintain a rhythm to the various team meetings.

Digital Roadmap

To provide the Digital Governance Council a plan for digital initiatives, Kirchner-King's PMO prepares a Digital Roadmap of key initiatives currently on target to plan for schedule and resources for each of the three digital initiatives (Customer, Manufacturing, and Foundation).

For each of the digital initiatives, key project timelines reflect significant project activities across four years. Figure 6.11 is an example of a digital roadmap

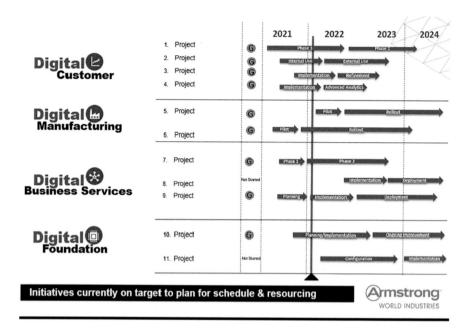

Figure 6.11 Digital roadmap.

template used. You will note that a color-coded status of projects reflects a green, yellow, or red status. In the template example, all projects are green except for two that have not started.

Compliance Checklist

The PMO developed a Compliance Checklist that identifies the documents required for each project phase and its purpose (see Figure 6.12), whether it is required (yes/no), and completion status. The Compliance Checklist's objective is to ensure that project teams reduce potential risk by following the project methodology. By identifying the required documents for each project stage, the project manager and project team have a roadmap of the documents needed, eliminating any missteps in the project execution process.

As you read through the document, you will notice that it is very detailed. It identifies the documents required for each of the six project phases, define, design, develop, deliver, and deploy, as well as documents required for *All Stages*. The checklist also includes document requirements for those projects that include capital appropriation and vendor involvement. Spend a few minutes reading the required documentation. You will realize that this checklist is comprehensive by identifying the needed documentation. Remember, project risk is one of the significant

Project Name:
Date:

Compliance Checklist

Stage	Document	Purpose	Required	Complete
Define	Project Charter	In the ServiceNow Demand, define Scope of the project (what, why)	Yes	
	ROM	Estimated cost of the project (how much)	Yes	
	Project Assessment	Document & help identifying Security Risks, SOX Implications & Technical needs of each project	Yes	
	Compliance Checklist	Documents required to meet project audit	Yes	
Design	Business Requirements	Expand on the project charter & list bulleted functional & non-functional requirements (what)		
	Project Plan	Tasks, milestones, dependencies, resources, hours & dates (how, when)		
	SOW	Delivery date, resources, hours & cost (who, when, how much)	Yes	
	High Level Design Document	Provide development team an overall picture of system architecture (how)		
	Functional Specification	Detailed specifications for program that will be developed (how)		
Develop	Technical Specification	Document programming work to assist in future support of code changes or trouble-shooting (how)		
	Unit/Integration Test Plan	Identify tests that will be done by A2S to validate the system		
	Updated SOX Narratives	Ensure SOX narratives are updated by owners	Yes	
	Define Change Management Process	Ensure a process is in place with any new application to identify changes moving to production w/change requestor, description of change, tester, change approver and dates.		
	User Documentation	Documentation that can be used by the business to understand UI fields & flows of system		
	Training Documentation	When A2S is providing training to the business		
Deliver	Acceptance Test Plan	Plan to identify business resources & test scenarios that will be used to validate project success		
	Business Sponsor/Test Sign-Off	E-mail approval from the business sponsor to accept the test results & approve implementation	Yes	
	Training Documentation	List of users trained on an application, training topic, date and type of access (read, write, etc.)		
	Implementation Plan	Detailed list of tasks to be executed for implementing the new system		
	SOX Implications Sign-Off	E-mail confirmation from SOX Narrative owner that controls were tested & SOX Narrative updated. Update SOX tab in ServiceNow Demand to reflect ServiceNow SOX review date and SOX approved by	Yes	
Deploy	Turnover Document	Communication to the Service Desk making them aware of a system change. Work with SD Member to fill out	Yes	
	Systems Documentation	A document to define the system architecture & flows to allow future support of the sytem		
	User Access Review (UAR)	Review all user access to ensure access requested = access granted		
	Project Close Out	Close ServiceNow Project, add implementation date to SN, close financials, ensure all issues are remediated	Yes	
	Project Team Recognition	Award from for anyone that went above & beyond on the project		
	Lessons Learned	Discussion & document to describe things that could have been done better during Project		
	Voice of Customer Form	Discussion with the Project Sponsor for customer satisfaction		
All Stages	Communication Plan	A plan to keep the steering committee, project sponsor & IT management up to date		
	RAID Log	Define risks, actions, issues and decisions that occur during the entire life-cycle of the project		
	Flash Report	Regularly updated Flash Report to share with the Project Sponsor		
	Meeting Minutes	Discussions, actions, next steps that occur during the meeting		
Capital & Vendor	Capital Appropriation	Get approval for the capital		
	MSA, NDA	Service agreement & non-disclosure agreement with Vendor		
	Vendor SOW	Defines work to be done, timing & cost		
	Bid Waiver	Reason we are not getting a competitive bid		
	Purchase Requisition	Approval to purchase services, hardware, etc.		

Armstrong
WORLD INDUSTRIES

Figure 6.12 Compliance checklist.

challenges for any project, especially a digital transformation project that leverages, in some cases, entirely new technology. The Compliance Checklist is a coach and mentor process that helps the team manage projects and make sure that all required documents are available for audit.

Tools for Managing Projects

One of the PMOs' significant responsibilities is providing processes, templates, and tools project managers and their teams utilize in executing projects. Identifying these processes provides consistency across the PMO of managing projects and the oversight needed to ensure project success. Every PMO organization includes project managers with varying skills and experience in managing projects. Experienced project managers have the insight and expertise, but project managers that do not have these skills need guidance and mentoring.

The PMO team provides a template that identifies the types of Tools for Managing Projects. Figure 6.13 is an example of such a template.

The template identifies the categories of tools the project manager must use in managing projects. These include flash reports, work plans, issue and dependency logs, and status reports that project managers use to manage projects. For each of these tools, the template provides a description, due date, where to file the associated

	PM Flash Reports	Workplans	Issue / Dependency Logs	Status Reports
Description	**Summary of Project Status** including key milestones and appropriate statuses, outstanding risks, issues, and dependencies	A comprehensive tool to help Functional Teams identify **key tasks**, execute against targeted activities and hold team members accountable	Enables functional teams to uniformly **track and manage issues and dependencies** through to resolution	**Summary of program status** including key accomplishments, plans for next period, upcoming milestones, outstanding risks, issues, and dependencies
Due	Mondays, 8:00 AM	Tuesdays, 12:00 PM	Tuesdays, 12:00 PM	Tuesdays, 12:00 PM
Deliver By	Load into Teams site URL: _insert link_			
Prepared By	Project/Program Manager	Functional designee or project/program manager	Functional designee or project /program manager	Program Manager
Used In	Sr. Mgr. Meeting and Weekly PM Meeting	Functional Team/Sub-team Meetings	Functional Team/Sub-team Meetings	ESC Meeting
Format	PowerPoint	Excel	Excel	PowerPoint

Figure 6.13   Tools for managing the project.

documents, who prepares each document, how it is used, and its associated format. Following is a description for each tool as reflected in the template.

> PM Flash Reports summarize *project status*, including key milestones and appropriate statuses, outstanding risks, issues, and dependencies.
> Workplans are a comprehensive tool to help functional teams identify the *key tasks*, executed against targeted activities, and hold team members accountable.
> Issue and Dependency Logs enable functional teams to track and manage issues and dependencies through to resolution uniformly.
> Status Reports provide a summary of the program(s), including key accomplishments, plans for the next period, upcoming milestones, outstanding risks, issues, and dependencies.

Deliverables: Workplans and Flash Reports

The PMO created a set of work plans and flash report templates that project teams utilize to update project status. David Sauder Manager-IT Portfolio Management, says that "…Issuing flash reports and issue and risk logs provides visibility and transparency to stakeholders on project progress."[1]

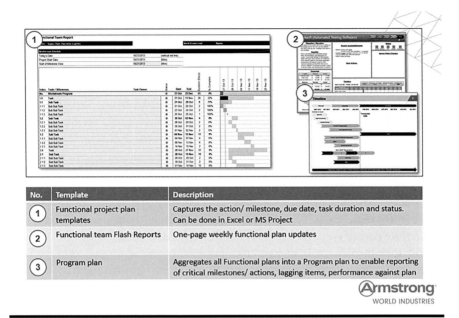

No.	Template	Description
(1)	Functional project plan templates	Captures the action/ milestone, due date, task duration and status. Can be done in Excel or MS Project
(2)	Functional team Flash Reports	One-page weekly functional plan updates
(3)	Program plan	Aggregates all Functional plans into a Program plan to enable reporting of critical milestones/ actions, lagging items, performance against plan

Figure 6.14 Deliverables: workplans and flash reports.

Figure 6.14 reflects examples of three types of templates project teams

Functional project plans capture the activities and milestones for a project and the due dates for these activities, task duration, and the current status. Most project teams utilize Microsoft Project as the application of choice and its import capability into project portfolio management applications (PPM) such as Planview, Oracle, ServiceNow, and SAP.

Functional team flash reports provide a snapshot overview of a project in a single slide. The project objective, a short narrative describing the project, and key financials are described on the left side of the template, while any recent accomplishments, next-step actions, a summary of the issues and risks associated with the project, and a timeline reflecting key project plan milestones. are described on the right side of the template.

The *program plan* aggregates all of the functional plans into an overall program that identifies the key workstreams and their associated activity dates. Examples include the program approach, high-level planning, detailed planning workstreams, and other program workstreams.

When projects are part of an overall program, it is essential to update management on the overall program status. The program plan template enables project managers to prepare a snapshot for all the key workstreams, timelines, and performance against the plan in a single slide. Updating management on the overall program status is necessary as it provides the visibility management requires in determining the status of the overall program and its associated projects.

Figure 6.15 is an additional example of a flash report template that provides summary information for a specific project ready for deployment. The flash report includes financial, stakeholders, project data, and timeline information. You will also note a status section where red, yellow, or green indicates security, resources, cost, schedule, and performance status.

Change Request Process

Figure 6.16 reflects the PMO process for processing change requests. Change requests are part of every project and can affect a product, process, service, or application. They involve scope changes, technology changes, additional tasks required within project scope, vendor changes, etc. To ensure that any request for changes is relevant to the project, the PMO created a *Change Request Process* to manage every change request's submission, review, and approval.

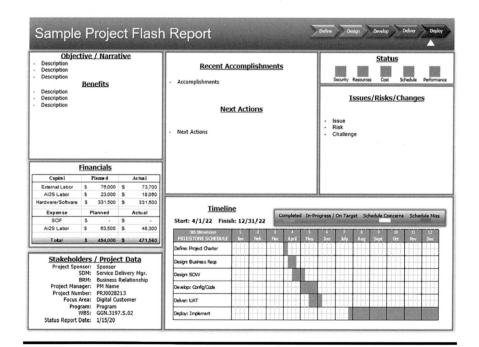

Figure 6.15   Flash project status report.

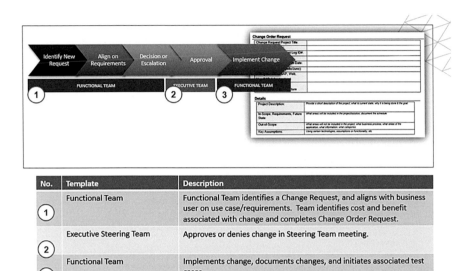

No.	Template	Description
1	Functional Team	Functional Team identifies a Change Request, and aligns with business user on use case/requirements. Team identifies cost and benefit associated with change and completes Change Order Request.
2	Executive Steering Team	Approves or denies change in Steering Team meeting.
3	Functional Team	Implements change, documents changes, and initiates associated test cases.

Figure 6.16 Change request process.

The *Change Request Process* identifies the following five phases: identify new requests, align on requirements, decision or escalation, approval, and implement change. The change request must have the concurrence of the business user to determine its business alignment. The request must also include relevant information regarding the description of the change, cost and benefit information, whether the change request is within or outside of the original project scope.

When completed, the requestor forwards the change request to the Executive Steering Team, for review, approval, or disapproval. Once approved, the functional team can implement the change.

Having a formal change request process ensures that everyone involved in the project understands the purpose of the change, its business value, and its impact on the project's overall success.

Project Closing Steps

Project teams are not always diligent in performing project closure activities. To help project teams perform their due diligence in closing a project, Sauder and his team developed a Project Closure Steps document that identifies the specific closure activities required (see Figure 6.17).

Project Closure Checklist

	Task	Completion Date/Notes
1	Make sure you have all User Sign-Offs filed in your Project SharePoint Site from the implementation	
2	Make sure you've communicated the change to the Service Desk (if necessary)	
3	Review your Compliance Checklist and make sure all required 5th Dimension documentation has been filed in your Service Now SharePoint site along with training and user documentation	
4	In your flash report, make sure it is showing the project in the Deploy phase. The timeline should be blue to show that it has been completed up to the project closure date	
5	In ServiceNow, change the Project Phase to "Deploy" and change the Project State to "Closed Complete"	
6	In ServiceNow, Dates tab, update the "Actual Implementation Date" to show the date you first implemented your project	
7	Change Project Status on SharePoint Documentation to "Closed" by right clicking on the Project Site or Document Set & select "Properties". Change Project Status to "Closed"	
8	If needed send a note to IT Supplier Management to reduce & close any Purchase Orders	
9	For Capital Projects send email to Melissa Rogati informing her of Beneficial Use Date and asking for the appropriate steps to be taken to close AR. Melissa may have additional questions	

10	Financials Checklist
	   System Operational?
	   All Good Receipts posted?
	   All Invoices Posted?
	   Commitments Zero?	

(A)rmstrong WORLD INDUSTRIES

Figure 6.17   Project closing steps.

Best Practices Metrics

Measuring the benefits of projects through a metric-based performance process is important in determining projects' business value. AWI captures project metrics at the project team level by measuring the traditional financial, milestone adherence, and schedule. Also, the PMO provides a series of reports to the Digital Steering Committees and Digital Governance Council that reflect the projects' business value.

Metrics are not always numbers. Metrics can also include helpful information leveraged on future projects. This is why the PMO also captures completed project data, such as issue and risk logs, in a Lessons Learned Library as part of the Compliance Checklist process. How is the Lessons Learned Library used? As Kirchner-King explains,

> For a merger acquisition project, I can access the library and see what issues, risks, and mitigation actions occurred that we could leverage on a current or new acquisition project. The Lessons Learned Library is a useful tool, and the PMO reviews every Compliance Checklist to ensure we properly capture project data so it can be of value for future projects.[2]

Benefit Metrics

Since digital transformation is a significant strategy, AWI updates its executive teams and investors via a simple one-page slide that communicates key metrics from its investments in the digital transformation program. Figure 6.18 reflects each initiative's digital initiative key metrics (Customer, Manufacturing, Business Services). These metrics reflect the projects for operational savings, net sales and cost of goods sold, if appropriate, gross margin improvement, and earnings before taxes data.

Every strategic initiative needs to provide business value. Otherwise, it is a poor investment of enterprise assets. Using a single slide to communicate the business value of these digital investments is an excellent communication tool.

Digital Dashboard

The digital dashboard (see Figure 6.19) offers an opportunity to provide the Digital Steering Committees and the Digital Governance Council an update on key project metrics for each of the three digital initiatives and the IT Foundational initiatives.

The digital dashboard provides a color-coded status for the projects associated with the three digital initiatives' business processes.

Investment Metrics

	Operational Savings	Net Sales	COGS Savings	Gross Margin Improvement	EBITDA
			Benefit		
Digital Customer 1. Program/Initiative 2. Program/Initiative 3. Program/Initiative 4. Program/Initiative	$X.x M				
Digital Manufacturing 5. Program/Initiative 6. Program/Initiative 7. Program/Initiative 8. Program/Initiative					
Digital Business Services 9. Program/Initiative 10. Program/Initiative 11. Program/Initiative					
3-year Value	$X.x M	$X.x M	$X.x M	$X.x M	$X.x M

Figure 6.18   Investor metrics.

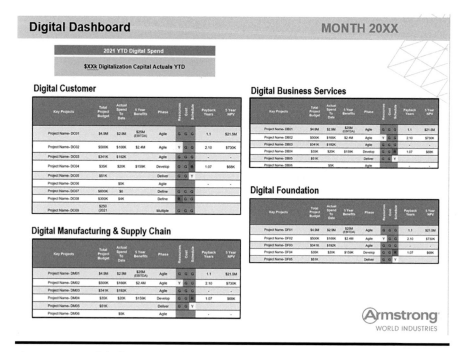

Figure 6.19   Digital customer dashboard.

Digital Dashboard for Each of the Three Digital Initiatives

Each of the four Digital Steering Committees (Customer, Manufacturing, Business Services, and IT Foundation) is responsible for providing oversight of its associated portfolio. To assist the Digital Steering Committees in reviewing its projects, the PMO group provides a digital dashboard. Figure 6.19 is an example of the digital dashboard for the Digital Customer initiative.

The dashboard identifies the financial benefits, project budget and actual spend, project phase, resource, cost, schedule performance for the project, and any associated comments for each project. The dashboard identifies the projects in the queue and key next steps as appropriate.

Chapter Summary

Digital Transformation initiatives succeed only if the underlying projects align to the transformation goals and are successfully executed and implemented. AWI has accomplished this through its digital Acceleration strategy designed around their 10-3-1 initiative. In Chapter 5, I discuss how this strategy supports the growth and productivity goal by identifying *ten* strategic optimization initiatives and three

Strategic IT Governance 2.0 Model

Figure 6.20 Strategic alignment – a balanced approach over time.

step-change outcome initiatives. AWI continues to stay focused on creating customer value while seeking a digital transformation that will disrupt the construction industry at large.

AWIs Digital Acceleration Transformation strategy is well on its way to changing the building products marketplace by leveraging the executive team and operational personnel's collaborative and teaming skills and incorporating the Strategic IT Governance 2.0 model's six key competencies into its digital governance strategy (Figure 6.20).

Citings

1. David Sauder/Phil Weinzimer interview February 19, 2020.
2. Dawn Kirchner King/Phil Weinzimer interview September 10, 2020.
3. https://www.cio.com/article/2395825/project-management-how-to-design-a-successful-raci-project-plan.html
4. Brent Lewis/Phil Weinzimer interview. September 29, 2020.
5. John Brabazon/Phil Weinzimer interview, September 1, 2020.
6. Craig Nadig/Phil Weinzimer interview March 4, 2020.

Chapter 7

How State Farm Transformed Its Governance Process to Improve Business Success

You cannot sit on your laurels when your company is number 42 on the Fortune 500 list. To maintain this position and hopefully move up to a higher ranking requires strong leadership, innovative thinking, and an organizational culture that thrives on challenge and change. Fortunately, State Farm leadership understands the changing dynamics in today's insurance industry. Over the past few years, State Farm has launched an IT transformation that recognizes technology's role in today's digital economy, where customers expect more personalized service. The IT transformation model implemented at State Farm includes many of the Strategic IT Governance 2.0 model principles. State Farm is an excellent example of how a large-sized company can navigate a transformation effort with executive leadership, collaboration, and a product delivery model that provides new and innovative services to its customers. I want to share with you a little historical perspective of the company, its IT transformation framework, and how its transformation model aligns with the six competencies of the Strategic IT Governance 2.0 model.

DOI: 10.1201/9781003317531-7

A Historical Perspective

Many of you may have never heard of George Jacob Mecherle, an Illinois farmer known as a very progressive and scientific farmer. At the age of 44, in 1921, Mecherle began selling tractors to farmers and realized that he had a real knack for selling. He also became aware of the higher cost of insurance for farmers. He was concerned that city insurance companies were "rooking farmers" with high premiums based upon city driving accident rates. So began his obsession with starting an insurance company. His plan was to sell automobile insurance to members of farm mutuals and their immediate families and those eligible for membership in such organizations. So, on June 7, 1922, G.J. Mercherle incorporated. To honor that date, State Farm celebrates Founders Day every year on June 7.[1,2] State Farm became a member of the Fortune 500 in 1995 when they allowed mutual companies to be part of the list, and since then, State Farm has always been in the top 50 companies.

To differentiate itself from other insurance companies, Mecherle adopted a variety of programs that provided financial strength to the newly founded company while at the same time providing unique benefits to its policyholders. Mecherle instituted a strict no-drinking-and-driving provision to reduce accidents. He also was sensitive to farmers' cash flow challenges so that policyholders could pay premiums in installments, the first program of its kind in the insurance industry. Eventually, his company became the largest property and casualty insurer in the United States and one of the 20 largest corporations on the Fortune 50.[2]

Today, State Farm has a net worth of 143.2B and ranks 42 in the Fortune 500 list of largest companies. Headquartered in Bloomington, Illinois, it sells property and casualty insurance, life and health insurance, annuities, and financial services products through its 19,400 agents, supported by 53,400 employees (Figure 7.1).[3]

State Farm believes that its shared values, quality service and relationships, mutual trust, integrity, and financial strength provide the foundation for its successful growth. Its vision for the future is

> To be the customer's first and best choice in the products and services we provide. We will continue to be the insurance industry leader and become a leader in the financial services arena. Our customers' needs will determine our path. Our values will guide us.[4]

George Jacob "GJ" *Mecherle* never imagined how the insurance industry would change by leveraging technology in new and innovative ways. Today customers are more technology-savvy and also demand superior service. As a result, technology is transforming how insurance companies interact with customers, perform daily activities, and even create new products and services.[5]

To meet the new digital customer, insurance companies have invested heavily in technology to leverage back-office operations and improve the underwriting process, claims, and marketing to enhance operational efficiency. McKinsey believes

State Farm – Fast Facts

- the #1 Auto Insurer[1] in the U.S. since 1942.
- the #1 Homeowners Insurer[1] in the U.S. since 1964.
- the #2 largest Life Insurer[2] based on policies in force in the U.S. since 2016.
- a leading Small Business Insurer[3] in U.S. Since 2014.
- a leading insurer of watercraft.
- ranked number 42nd on the 2021 Fortune 500 list of largest companies, based on revenues.
- State Farm offers about 100 products.
- Approximately 19,400 agents.
- Approximately 53,400 employees.
- State Farm has 87M policies and accounts in force in the U.S. (Financial Reporting & Analysis - U.S. only as of 12/31/2021).
- About 60% of State Farm households have more than one product.

Figure 7.1   State Farm – fast facts.

Source: https://www.statefarm.com/about-us/company-overview/company-profile/fast-facts#:~:text=ranked%20number%2036th%20on%20the,largest%20companies%2C%20based%20on%20revenues

the insurance companies that want to maximize the digital era will automate 50–60 percent of their operations organizations for new ways of working. To accomplish this is to form interdisciplinary teams that integrate technology and operations organizations more collaboratively. That's the approach State Farm is taking – using technology to complement the human connection their agents and employees have with customers. Companies that undertake this kind of change requires significant efforts, *but those that make this shift could see a significant drop in expense ratio and time to market; in turn, they may be able to make more investments, reduce prices, and improve profitability.*[6]

State Farm is one of the insurance companies that recognized leveraging technology in new and innovative ways as one way to continue to meet customer needs. An example of this was in 2018 when State Farm Ventures launched a $100 million venture fund. The goal was "to invest in startups developing technologies and products to fulfill customer needs in ways they wouldn't think possible with their insurance company".[7] The program is led by Michael Remmes, Innovation Executive, State Farm Ventures. *The goal is to focus on several key areas to provide customers with new and innovative products and solutions.*[7]

State Farm Ventures is just one of many examples of how State Farm decided to leverage technology. As State Farm began to invest heavily in technology in new and innovative ways, its executives recognized that the information technology organization's traditional role needed to change as it leveraged technology in new and innovative ways. Thus began the digital transformation journey to reengineer the technology into a more strategic, collaborative, and innovative organization.

The State Farm Digital IT Transformation Journey

Suppose your company understands that technology is a business driver in today's global marketplace. In that case, you need a CIO like Ashley Pettit to help lead the journey. Pettit is CIO and Senior Vice President of Enterprise Technology for State Farm. She has dedicated her career as a CIO to transform how business and technology align to enable State Farm to Scale and rapidly adjust to changing markets and reduce costs, inefficiencies, and redundancies (Figure 7.2).[8]

Pettit has an illustrious 30-plus-year career at State Farm, holding numerous positions in the information technology organization. Pettit started in the software development organization as a developer, technical lead, business analyst, manager, and director. She quickly moved up the ranks as Assistant Vice President-Systems Head, Infrastructure & IT Operations, Vice President-Systems. Pettit was promoted to Sr. VP in 2017 and named CIO in 2019.[8]

Pettit partnered with her peer, Fawad Ahmad, SVP, and Chief Digital Officer, to transform the Information Technology organization dramatically. Her promotion to CIO coincided with State Farm executives recognizing the greater importance of leveraging technology and business growth opportunities. In mid-2017, State Farm senior executives asked Pettit to lead an effort to look at the efficiency and effectiveness of the information technology organization. At that time, the information technology organization recognized the need to improve strategic alignment and partnerships with the business toward joint outcomes. "…we were slow to deliver. We were told that IT cost too much, the technology takes so long to implement, and IT doesn't seem to be strategic and aligned to business strategy".[9] When it came to execution, "…we experienced the traditional metaphor of business requirements hurled over the wall to IT, and things just took too long to get done. Sometimes we solved the wrong problem due to a lack of collaboration."[ibid]

State Farm uses the Show Back-back method to allocate IT costs to business units like many IT organizations. The details included in these allocations can sometimes

Figure 7.2   IT Ashley Pettit.

be challenging to understand as they contain IT speak that is difficult to know if you aren't familiar with technical jargon. This was the case with the business units at State Farm. In speaking to many CIOs, I've found their comments interesting. "I know we need IT, but I don't understand why it costs so much. Or even better. I know we need IT, and I pay the bill without understanding the detail." These comments impact the trust relationship between IT and business units and lead to the notion that IT is just a cost center.

Pettit wanted to improve the relationship between IT and the business units. Her goal was to move the typical IT allocation cost conversations from *I don't understand these costs* to genuine business dialogue.

Here's how Pettit describes the goal. "Instead of a business unit leaders just paying the IT allocation cost without truly understanding the detail, I would like to have a conversation where we could discuss the cost of IT applications that support business processes and have a productive dialogue. Why the costs for a particular application so high? How can we invest more capital in improving the application that supports the business processes?"[ibid]

Pettit also wants to elevate the conversation where we can discuss

> how are we making investment decisions? Do we have transparency to understand costs? How do we eliminate duplicate costs? What technology can we retire without impacting business results? How do we measure the ROI of IT investments and communicate to the business to understand how technology is driving business results?[ibid]

Over six months, Pettit and her team gathered information, analyzed, ad assessed the information technology organization. They identified four key areas that formed the framework for an IT transformation to improve its value to the business.

Figure 7.3 is a graphic of the IT Transformation Framework and the four key areas that comprise the framework. The four key areas are strategic alignment, delivery speed, cost efficiency, and operating model.

Following is a brief description of the objectives for each of the four key components.

Strategic Alignment: Adopt an outcome-oriented, integrated plan with active business support.
We need to improve our process of aligning our projects to business strategy and measuring business outcomes with active involvement and business personnel support.
Delivery Speed: Right speed for tight solutions thru viable products and delivery automation.
We can do much better with improving our delivery speed by viewing products instead of projects, automating some of our delivery activities to optimize our people and technology investments. We can also improve cost transparency for the

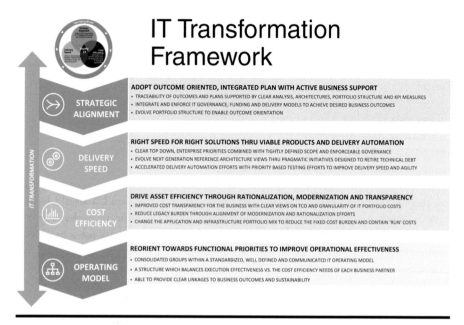

Figure 7.3   IT transformation framework.

business by looking at a total cost of ownership of asset portfolio instead of individual cost slides to provide business units true cost of ownership.

Cost Efficiency: Drive asset efficiency through rationalization, modernization,
and transparency.

*We can we improve our work flow, disciplines, and processes for solution design,
delivery, architecture to more efficiently deliver value to the business faster.*

Operating Model: Reorient towards functional priorities to improve operational
effectiveness.

*How can we improve our operating model to improve how the business and IT
interact with each other? We can better organize IT to pair off with business areas,
align more directly with business personnel, have better end-to-end views, and
upskill personnel.*

As I mentioned earlier, the State Farm IT Transformation Framework contains
many of the Strategic IT Governance 2.0 model principles. Figure 7.4 illustrates the
State Farm IT Transformation Framework's four focus areas and how it aligns with
the Strategic IT Governance 2.0 Framework's six competencies. Notice that each of
the six competencies of the Strategic IT Governance 2.0 Framework connects with
one another and, in fact, relies on each other to gain the benefit of a Strategic IT
Governance 2.0 governance model. One cannot have an effective governance model
without all six competencies working in harmony. And this is true with the State

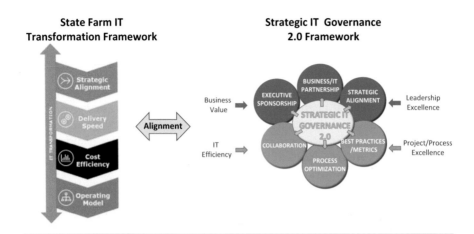

Figure 7.4 State Farm and Strategic IT Governance 2.0 alignment.

Farm IT Transformation Framework. State Farm requires each of the Strategic IT Governance 2.0 Framework's six competencies to succeed at the transformation.

Let us explore each of the four State Farm IT Transformation focus area objectives and identify the significant Strategic IT Governance 2.0 competencies required for success.

Strategic Alignment: Adopt an outcome-oriented, integrated plan with active business support

Executive sponsorship and a business and IT partnership are imperative to accomplish strategic alignment at State Farm. How else can State Farm adopt *an integrated plan with business support?* Additionally, personnel must effectively collaborate across organizational boundaries and improve the processes and metrics to measure the success of the portfolio of projects that support its 100 products and associated services.

Delivery Speed: Right speed for right solutions thru viable products and delivery automation.

State Farm must optimize their processes to identify the right products and associated services to accomplish this objective. They must also incorporate a robust set of best-practice metrics to measure progress and incorporate agile practices to rectify off-course errors. And finally, increasing delivery speed requires automation of manual processes to improve delivery speed and agility. And let us not forget that improving delivery speed is not a single person's job, but personnel involved in delivering products and services to collaborate actively.

Cost Efficiency: Drive asset efficiency through rationalization, modernization, and transparency.

Process automation, best practice metrics, and collaboration are necessary to achieve asset efficiency through rationalization, modernization, and transparency. State Farm integrated several Apptio solutions to provide IT Assets visibility, transparency, and cost detail. "This helps organizations make smart decisions as they analyze, optimize and plan technology investments that will transform the IT operating model."[10]

Most importantly, the information derived from the Apptio solutions provides meaningful metrics to business personnel and results in more refined business discussions regarding the use of IT assets by business units. As Pettit summarized, "the lack of understanding the cost of IT assets hampered the company's efforts to roll out the digital products that State Farm customers wanted" (ibid.). Providing business unit managers with IT costs in a language they can understand is very beneficial. It results in the transparency needed to have a more meaningful dialogue of the cost of the IT assets to support their business processes. This benefits a more collaborative business discussion between IT and business personnel, improving asset utilization and improved efficiency. Here's an example. A State Farm IT Manager presented a business unit manager with a new, more transparent cost report that reflected the IT costs that supported his business unit. The business unit manager had a general idea of the IT costs to support his business unit. When presented with a new Bill of IT cost report, the manager quickly realized that the IT costs were almost five times higher than previously thought. As a result, more meaningful conversations began to determine the cost of the IT investment required to support the business unit processes. "Transformation has allowed me to step into a space of creativity, autonomy, and innovation," said Mellainee Johnson, a Scrum Master in the State Farm Enterprise Technology Department. "With product ownership, we can connect the world of IT and Finance by leveraging Apptio as a mechanism for making more informed IT cost decisions. Before the transformation, work seemed to be monolithic. However, through this change. I have had an invaluable opportunity to learn, grow and make a daily difference for State Farm by delivering measurable product-specific results."

Operating Model: Reorient toward functional priorities to improve operational effectiveness.

Improving the effectiveness of IT requires a revamp of the existing structure to reorient toward a more functional and operationally effective IT organization and ensure that IT activities are linked to measurable business outcomes. The goal is to move from an IT organization traditionally viewed as a cost center to a business partner and contributor to achieving State Farm's business strategies and associated goals and objectives. To accomplish this requires collaboration between business and IT, optimization of processes, improved metrics, and a business/IT partnership that is more collaborative. Additionally, this also requires upskilling IT personnel to improve their ability to speak the language of the business, improve IT operational processes, and incorporate a new set of metrics that tie IT activities to business outcomes. One of the Apptio solutions (ApptioOne Billing) provided business partners "...*d*eeper insights into how their demands and desires shape IT budget and spending."[10] Finally, a reoriented IT operating model requires a governance model that, as described in Figure 7.3 *balances execution effectiveness versus the cost efficiency needs of each business partner.*

How State Farm Incorporates Strategic IT Governance 2.0 Competencies to Achieve IT Transformation

The previous section identified how the State Farm Transformation Framework aligns with its six competencies with the Strategic IT Governance 2.0 model. The following explains in more detail about how each of these competencies is utilized at State Farm to transform their IT organization into a collaborative business partner.

Executive Sponsorship/Business IT Partnerships

Executive sponsorship for the IT transformation was a given at State Farm. As discussed earlier in this chapter, the Executive Team asked Pettit to lead an effort to improve the efficiency and effectiveness of the information technology organization. This level of support provided the foundation for Pettit and her team to embark on the transformation effort. Executive sponsorship is imperative if any company embarks on an IT transformation. Pettit realized that for the transformation to be successful, she needed to partner with Fawad Ahmad, Sr. VP and Chief Digital Officer. He discussed the need for the transformation.

> State Farm has undergone several customer-driven transformations. We evolved to add more products, more capabilities with our contact centers, and of course, the current push to digitize how we work so that we are all able to maximize our ability to help more people in more ways. This transformation is truly an enterprise approach, where our business, technology, and support teams are all aligned through common goals. Agility, pace, and analytics are the new currency for us. We are taking a true end-to-end view of what it takes to attract and retain customers while creating delightful experiences for them. There is a recognition that when we also create the right physical and virtual environments for our agents and employees, they, in turn, are able to create that seamless experience we aspire to enable for our customers.

Pettit explains the need for reorganizing the IT organization.

> We had multiple technology teams interfacing with numerous areas of the business. I led a transformation study producing recommendations. When Fawad and I committed to the transformation, we formed one

> IT group and engaged and partnered with the business. It was a "One Team" concept. We had broad top-down support from the CEO and COO.[Ibid]

Pettit and Ahmad reorganized three business units into the newly formed Enterprise Technology Department. The three business units were the Systems Department (tradition or core IT), State Farm Digital, an early venture into agile and product management, and the Integrated Solutions Department, a blended team of tech and business intended to serve as an accelerator for the transformation.

The challenge, however, is to bring about a partnership between IT and the business that drives business outcomes. Building a business and IT partnership can succeed only if you provide a common goal. One of the major changes incorporated at State Farm is focusing on products versus projects. *(Author's note: more about moving to a product vs. project focus later in this chapter.)* When State Farm moved from a project to product focus, a lot needed to change. These product teams included both IT and business personnel. Ahmad understood that these teams needed some key principles that would bond the group and maintain their focus in developing a common goal of creating the best products State Farm can offer its customers. So, he asked his Digital Technology Group team to develop a list of key product team principles. "When we moved to a product-centric model, we identified some key principles to help the teams partner more effectively by maintaining a common focus.[Ibid] Figure 7.5 identifies some of these key principles.

Improving the partnership between IT and the business requires a basic understanding of how each area provides value. Unless there is a common language and culture, this will be difficult. Traditionally, IT personnel are very good at technology speak and technical skills but may be less adept at speaking and understanding the language and culture of the business. One of Pettit's most significant challenges was changing the skills and mindsets of IT personnel.

> We were entrenched in technology, and we sometimes couldn't speak the language of business. Here's an example. When we implemented Apptio, we determined the total cost of ownership (TCO) for our IT assets. Previously this had been a challenge to convey between IT and the business. Still, Apptio allowed us to use the same data to connect IT, our business areas, and finance, which helped each group better understand the information from the ' 'other's perspective. We started a training program to help our IT teams better understand the cost of ownership of their product and understand and speak the language of the business, or as we say, business-speak. We started with an IT team with strong relationships with their business peers to build momentum for our training program. This program helped our IT personnel better communicate with their business partners.[ibid]

- Focus on your customers and their needs

- Know your product (inside and out)

- Share ideas openly and do not hesitate to disagree professionally

- Focus on experiences vs process

- Value team-level empowerment and decision making

- Discover and innovate your products

- Delivery value in smaller pieces and do it often

Figure 7.5   Key product team principles.

IT personnel participate as active members of business teams through a unique mix of physical co-location and virtual collaboration with business personnel. This enables IT personnel actually to see how business personnel use IT applications. "I was amazed to see how many of our technology personnel didn't know how business personnel uses our IT solutions in their daily work activity," said Pettit.

> To help build a long-lasting partnership with the business, we implemented a program where we identified product owners for specific IT assets and paired them with the corresponding business owner. This joint owner-ship model created a shared line of sight and enabled the IT and business owner to more effectively partner in managing the product group.[ibid]

Randy McBeath, an Enterprise Technology Executive at State Farm, summarizes the benefit of the IT Strategy Decision Investment model and how it brought about a business and IT partnership.

> Now that we are focusing on products instead of individual projects, we can align each product strategy to our technology investments, focusing on creating more value for our customers at the same time, we work with the business executive responsible for each product developing a product roadmap, architecture, and partnership strategy to optimize technology investments. We're still on our journey. Our employees and business part-ners are becoming more comfortable working in a product management world, and we continue to make iterative adjustments to our processes.[11]

Strategic Alignment

Strategic alignment ensures that selected projects directly link to the business strat-egy, goals, and objectives. To truly embrace the meaning of strategic alignment requires a thorough understanding of how the company works, its business unit goals, and how personnel perform daily work activities to support the business. Randy McBeath is one of these individuals.

Randy McBeath is an Enterprise Technology Executive at State Farm and has extensive experience leading and delivering multiple initiatives within State Farm. He graduated from Illinois Wesleyan University with a bachelor's degree in accounting. He continued his professional education and completed a number of certifications. He is a Certified Public Accountant (ALMI), Fellow, Life Management Institute (FLM, Chartered Financial Consultant (ChFC), Chartered Life Underwriter (CLU), and Chartered Property Casualty Underwriter (CPCU). One can say that McBeath understands the insurance industry.

McBeath has served in numerous roles at State Farm during his 25-year career. His first 16 years provided him with a good foundation of learning the insurance business. He started as an accounting supervisor in Florida, then moved on as a claim representative in California. He also worked as an accountant in the Accounting Procedure department before moving on to be a project manager and service manager in the Systems Department and an executive manager in the Property & Casualty underwriting consultant. In 2015, McBeath was named Assistant Vice President in the Integrated Solutions Department. A few years later, in 2018, he was promoted to his current role as Enterprise Technology Executive-Planning & Management.

McBeath was part of the cross-discipline leadership team that helped develop the new IT Investment Process. Figure 7.6 depicts the framework for the Strategy Investment Decision Model.

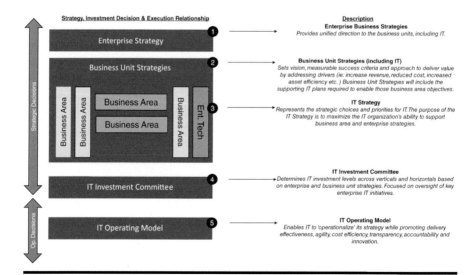

Figure 7.6   Strategy decision investment model.

The model is a multilayer framework that depicts the enterprise business strategies' alignment with business unit strategies, the IT investment committee, and the IT operating model. Following are the objectives for each area.

Enterprise Strategy: *Provides a unified direction to business partners and IT of the enterprise strategy and its underlying goals and objectives.*

Business Unit Strategies: *Sets vision, measurable success criteria, and approach to delivering value by addressing key drivers (i.e., increased revenue, reduced cost, increased asset efficiency, etc.). Business Unit Strategies include the supporting IT plans required to enable those business unit objectives.*

IT Investment Committee: *Provides oversight to ensure that IT investment levels across verticals and horizontals are based upon enterprise and business unit strategies.*

IT Operation Model: *Enables IT to operationalize its strategy while promoting delivery effectiveness, agility, cost efficiency, transparency, accountability, and innovation.*

The cross-functional team included McBeath and personnel from different business units, finance, and technology. During the planning sessions, the team agreed that the core objective was to develop an IT Investment Management approach that replaced the historical processes and emphasized a greater strategic alignment between IT and business leadership.[11]

Before the Strategy Decision Investment Model, State Farm did not have an overarching enterprise-wide IT strategy. Instead, there were multiple strategies and priorities within the different business areas. A robust Portfolio Management process governed projects from the numerous product lines (auto, home, Life, etc.). The challenge faced by State Farm IT was connecting hundreds of projects to each of the dozen State Farm companies depicted in Figure 7.7.[12]

As McBeath describes it, "We had a process for aligning and managing projects. PMO set up a portfolio, criteria, and prioritization models. But we spent more time managing the process than diving deep into the work product."[ibid]

We struggled at times to track work effort. Our funding model was based on a 12-month cycle. When we recommended priority to the C suite, it was difficult for the C suite to understand the work effort and to drive business results? Our challenge was to get C suite to understand we were doing the right things. We would go through a prioritization exercise. We would identify a prioritization score by identifying the business value and multiplying it by the revenue impact. This was very subjective, and we needed a better way.[ibid]

The new Strategy Investment Decision Model is a more relevant model to manage IT investments. Firstly, the enterprise strategy and business unit strategy align with

State Farm® Companies

- **State Farm Mutual Automobile Insurance Company**
- **State Farm Life Insurance**
- **State Farm Life and Accident Assurance Company**
- **State Farm Fire and Casualty Company**
- **State Farm Indemnity Company**
- **State Farm Guaranty Insurance Company,**
- **State Farm General Insurance Company**
- **State Farm Florida Insurance Company**
- **State Farm Lloyds**
- **State Farm County Mutual Insurance Company of Texas**
- **State Farm Investment Management Corp.**
- **State Farm VP Management Corp.**

Figure 7.7 State Farm companies.

one another. And secondly, the investment committee ensures that IT investments align with the business unit strategies.

> When the highest leaders in our organization make these decisions, and when you have that type of message being shared consistently from the top down, and aligning with enterprise priorities, it makes it much easier for the rest of our leaders to understand the importance of the changes and execute on them.[ibid]

A significant shift occurred at State Farm as they moved from a project to a product focus. As McBeath describes it, "…this was an emerging trend in the industry. We don't identify projects. We determine what products we have and how much we need to allocate to each product."[ibid]

Many businesses manage projects that support business needs. However, when you have over a dozen companies with hundreds of business units and thousands of projects, looking at projects is comparable to the idiomatic expression *missing the forest for the trees*. You lose the detail. It's far down the food chain. State Farm decided to move from a project focus to a product focus. Rather than focus on the hundreds of projects, State Farm executives focused on the 100+ products provided to customers and determined the IT investments required to improve the product's value. This turned out to be a more strategic view and provided State Farm with relevant data on IT investments to improve customer value.

This shift to products from projects had enormous implications for the IT Operating Model. IT organizations were restructured to a product model. Before, personnel assignments were by the project. Now technology personnel are assigned by product.

Brett Weber is an Enterprise Technology Executive at State Farm responsible for IT Risk and Compliance. He believes

> That a focus on product versus projects helps our team to own things, be more proactive, and create two-way dialogues between IT and business units that result in better products for our customers. Moving to a product focus helps us align our top priorities. It helps push our thinking, leading us to be more innovative. We have consistent IT and business personnel teams working together, having business results reviews vs. tactical project discussions with a product structure. Strategically, moving to a product focus aligns technology and business plans and helps people see that IT is run as a business with financial metrics and a business management approach leading to a more collaborative working environment with our business peers.[13]

State Farm Drive & Save™ is one of these products enabled by technology investments. It rewards drivers based upon their driving habits and miles driven. A downloadable app is connected to a Bluetooth beacon provided by State Farm and automatically records your driving trips. The application offers discounts on your auto insurance based on your driving data and tips for improving your driving behaviors.[14]

Ritesh Saraf is one of the State Farm Enterprise Technology Executives and played an important role in establishing product teams in the IT organization. He describes an example of one of the product teams.

> We have different product teams, each with specific capabilities for the products they support. Our insurance telematics program comprises different sub-products, each with its own product technology team. For example, in our Drive Safe & Save™ program, we have sub-product teams for user interface, back-end services, data/infrastructure, hardware, etc. And all of the sub-teams roll up under the Drive Safe & Save program, part of the Property and Casualty business operation.[14]

An organization that evaluates approves, and implements projects on an individual basis could overlook scope and other enhancements that would improve the value of the product the project supports. This leads to unnecessary additional scope and features through additional projects, resulting in more time, more money, and additional resources, all of which could be used for other technology investments. This is why moving to a product view provides State Farm the ability to strategically look at each of its 100+ products and identify the technology investments that would provide the greatest business benefit and customer value. Additionally, it provides an opportunity for the IT organization to work strategically with business unit management and collaborate more effectively, building a trust-based relationship elevating the IT to a value-based strategic partner.

"Through strategically aligning business and technology functions, the traditional roadblocks have been removed, and a continuous delivery strategy was born," said State Farm IT Governance, Risk & Compliance Analyst Mitchell Tielke.

> Business teams work personally with their technology partners to avoid undue delays in communication, resulting in more accurate functional requirements and targeted key performance indicators. While transformation will never truly be complete, I am encouraged at the direction our enterprise is heading and look forward to growing alongside it.

McBeath describes that project prioritization for projects occurs at different product structures. "We have products, product suites, and product areas.

Product Area – A group of related product suites that align with a business line. (e.g., Life)
Product Suite - A group of related products.
Product - A piece of work or functionality that delivers measurable business value and can be owned from initiation to sunset by a small, persistent team.

> Example: The Life Insurance technology area (*Product Area*) ➔ Life Quote, Purchase, and Application (*Product Suite*) ➔ Life Quote (*Product*)

Product groups work with their business areas to prioritize based on the problems and business outcomes they are trying to achieve, which also needs to be in alignment with our overall enterprise objectives."

McBeath summarizes the benefit of the IT Strategy Decision Investment model.

> Now that we are focusing on products instead of individual projects, we can align each product strategy to our technology investments, focusing on creating more value for our customers. And at the same time, we work with the business executive responsible for each product developing a product roadmap, architecture, and partnership strategy to optimize technology investments. We're still on our journey. Our employees and business partners are becoming more comfortable working in a product management world, and we continue to make iterative adjustments to our processes.[11]

"Initially, the transformation was uncomfortable for a lot of us, including me," said Infrastructure Analyst Jon Guidry.

> Many unknowns were going into it, making us afraid of what might happen. Ours was an organization that almost never drastically changed. Once the new product management model was implemented, it took us some time to acclimate because it was so new and unfamiliar. Now that we have been doing this for several years, I can definitely say that the product management model helps us move faster.

Collaboration/Process Optimization

Integral in every IT Transformation is teamwork and process improvement. These two principles are necessary when an enterprise recognizes technology as a critical component of a business strategy. Traditionally, IT organizations are viewed as cost centers and not necessarily well integrated into the business processes that support a company's products and services. If you don't believe this, look at how many corporations have the IT organization physically separated from the central business campus. I've seen this firsthand dozens of times. Collaboration and process optimization are critical to its success when the goal is to transform IT into a strategic business partner.

Pettit recognized that collaboration and process optimization were critical to State Farm's IT transformation as a strategic CIO.

> Finance leads our strategic planning process. To build collaboration and process improvement, we leveraged finance to lead the process to help define the business outcomes we wanted to achieve. For example, take claims. If customer claims are not processed efficiently, our customers get frustrated. So we used the finance organization to broker a process between IT and business personnel to work together to define the business outcomes required to improve the claims process. Having finance take the lead to bring IT and business personnel to work collaboratively to solve business challenges is the right way to build trust.[9]

Pettit provides another example: "Take our product development process. Instead of IT and business personnel planning in isolation, we first worked together to define the specific business outcomes we wanted to achieve. We then worked together to determine the tactics needed to achieve these business outcomes."[ibid]

Ahmad expanded collaboration across the business by holding monthly joint meetings with technical and business teams to discuss project status. Are we on track?

Are our targets changing? What has changed in the last month that would impact the project? These are some of the questions these joint business reviews address. Holding monthly meetings provides a cadence of collaboration and allows the teams to be more dynamic in validating product strategy and delivering customer value.[ibid]

Earlier in this chapter, Randy McBeath was part of the cross-discipline leadership team that helped develop the new IT Investment Decision Model The team included McBeath and personnel from different business units, finance, and technology.

> During our planning sessions, we agreed that our core objective was to develop an IT Investment Management approach that replaced the historical processes and emphasized a greater strategic alignment between IT and business leadership. We jointly collaborate on the business needs and problems that business units are trying to solve and figure out how to develop technology solutions to accomplish those objectives.[11]

Additional IT executives participated as Ahmad expanded the collaboration and process optimization process at State Farm. Jeff Bertrand is an Enterprise Technology Executive-Architecture & IT Services at State Farm. Bertrand has a bachelor's degree in computer science, and minor in business, and a master's degree in business administration. He started his career at State Farm in 1985 as a data processing trainee and then as a project manager and PMO manager in subsequent years. He established the Future State Technology program. In 2014, he was promoted to assistant vice president and senior IT architect role, and in 2018 promoted to his current position of Enterprise Technology executive.

In his current role, he reports to Pettit CIO. Bertrand has oversight of the IT Architecture and IT Services organization. His initial assignment was to bring together the IT Architecture and IT Services organization to improve operating efficiency.[15] Bertrand focuses on defining and governing architectural direction, defining and managing standards and practices, and driving to consolidate roadmaps and metrics. His key focus areas in IT Services include the services, tooling, and techniques to manage test enablement and solution delivery and engineering.

> We were more command and control instead of listening and innovating. The challenge was to refocus and rebuild the relationships between solution delivery and engineering teams within IT from what we do TO them to do the right things FOR them. We didn't understand the value of our consumers from an architectural and IT services perspective.[ibid]

One of Bertrand's goals was to improve collaboration between the business and IT personnel. Remember, one of the goals of the IT transformation was to develop more of a focus on business outcomes and the value State Farm provides its customers. Historically these two business areas were not as collaborative as they needed to be, and Bertrand wanted to find a solution to integrate a common culture between these two areas. "We needed these two business areas to have some shared objectives so that they could work better with one another in a more collaborative way focusing on business outcomes.[Ibid] Bertrand's solution was to create a two-day workshop where business and IT personnel identify key objectives and business results as an initial foundation for developing a collaborative working relationship. Bertrand wanted to introduce the concept of Product Management to the two groups to elevate the conversation from working on projects to develop products. Product management focuses on new product development, business justification, planning, verifications, forecasting, pricing, product launch, and marketing of a product or products at all stages of the product lifecycle. Traditional discussions between these two organizations were too tactical. Remember the previous discussion around *seeing the forest for the trees.* Well, this often happens in organizations where personnel lose sight of the bigger picture. Introducing the notion of Product Management elevates the conversation.

Figure 7.8 is the agenda for Bertrand's two-day workshop on How Product Management and Agile Principles Can Accelerate Collaboration at State Farm.

During the two-day workshop, business and IT personnel teams work together to understand the role of product development and how IT and business personnel can work together using agile principles to develop products. One of the tools used in the workshop is a product canvas; a storyboard that conveys what your product is and how it is strategically positioned. A product canvas is a planning tool designed to help build products with a great user experience focusing on feature development. It combines agile methodologies with UX principles to help validate product solutions. Figure 7.9 is an example of a product canvas.

Using the concepts of a product canvas, teams can develop a business case for a product using a single storyboard image. Agile principles are incorporated into the product canvas process to help teams collaborate efficiently. Bertrand says,

How Product Management and Agile Principles Can Accelerate Collaboration at State Farm

- **Day 1:**
- Welcome
- What is a Product7
- Discovery & Delivery
- Product Teams
- Product Managers
- Five PM Responsibilities
- Agile & Product Management
- Objectives & Key Results (OKRs)

- **Day 2:**
- Data & Measurements
- Product Discovery
- Discovery Techniques
- Discovery Principles
- Design Thinking
- Experimentation

Figure 7.8   State Farm collaboration workshop.

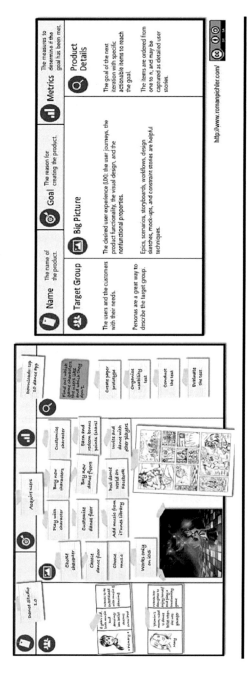

Figure 7.9 An example of a product canvas.

"Using agile concepts during the workshop allows the group to discuss user experiences and develop ideas that can be incorporated into the product design" (ibid.). This type of activity helps build a bridge between business and IT personnel to work together to achieve a common goal. It also helps teams create products agree on what the product does, define a great user experience, and identify value to customers. Many product development teams utilize user experience (UX) to incorporate user feelings and experiences in the design of a product.[16] Five important UX design principles are design, feedback, digestibility, clarity, and familiarity.[17] These are important concepts to keep in mind when developing products for customers.

Design – Design for your users-not for yourself,
Feedback – Provide feedback- a response to users' actions,
Digestibility – Provide small chunks of data
Clarity – Don't confuse customers
Familiarity – don't make users overthink

Remember, the objective of UX design is to "focus on users throughout the design process, know where you are in the design process, usability first, and less is more."[ibid] The goal is to focus on the customer and their needs, wants, and desires. Doing so provides a more value-added product.

Bertrand goes beyond just having the teams work on product canvases. "We even have the teams write an internal press release and discuss how moving from a project to a product focus is the right approach."[15]

In addition to the workshop, Bertrand uses other tools to build collaboration. "The workshop is just one tool we use to improve the cooperation between IT and business personnel. We also continue to expand and improve our software toolset supporting more effective associate virtual collaboration and enhanced productivity. Some example products we use include Microsoft Teams, Yammer, Zoom and Mural."[ibid]

As collaboration continued to expand collaboration across State Farm, a significant area of focus was Property and Casualty Claims and its underlying processes as they are integral to customer engagement and brand success. Ritesh Saraf is the Enterprise Technology Executive for Property and Casualty Claims. Saraf joined State Farm in 2016 and led customer experience teams in Claim, Bank, Billing & Payments, and State Farm.com. He has successfully established 22 product teams, created roadmaps, and delivered roadmaps that lead to incrementally better outcomes. Educationally Saraf has graduated with a degree in industrial engineering and has two master's degrees in science and business administration. So it is fair to say that Saraf understands the power of collaboration amongst teams from IT and business partners.

Saraf understands the importance of collaboration.

> It is essential to have both business and IT personnel participate together in teams. I use the phrase "2 in a box" to represent the merger of IT and business personnel working together to solve business challenges. We have teams engaging with business partners in planning sessions, strategic mapping outcomes, defining goals, developing product roadmaps. For example, in one of our claims teams, our business partners define business needs and desired results. We have weekly working sessions that include business and IT organizations personnel to define the tactics. Our teams engage heavily in planning, outcome management, and accountability. This partnership between IT and the business helps us focus strategically on providing our customers with the best products and services.[18]

Saraf explains more about the transformation.

> *When we began this transformation journey of improving the claims process, our team recognized that we needed to be more efficient and responsive to market needs. We know that we need to improve.* We needed to listen and work across organizational boundaries, business and IT fully integrated into one team throughout the lifecycle of our work. As we shifted to joint accountability and co-ownership, the magic happened. It's now a much better environment as we focus on providing the best claims processing services to our customers.[ibid]

Collaboration is ubiquitous across State Farm. Following is another example. Mahesh Chandrappa is the Enterprise Technology Executive – Digital Assets & Strategy at State Farm. He is responsible for leading digital transformation, analytics, and experimentation for Claims, Bank, Billing and Payment, Web and Mobile, Data capture, and validation in Adobe analytics for State Farm Digital. He also manages the department budget and scorecard. Chandrappa has a degree in electrical and electronics engineering and an MBA.

His team conducts planning sessions with business and technology partners to define business outcomes and measurable scorecards. "I focus heavily on product adoption with the team," Chandrappa said.

> We make it happen with the same scorecard and goals, with everyone marching in one single direction. State Farm is a huge organization, and the challenge is for our teams to have common accountability as we work together to provide the most value to our customers.[ibid]

When Chandrappa works with teams, the goal is to define the desired business outcomes. The business is responsible for determining the business problem and desired business outcomes, and the team works collaboratively to translate these two drivers into a realistic solution.[ibid]

Claims is another area where collaboration is part of daily work activities. Randy McBeath, an IT Technology Executive, discusses how the new transformation model integrates collaboration and process optimization to the relationship between the IT organization and State Farm business partners.

> There is an Enterprise Technology area that interfaces with our Claims area, and they are structured to connect with and focus solely on the technology needs with Claims. They establish working relationships at various levels, from executive to manager to the analyst level, to promote dialogue back and forth. We customized our structure to map easily based upon our business areas. We created the pillars inside Enterprise Technology to better align with our business areas and build and strengthen our relationships with business area counterparts to address their technology needs better.[11]

Pettit, Ahmad, and their team have a keen sense of the marketplace, understand customer expectations have changed, and see the need for State Farm to interact with its customers on a more personal level.

> We want to engage our workforce and modernize technology and data to improve and personalize customer experiences while innovating and finding new ways to help people. Two key objectives of the IT transformation were to improve strategic alignment across business and technology units and to change how technology solutions were built and delivered fundamentally. The teams relied heavily on improving collaboration and process optimization to achieve these outcomes by learning to work as "one team" across organizational boundaries and emphasizing a growth mindset.[9]

Best Practice Metrics

Why are metrics important? Metrics are a key component of The Strategic IT Governance 2.0 model or any transformation model. Whether you believe the original quote is from Peter Drucker: "If you can't measure it, you can't improve it." Or from W. Edward Deming: "you can't improve what you can't measure" Metrics are an important way to measure progress. State Farm uses metrics to measure the success of the IT Transformation in different ways.

Pettit shares her thoughts on the need for metrics.

> To achieve and sustain improvement over time requires constant atten-
> tion. Our focus was to ensure that we had a balanced set of metrics to
> track our progress, build momentum towards bold goals, and identify
> any unintended consequences along the way. And visible metrics build
> confidence in our plan as it provides visibility into the value delivered
> through IT investments.[ibid]

Chris Lay is the Manager of Data Analytics and sees the value in metrics. "The
scorecards we use become key to supporting collaboration and leaders' transparency about progress toward outcomes and challenges impacting progress through
monthly discussions and reports in business review meetings," Lay says. "But, they
also help maintain alignment with the highest-level enterprise priorities and the
overall transformation of the IT department." For example, on each scorecard,
the outcomes and measures are organized according to alignment with the department's transformation goals, Customer Experience Excellence, Data & Analytics
Process Automation & Business Simplification, Profitable Growth, Self-Service, and
Technology Advancements. Through these transformation goals, measures are connected to an overall transformation scorecard, used by senior executives to evaluate
the success of the overall transformation. More tactically, the scorecard outcomes
help individual product teams identify features and prioritize work that helps to
deliver the intended results. These measures help senior executives evaluate the outcomes driven by the changes taking place.[19]

Some examples of these measures include:

Customer Experience Measures:	Auto Customer Experience Score, Net Promoter Score
Agent & Workforce Measures:	Employee Engagement, Agent and Employee Change Fatigue, Developmental Opportunities
Technical Measures:	Systems Availability, % of Data Migrated to Strategic Platforms

The Enterprise Technology Executive – Architecture & IT Services at State Farm
Jeff Bertrand discusses how metrics help teams. "We use quantitative metrics to
help teams understand how well they deliver changes to their product and potential
areas for improvement, and new opportunities to create value." Following are some
examples of metrics identified in one of the reference handbooks used in the two-
day collaborative workshop.[20]

<u>Deployment Frequency</u>: The number of days between production implementa-
tions for software.

Lead Time: The number of days it takes from when a customer makes a request (e.g., for a new/updated feature) to satisfy the request (in production).

Delivery Lead Time: The number of days it takes from when the work actually starts (coding) to when it is implemented to production.

Adverse Change Fail Count: The number of changes in production that result in failures or defects (sometimes resulting in code pull-back from production).

Mean Time to Recover: (Restore): Average time to restore service.

Figure 7.10 represents an example of State Farm key metrics in a dashboard that depicts changes in deployment frequency and delivery lead times from the prior month.

To identify metrics to measure the success of the IT Transformation, Pettit needed to overcome the cost transparency challenge. The IT organization did not effectively identify the total cost of ownership of IT assets. This is important if you want to communicate the cost of supporting the technology that enables its business processes to a business unit. Cost transparency was a key challenge. Pettit overcame the challenge by implementing a few solutions from Apptio, the Bellevue, WA, global technology company.

Figure 7.10   An example of key metrics.

These solutions help organizations make smart decisions by analyzing, optimizing, and planning technology investments that will transform the IT operating mode.[19] The Apptio solutions provided State Farm the ability to achieve greater cost transparency of their IT investments and "actionable insights to connect technology investment decisions to drive better business outcomes."[ibid]

McBeath explains how Apptio provided value.

> The challenge was to find an effective and efficient way to measure the total cost of ownership of the IT assets that support the business. Using Apptio solutions enables us to answer some important questions. What is the total cost of ownership and the individual components for our customer order entry system? What can we do from a technology investment to improve the system's value? How do we decide what work to do/What are the top priorities of work? The ability to have this information enables us to change our entire relationship with our business partners. We can have a strategic business discussion about the technology investments required to achieve our business goals and objectives.

Pettit believes that implementing Apptio to provide cost transparency has changed the dynamics of how IT works with business partners. "It's more of a collaborative strategic relationship where we work together to determine the most optimum technology investments to achieve the business goals and objectives," she says.[9]

Identifying business outcome metrics is an area that is starting to emerge across the business landscape. IT organizations typically use efficiency metrics to measure their success in implementing projects. These usually include scope, schedule, and budget measures. Utilizing efficiency metrics without considering the business value of the project is counterproductive. A project sponsored by a business unit that doesn't align with the company strategy isn't a good investment even if the project is on time, within scope, and within budget. I'm sure you would agree with this. Identifying business outcome metrics that measure business value is a measure of effectiveness, where scope, time, and financials measure efficiency.

The IT Enterprise Technology Executive – Architecture & IT Services Jeff Bertrand talks about business outcome metrics.

> Objectives and key results (OKR) is an important metric for us at State Farm. We created a 3-hour workshop where we work with business partners and Enterprise Technology to accomplish more together - to say, "what are OUR objectives and key results? and the outcomes?" We are trying to become more outcome-driven. We try to start at a higher level and then drill down. We include a whiteboarding exercise where we together figure out our objectives, stakeholders, why they care, the results/outcomes, and how we will measure results. We ask the team, what are the business outcomes we delivered? Are we capturing them correctly? Are we improving the business? Where can we provide more

value? When you drill through using the OKR mindset, it forces you to talk in measurable and tangible ways related to business outcomes.[15]

Pettit describes how Ahmad brought a discipline of using metrics to help the IT organization track and show the value provided to the business. "He built accountability by holding weekly and monthly reviews where we track progress, risks, dependencies using a common set of metrics."[9]

Lay, who manages the Data Analytics organization, talks about scorecards.

> The scorecards developed collaboratively between business and technology are key for these monthly reviews. Every week, there are business review meetings in which business and technology executives and directors come together to discuss scorecard results – measures of outcomes progress. Every scorecard is assigned to one of the weeks in a month to be featured.
>
> At those meetings, leaders discuss the scorecard results and the business insights explaining changes in the data. These conversations help them discuss whether targets are set aggressively enough or too aggressively, what can be done to provide lift when targets are being missed, and evaluate which tactics (technology changes, business process changes, etc.) influence the results most successfully.[19]

The Digital Experience Team tracks metrics on a scorecard. Examples of some discussed in these meetings include the following.

> Registered Customers Active on the State Farm Mobile App: Measures digital penetration with permanently registered customers.
>
> Digital Self Service Completion Rate: An average score of customers completing digital transactions using self-service capabilities to take action on an existing policy or account or by a customer or prospect that could lead to a new policy or account.
>
> Digital Insurance Quote Starts: Count of auto and fire (property) insurance quotes that are started and calculated online.

Each of these measures, along with many more on scorecards across the department, is tracked against targets set and examined regularly to determine if the work is driving the desired outcomes.

Summary

The transformation effort led by Pettit and Ahmad and implemented by very capable IT and business personnel working collaboratively has positively impacted State Farm's business results. As Pettit describes:

At the highest level, there is heightened accountability in the business. We are all rowing in the same direction and laser-focused on a common outcome as one team supporting each other in executing the State Farm business strategy. We've seen incredible strides in both the speed and customer-focus of our technology deliveries.[9]

Today, business and technology are increasingly interdependent at State Farm, and the Transformation effort resulted in IT delivering technology changes at a rate of 3x more than previously experienced. IT and business personnel teams are aligned with one mission that enables State Farm associates to personalize the customer experience seamlessly and efficiently.

Pettit and Ahmad's transformation model incorporates the six components of the Strategic IT Governance 2.0 model. The transformation enables IT to partner with business partners to effectively implement technology to support business goals and objectives and help State Farm provide superior products and services to its customers.

State Farm was very gracious in providing me with information on the transformation, and the following is my summary of the key benefits State Farm derived from the transformation.

- Today, business and technology are increasingly interdependent.
- At its core, product management is about developing technology and measuring its success from a user-based perspective.
- This new, agile approach aligns perfectly with the customer-first philosophy at State Farm.
- There have been incredible strides in both the speed and customer-focus of technology deliveries.
  - The agile-based product team methodology is delivering at a pace never seen before.
  - Shifting into new ways of working together has resulted in a 3x improvement in delivering technology changes to the business than our previous approaches.
  - State Farm is building technology differently to prioritize customer experience into product solutions.
- The engagement model fundamentally changed how business and IT interact daily.
- IT incorporates more agile delivery concepts in a more dynamic way delivering more value to the business faster than ever before.
- As the competitive environment evolves, IT can be a flexibility lever in using technology to adapt to changing business dynamics.
- What are the enterprise outcomes we're driving – how do we have shared incentives across business and IT groups.

- Leveraging the Finance organization allowed our business and IT relationships to blossom in a new way with more collaboration across business areas.
- Business and IT are not separate anymore – both organizations align with one mission: enabling our associates to personalize the customer experience seamlessly, efficiently.
- Our digital and technology transformation has allowed business areas and IT to align better with its business goals, which translates to better customer experiences.

Citings

1. https://www.statefarm.com/about-us/company-overview/company-profile/state-farm-story
2. https://en.wikipedia.org/wiki/George_J._Mecherle
3. https://www.statefarm.com/about-us/company-overview/company-profile/fast-facts
4. https://www.comparably.com/companies/state-farm/mission
5. https://global.hitachi-solutions.com/blog/insurance-technology-trends
6. https://www.mckinsey.com/industries/financial-services/our-insights/the-insurance-switch-technology-will-reshape-operations
7. https://newsroom.statefarm.com/launch-of-state-farm-ventures-llc/
8. https://www.linkedin.com/in/ashleypettit1/
9. Ashley Pettit/Phil Weinzimer interview-February 19, 2020.
10. https://www.apptio.com/blog/apptio-empowering-state-farms-digital-transformation/
11. Randy McBeath/Phil Weinzimer interview May 27, 2020.
12. https://www.statefarm.com/about-us/company-overview/company-profile/state-farm-companies
13. Brett Weber/Phil Weinzimer interview June 7, 2020.
14. https://www.statefarm.com/customer-care/download-mobile-apps/drive-safe-and-save-mobile?cmpid=ps:google:auto:National%20-%20Brand%20-%20Auto%20-%20BMM:Drive%20Safe%20%20Save:drive%20safe%20save:Broad:B&gclid=Cj0KCQjwyN-DBhCDARIsAFOELTk0-ZUlTdOnAttuRCh97RklfOSWsBf6mcX3GIZuXLb9nNIKyqFbSsIaAuNkEALw_wcB&gclsrc=aw.ds
15. Jeff Bertrand/Phil Weinzimer Interview, June 4, 2020.
16. 103 https://uxplanet.org/5-principles-of-ux-design-d1579e7267db
17. UX Planet, 5 Principles of UX Design, Showrin Barua, November 2, 2019, https://uxplanet.org/5-principles-of-ux-design-d1579e7267db
18. Ritesh Saraf and Mahesh Chandrappa/Phil Weinzimer Interview, June 2, 2020.
19. Chris Lay and Phil Weinzimer interview, July 16, 2021.
20. Accelerate: Building and Scaling High Performing Technology Organizations; Fendici E-Books; Nicole Forsgren; Jez Humber; Gene Kim; ISBN 9781942788331.

Chapter 8

How the State of Georgia Implemented a Governance Solution Saving Millions of Dollars Each Year

The State of Georgia is one of the fastest-growing states in the United States. And as you can imagine, the State requires a technology organization that is visionary, innovative, and agile in anticipating the technology needs of its state agencies that provide services to its private and business citizens. Fortunately, the Georgia Technology Authority (GTA) manages the technology and infrastructure for the State has the leadership, personnel, and a strategic plan that helps guide Georgia's technology investments to serve state priorities securely and efficiently.

Calvin Rhodes is the Chief Information Officer for the State of Georgia and Executive Director of GTA. Rhodes is one of the longest-tenured CIOs of all 50 United States and has successfully built a first-class technology organization. I've met Rhodes several times during the past ten years and can tell you from personal experience that his focus is on providing the best technology that enables State agencies to deliver the best to Georgia constituents. Rhodes retired on June 30, 2021.

Rhodes joined GTA in 2011 from Paladin Investments, a private investment company he established. His bio on the GTA website speaks of his business acumen. Rhodes joined GTA and "*leads the State's public/private partnership IT transformation and consolidation effort. The initiative has strengthened security, modernized infra-structure and networks, improved reliability, and increased transparency in the State's IT enterprise. Building on its successes, the State has evolved its service delivery model to enable State Agencies to more easily benefit from changes in the IT marketplace. Mr. Rhodes and his team promote an enterprise approach to technology by establishing statewide policies, standards, and guidelines based on industry best practices and federal requirements".*[1] GTA follows the Governor's strategic plan to help Georgia's technology investments serve state priorities securely and efficiently. In August 2019, GTA published an updated Georgia Enterprise IT Strategic Plan.

The updated plan assists Georgia state government technology and business leaders in making informed technology decisions for their agencies. It establishes focus areas and goals for the State's IT enterprise through 2025.[2]

To provide you with insight into how Rhodes's organization focuses on providing the most optimum technology to drive improved State Agency services, Figure 8.1 is the GTA Technology 2025 IT Vision. The 2025 vision is, "by 2025 Georgia agencies will leverage data to provide digital services for a broad range of citizens' needs and work closely with the private sector under a mature security strategy."[2]

The 2025 IT Vision identifies five key strategies and for each the associated goals in the near-term, mid-term, and long-term timeline.

The GTA recognizes that technology comes with risks, and sound planning and project execution are critical to minimizing those risks. One of its key visions is "to provide a transparent, integrated enterprise where technology decisions are made with the citizen in mind."[3] One of the essential organizations within GTA is the Sourcing Management Organization (SMO) which manages the Georgia Enterprise Technology Services (GETS) Program, which is the public–private partnership providing infrastructure systems that support over 100 state agencies.

Please take a moment to look at Figure 8.1, previously discussed. Each of the five strategies impacts the SMO, but one, in particular, is very specific and aligns directly to the charter of the GETS Program.

■ Continue to improve the delivery of technology services: I draw your attention to the near-term goal that states *establish a mega IT project governance baseline* and the mid-term goal to *increase cost-effectiveness and access to technology-enabled services for agencies.*

Dean Johnson, Chief Operating Officer, leads the 20-plus personnel in the SMO. Figure 8.2 provides you with two high-level GETS organization charts. The first chart reflects Johnson's COO Office. The second reflects the Gets Integration & Technology Office organization. Most of the GETS staff provides technology direction and day-to-day management and oversight of the Infrastructure services provided through the GETS platform to State Agencies. Johnson also has a PMO office that oversees the GETS Program's portfolio, projects, and programs. Dean resigned from his position in June 2021. He currently is Senior Executive Government

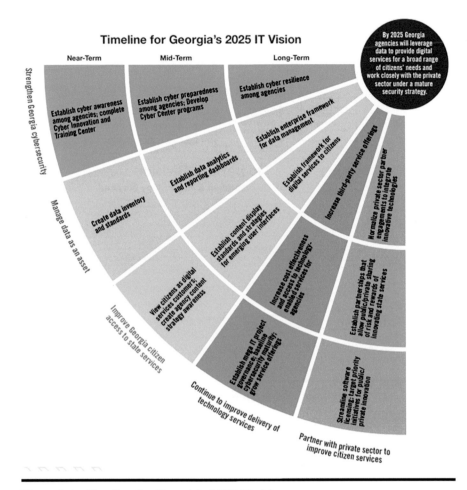

Figure 8.1   Timeline for Georgia's 2025 IT vision.

Advisor, Public Sector, North America, at Ensono, a managed service provider that empowers clients in various industries to achieve business outcomes through purpose-built, workload-optimized technology solutions.

(Author's Note: This chapter is based on interviews with Dean Johnson before his resignation from GETS and the Georgia Technology Authority.)

The GETS delivers Infrastructure Services to State Agencies. The SGO provides oversight of GETS governance and processes, is responsible for An Administrative Services organization and Sourcing Governance Organization, supports the COO office for the GETS contract administration, and leads the market testing and rebid activities to contract for new and/or rebid existing services.

(Author's Note: More detail on the PMO further in this chapter.)

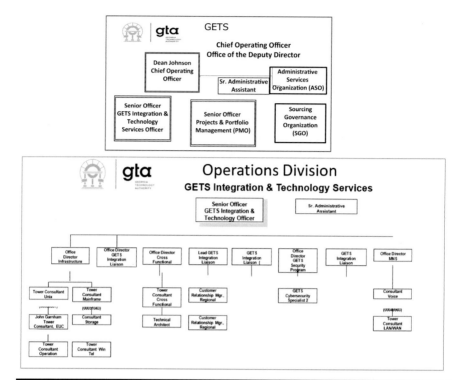

Figure 8.2 GETS high-level organization chart: COO office and integration & technology services.

Johnson and his team recognize that technology comes with risks and that sound planning and project execution are critical to minimizing those risks. As a result, Johnson and his team transformed an insourced infrastructure services model to an outsource infrastructure model through a services governance process for managing the technology and associated infrastructure that positions the State of Georgia to continue its rapid growth.

Following is some background that led to a new outsourced infrastructure model, the governance process to manage outsourced infrastructure vendors, and the alignment of the GETS governance model to the six components of the Strategic IT Governance 2.0 model.

Background

The State of Georgia is the place to live as it is one of the fastest-growing states in the United States. With a growth rate of 14.4 percent, Georgia's growth rate is 1.5 times greater than the average US population growth rate. And the forecast is for the population to grow by 17.7 percent by 2030. Besides being a great place to live, corporations enjoy making Georgia their home. United Parcel Service, The Home

Depot, Delta Airlines, The Coca-Cola Company, Arby's, and many more make Georgia their corporate home. And it's not only the large companies that make Georgia their home. The State is ranked #10 in Growth Entrepreneurship, scores an "A," and ranks in the top 5 for small business friendliness. And many Georgians are more educated. Nearly 30 percent of Georgians have a bachelor's degree, at a minimum, and 1 in 10 have a master's degree or higher.[4]

The Georgia Technology Authority (GTA) currently manages the delivery of IT infrastructure and managed network services to 1,200+ state and local government entities, including 14 Executive branch agencies, representing approximately 70 percent of all IT expenditures within the State of Georgia. IT infrastructure services encompass cloud, email, mainframe, print, servers, service desk, end-user computing, backup and recovery, disaster recovery, and security. Managed network services include the State's wide and local area networks, voice, cable and wiring, and conferencing services. These services provide shared services through a public-private partnership called the Georgia Enterprise Technology Services (GETS) (Figure 8.3).[6]

Dean Johnson is COO for Georgia Technology Authority. He is responsible for leading Georgia's GETS Program (Georgia Enterprise Technology Services), which provides technology services to state government entities. Johnson is accountable for ensuring that service levels for privatized services are maintained and continually improved, and problems with the day-to-day delivery of services are minimized. He also oversees the quality of service, customer satisfaction, and planning and forecasting of service consumption. Johnson works closely with agency and service provider leadership to identify, recommend, develop, implement, and support cost-effective technology solutions that adhere to statewide enterprise standards and meet future business needs.

Johnson has more than 35 years of experience providing information technology services within the public and private sectors. He has an extensive background in technology and state government. His experience includes overseeing and directing various IT departments that provide production control, security of mainframe applications, network engineering, development, network administration, network

State Agencies receiving the full complement of all IT services provided by the GETS program

- Department of Administrative Services
- Department of Behavioral Health and Developmental Disabilities
- Department of Community Health
- Department of Driver's Services
- Department of Revenue
- Department of Public Health
- Governor's Office of Planning and Budget
- Georgia Department of Corrections
- Georgia Bureau of Investigation
- Georgia Technology Authority
- Department of Juvenile Justice
- Department of Human Resources
- Department of Natural Resources
- State Accounting Office

Figure 8.3 State Agencies receiving the full complement of all IT services provided by the GETS program.

Figure 8.4   Strategic IT governance 2.0 model.

security, data center, disaster recovery, telecommunications, email, and help desk support.[5]

In 2007, GTA leadership recognized that the State required a more modern and agile infrastructure to service the growing needs of its citizens and businesses. State Agencies need to be prepared to support the increasing demand for services from citizens and companies with such a rapidly growing population. This requires an agile infrastructure that maintains control and stability of the technology systems. More importantly, GTA realized that transforming into an agile and effective service organization required outside help. The GTA leadership team needed to develop a new governance model to accomplish this transformation. Once developed, Johnson led the effort to implement the new governance model that became one of the key ingredients that led to the success of the GETS program.

The model he developed aligns closely with the six competencies of the Strategic IT Governance 2.0 model, as represented in Figure 8.4.

Following is Johnson and his team's journey to successfully deliver superior infrastructure services to the state agencies and, ultimately, Georgia's citizenry.

Executive Sponsorship for a New Governance Model

Johnson knew the transformation was going to be a journey. As Dean Johnson explains,

> We had several challenges. We had an aging infrastructure, a thinly staffed organization, personnel who lacked the technology skill set or couldn't keep up with technology standards and processes. We didn't have a safe, secure, and reliable environment to deliver IT services. Each of the 14

Executive branch agencies that make up approximately 70 percent of the State IT budget ran their IT shops independently (infrastructure, networking, and user computing), buying their own IT equipment. Each state agency had an IT organization with personnel managing projects. We needed to be more agile and improve our ability to maintain control and stability of the Agency's infrastructure. Personal computers were 8-10 years old, servers 10-12 years old, and technologically outdated. Everyone was doing their own thing, and GTA leadership knew that the State was at significant risk. We desperately needed to pull ourselves up by the bootstraps, but we didn't have the expertise in-house.[7]

In 2007 GTA, with approval from the State Legislature, contracted with TPI of Woodlands, Texas, a consulting company, to assess GTA's infrastructure services and provide recommendations. The consultants recommended that GETS contract with private companies to address the challenges of the Information Technology organization. A critical success factor was the executive sponsorship of the Governor's office. This was a crucial milestone in proceeding with the IT infrastructure transformation. GTA leadership received approval from the Governor's office to proceed with a solicitation of outsourcing of the IT infrastructure and managed network services. This solicitation to outsource the infrastructure services included all the data centers, end-user computers, print, mail, and other IT infrastructure services.

Our goal was to transform from an organization that uses in-house resources to perform the day-to-day infrastructure activities to an organization that manages and oversees the work and becomes a service management organization by managing contracts, people, processes, and technology.[ibid]

Developing the GETS Outsourced Infrastructure Service Model

In 2008 GTA solicited bids to the IT market to provide infrastructure services. By November 2008, GTA leadership signed contracts with IBM and ATT to provide infrastructure support services to Georgia. Over the next several years, infrastructure services improved dramatically.

We moved from infrastructure being a Capital expense to an operating expense. Moving from Cap ex to Opex was a major improvement. It's a more predictable spend model and enables us to manage budgets more efficiently. We utilize industry standards best practices and have a more reliable infrastructure and well-governed environment. Now we have a perpetual refresh of laptops and tablets every three years, servers every five years, and networks every 5, 7, or 10 years as needed. Before outsourcing infrastructure, each Agency ran its own IT shop but didn't have its own IT budget. As a result, there was never enough money for infrastructure as large state programs, such as family services, child support services, and other health services programs were taking all the money.[ibid]

IBM managed the infrastructure, and ATT managed Network services (LAN, WAN, and voice services). Johnson renamed his organization to Sourcing Management Organization (SMO) from Service Management Organization (SMO) to more appropriately reflect the management of and continual process of reassessing the market for outsourced services. Over time the SMO became highly skilled and efficient in procurement and sourcing services.

Over the following number of years, IBM and ATT performed well. IBM performed various infrastructure services such as mainframe, servers, storing data, end-user computing, print, comprising the entire spectrum of infrastructure services, as well as service desk and chargebacks. IBM even maintained the Configuration Management Data Base (CMDB). IBM performed all the back-office cross-functional activities in addition to day-to-day infrastructure services.

Many organizations during this period embarked on outsourcing and began to recognize that some of the service companies would sometimes become complacent and, as a result, services suffered. Johnson didn't want to be in this position. So fast-forward to 2015, when Johnson recognized the need for a vendor that would provide the necessary oversight and management of IBM and ATT in the performance of their outsourced services. This type of service is known as a Multisourcing Service Integration model (MSI). A Multisource Service Integrator is responsible for coordinating and overseeing the delivery of services by multiple providers. GTA chose Capgemini as its MSI vendor.[8] With this model in place, GTA still maintains responsibility for service provider direction, oversight, and management. "It was a game-changer for us," says Johnson, as it created more visibility and transparency for the infrastructure services the GETS program is responsible for providing to State. As a service integrator, Capgemini delivers independent oversight to infrastructure services: service management processes and systems that include billing, service desk, service catalog and request management, and risk and security management, among other services for the State of Georgia.[4] As part of its service offering, Capgemini provides metric-based reports on the services provided by IBM and ATT. In effect, Johnson is very aware of outsourcing complacency syndrome when outsourcing companies become complacent in their service offerings, even with the Capgemini MSI model. And Johnson was also mindful that the approach to *placing all your eggs in one basket* comes with risk. In 2015, Johnson led the effort to recompete the IT infrastructure and managed network services contracts. This enabled

Johnson's GETS organization to break up the infrastructure outsourcing services contracts to industry leaders.

- AT&T – LAN, WAN, and Voice Services
- Atos – Managed Security Services and Mainframe (2 separate contracts)
- NTT Data – End User Computing
- Unisys – Server Services (includes many different towers like Data Center Mgnt, Messaging, Servers, Storage, Cloud Broker Services, etc.)
- Xerox – Print to Mail

With Capgemini providing its MSI services, this allowed the GTA SMO to apply appropriate oversight, Governance, and management to ensure that all the service providers perform to their best abilities.

The journey to transform the GETS organization from an in-house provider of infrastructure services to State agencies into an outsourced services organization was a significant transformation. Figure 8.5 reflects the success story of the GETS organization. The consolidation of the IT infrastructure replaces aging infrastructure, ensures a robust disaster recovery, delivers a stable operating environment, provides for a well-governed IT enterprise, and safeguards security.

GETS Services Platform

Johnson and his team realized that the technology landscape changes dramatically, and the IT infrastructure needed to adapt to the state agencies' ever-changing IT needs. The GETS IT infrastructure platform, developed in 2015, is more of a

A 10-year success story

The Georgia Enterprise Technology Services (GETS) program continues to meet the goals that originally motivated centralization in 2009:

- Consolidate IT infrastructure
- Secure state data
- Ensure a stable operating environment   **ÓGETS**
  Georgia Enterprise Technology Services
- Ensure a well-governed IT enterprise
- Replace aging infrastructure
- Ensure robust disaster recovery
- Ensure adherence to industry standards

Figure 8.5   GETS' ten-year success story.

Built to suit fast-changing IT needs

- GETS platform features plug-and-play model
- Allows quick response to changing needs
- A single business approach using multisourcing service integrator's tools, across multiple IT service providers
- Strong governance structure capitalizes on heavy engagement from agencies served
- Emphasis on service delivery, innovation, and transparency
- As the state's IT services broker, GTA matches agency business needs to best-suited services from IT market

Figure 8.6   GETS – built to suite fast-changing IT needs.

plug-and-play model that allows for quick responses to the changing needs of state agencies. The model is a robust governance structure that relies on collaboration between the agencies, GTA, MSI, and GETS services providers to provide excellent service delivery, innovation, and transparency. And, as you can see in Figure 8.6, the GETS Services Platform emphasizes a business model that focuses on the state agency business needs by applying the best-in-class technology from the IT market.

The GETS Services Platform provides infrastructure services to State Agencies and is supported by the GTA Sourcing Management Organization.

Capgemini provides the Multisource Service Integrator (MSI) services to the State Agencies by providing standard processes and tools sets. In addition, they provide service performance management services overseeing the outsourcing providers (ATT, Atos, Xerox, etc.) as represented in Figure 8.6 as Service 1, Service 2, Service 3, etc.

Johnson is a big believer in continuous improvement. With the GETS Services Platform in place, GTA needed to develop a revised governance model to provide oversight and transparency for efficient infrastructure services to the various State agencies. Over the years, the GTA team developed a governance model that provides increased service levels to State agencies while reducing service delivery costs.

The GETS Governance Model

Figure 8.7 represents the GETS Governance Framework and Escalation Paths, consisting of a three-level framework. A series of forums (committees) align at an Executive, Enterprise, or Workstream Governance level. Following the graphic is a summary of the committees and their area of focus.

Governance Framework and Escalation Framework

Joint Forums Escalation, Decision, & Information Flow

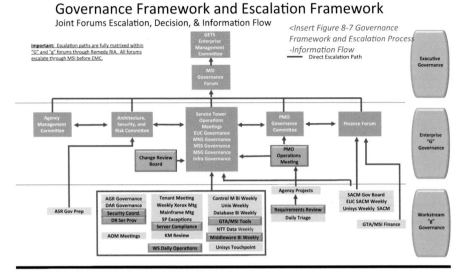

Figure 8.7 GETS Governance framework and escalation framework joint forums escalation, decision, and information flow.

Executive Governance: Strategic Level

GETS Enterprise Management Committee focuses on strategic oversight and alignment of the GETS program to the GTA and Agency business needs. The Capgemini and all service provider senior executives and GTA representatives have a monthly meeting. The GETS COO is the chair, and Capgemini is the co-chair.

MSI Governance Forum is a monthly meeting of key GTA and Capgemini leadership, focusing on Capgemini activities related to their oversight governance responsibilities. The Forum also acts as an escalation forum when issues and risks cannot be resolved at lower levels and are escalated to the MSI Governance Forum.

Enterprise "G" Governance – Operational Level

Agency Management Committee meets monthly and is chaired by GTA SMO leadership and co-chaired by senior management from one of the fourteen agencies that receive all their Infrastructure services from GETS. (There are approximately 88 other State Agencies that receive partial service but do not participate in Agency Management Committee meetings.) The co-chair rotates amongst Agency senior executives once a year, usually the CIO.

Architecture, Security, and Risk Committee meets monthly and is chaired by GTA and co-chaired by Capgemini. The focus of this Forum is Architecture, risk, and security standards and procedures. Attendees include a large audience as the subject matter crosses over many State Agencies. Any Agency attendee can discuss items where the Agency may have a new architecture, security, or standards and procedures that affect technology that GETS provides.

Service Tower Operations Meetings are individual meetings for each Service Tower. A Service Tower is a grouping of services provided by outsourced vendors. For example, GTA chairs the Managed Network Services (MNS) Tower Operations meeting. Managed Network Services comprise WAN, LAN, and Voice services that AT&T manages. Capgemini currently co-chairs these meetings. Attendees include members of AT&T (service tower provider for MNS, GTA, and Capgemini. The MNS Tower Governance meeting covers many topics, including SLA attainment, operations issues and actions, operational reporting, and project-related updates and issues. These same topics are covered in each of the primary Operations meetings listed below.

Following is a listing of the Service Towers and the services provided.

> EUC Governance – end-user computing services, including desktops, laptops, and tablets
>
> MNS Governance – managed network services, including LAN, WAN, and Voices services
>
> MSS Governance – managed security services, including security awareness training, SOC, SIEM, eGRC, and VMS
>
> Messaging Governance – messaging services covered under O365
>
> INF Governance – infrastructure services including server, mainframe, print to mail services
>
> AOM Meetings – Agency operations meetings focus on incidents, changes, projects, operational issues, etc., as well as communication about upcoming services

Change Review Board is an operational board that focuses on stringent change control.

The change review board is chaired by the GTA Cross-Functional Manager and co-chaired by Capgemini.

PMO Governance Forum focuses on escalated project issues, enterprise actions, and prioritization for Agency and Enterprise driven projects and programs. In addition, the PMO Governance Forum reviews SLA performance and PMO key performance indicators to help drive the right behaviors, focusing on continuous improvement. GTA PMO Office chairs the committee that meets biweekly. Attendees include key stakeholders and decision-makers from GTA, each service provider, and the MSI.

PMO Operations Meeting focuses on portfolio health, project issues, and key metrics related to Agency and Enterprise driven projects and programs. This meeting facilitates decisions, provides a forum for communications about upcoming features/changes, etc. GTA PMO Manager chairs the committee that meets biweekly, and attendees include project management stakeholders from each service provider and the MSI. Tenant Meeting is a specific group of GTA, service providers, and agency attendees using the Office 365 system. Around 2015, GTA moved into a single Office 365 tenant instance, and GTA needed a specific Forum to address any changes to Office 365 that could impact all of the affected agencies.

Workstream 'g' Governance

These meetings are what are called little g governance meetings because they are at the lowest workstream level of our governance model. These meetings happen weekly and are usually held between a GTA SME, a MSI SME, and potentially an STP SME counterpart. These operational meetings focus on day-to-day risks, actions, issues, and decisions needed to keep the operations moving for any aspect of the GETS services. As you can see, there is a comprehensive framework to cover all aspects of the GETS Program services, and each one of these has a place to escalate within the Enterprise Governance structure (Figure 8.8).

AGR Governance
DAR Governance
Security Coordinator
DR Ser Prov
AOM Meetings
Weekly Xerox Mtg
SP Exceptions
Server ComplianceKM Review
WS Daily Operations
Control M Bi Weekly
Unix Weekly
Database Bi Weekly
GTA/MSI Tools
NTT Data Weekly

Figure 8.8   Little G meetings.

Middleware Bi Weekly
Unisys Touchpoint
Agency Projects
Requirements Review
Daily Triage
SACM Gov Board
EUC SAACM Weekly
Unisys Wekly SACM
GTA/MSI Finance

Business/IT Partnership/Collaboration

Johnson and his team focused on building a governance model that incorporated a collaborative partnership between the GETS organization, outsource providers, Capgemini, and State agencies. These organizations needed to function as one team to deliver infrastructure services with the highest quality at optimum costs. Here's how Johnson and his team structured the GETS Governance model to build a GETS/Capgemini/Agency partnership referencing the three-layer model in Figure 15.7.

Strategic Alignment

Unlike many private sector companies, the GETS organization has unique features in its delivery model for infrastructure services. Fourteen State Agencies receive all their infrastructure services from the various outsourcers contracted by GETS. In comparison, some of the other 88+ agencies receive some of its infrastructure services from these outsource vendors. And the Capgemini MSI group oversees the outsourced vendors that provide infrastructure services to these State Agencies.

Each state agency has its own IT organization, and PMO group that identifies and tactically manages projects for its Agency. The agencies are responsible for the applications that support their business. Projects are sometimes managed through a centralized PMO organization with the agencies and in other cases, through business leaders. It is up to each Agency to ensure that the projects they are undertaking align with their Agency's strategic goals. This process is different from Agency to Agency.

Every project that is broader than a single agency initiative and has a state enterprise goal or objective is required to map back to the State's strategic goals and/or objectives. So, in other words, each executive branch agency that GTA works with is required to align to GEMS on projects that align to statewide objectives.

The GETS organization has a PMO organization responsible for aggregating all governance processes that support the Capgemini MSI services and is ultimately responsible for successful project management outcomes. Erica Keller is the PMO Officer at Georgia Technology Authority and manages the GETS PMO function.

The GETS organization reviews all project requests submitted from State agencies. Keller explains the process.

> When a project request is received, we utilize our complexity matrix tool to perform an initial triage to determine the size and complexity of the project. We use this process to understand the level of project management required and also determine the type of SLA we will apply to the project
>
> Part of the collaboration that helps GTA and the agencies achieve the most success is based on our understanding of the business impact/goals a particular project request achieves. To perform this triage, during the project intake process, the Agency completes a business case to determine the general project scope and assess business impact to the Agency and the strategic alignment. This step helps the GETS team understand how the project meets the Agency's goals and helps us be a better partner in delivering services.[9]

Figure 8.9 shows that the GETS Complexity Matrix is a tool used by agencies to determine the project complexity.

As you can see from the Complexity Matrix, several characteristics determine the size of the project. Each characteristic is assigned points, from 1 to 3, depending on the response. A total score of 0–3 points is considered a small project, 4–7 points are considered a medium project, 8–11 points is regarded as a large project, and a score of 12 points or greater is regarded as a huge project.

The size and complexity matrix drive the amount of time allowed for designing, costing, and planning activities and the project management rigor and methodology used to manage the projects. For low-complexity small projects, often pre-approved designs and standard pricing are used, so the projects are moved directly to implementation. There are many steps for design reviews and proposal writing, and approvals are not needed. Whereas for highly complex, very large projects, every step from initiation and planning through implementation and closing is completed, and stage gates are applied after each step to ensure success. And this happens no matter whether the project utilizes an agile or traditional waterfall approach.

The characteristics used in the complexity matrix represent potential risk areas that increase the difficulty of the project. The number of outside vendors, how many geographic locations, applications requiring support, technical complexity, and system complexity are elements of a project that can increase the complexity and potential risk for success. And the PMO organization needs to apply the appropriate project management processes to manage the level of complexity.

Name:				Date:	5/29/2021
Agency:				Agency Requestor:	
Requestor #:				Requestor Email:	
Project Name:				Request Number:	
SIZING:		SMALL		Proposal Turnaround:	10 BDs
Characteristics	0 Points	1 Point	2 Points		Score
Outside Vendors (3rd Party)	1	2	3		0
STP's Involved	1	2	More than 2		0
Geographic Locations	0-3	4--14	15+		0
Number of devices/Users	0-39	40-79	80+		0
Agencies Involved	Work group within agency	Agency-wide	More than one agency or government level		0
Time to Deliver*	Less than 6 months	6-12 months	More than 1 year		0
Requires App Support	Minimal change or simply adds functionality to existing system	Moderate change or modifies systems now in use, but does not change work process	Significant change or work methods of agency personnel and/or delivery of services to agency clients . This includes AT&T HVS and Firewalls.		0
Impact outside Agency	Low Political Low Visibility	Medium Political Medium visibility	High Political High visibility		0
Technical Complexity	Standard, proven GETS technology	Proven at Industry or State Level, but new to GETS	Emerging, unproven or new to the state		0
System Complexity	Stand-alone system	Some integration with another system	New system which needs to integrate with several others, and/or they are critical systems. This includes AT&T HVS and Firewalls.		0
			Total:		0

*Estimate

	SMALL	0-3 Points	
	MEDIUM	4-7 Points	
	LARGE	8-11 Points	
	VERY LARGE	12 Points or Greater	

Figure 8.9   GETS complexity matrix.

Process Optimization/Collaboration

Johnson is a big believer in optimizing processes and creating a collaborative team environment where personnel work together to provide the best possible infrastructure services. Johnson accomplishes this with a focused work ethic and dedication to continuous improvement.

As previously discussed, the GETS Infrastructure delivery model includes six vendors over seven GETS contracts. All other vendors have a one-to-one relationship, each providing a specific infrastructure service to State agencies. To ensure that these outsourced service providers deliver infrastructure services with the highest quality, GETS contracted with Capgemini to provide Multi-Service Integration Services (MSI) to provide overall governance over the outsourced infrastructure service providers. The GTA Executive Management Committee has responsibility for the overall governance of the infrastructure. The GTA PMO has overall project governance. Fourteen Executive branch State Agencies across 27 governance forums interact with GTA and Capgemini services organizations that receive infrastructure services.

As you can imagine, the network of different organizations involved in delivering and governing infrastructure services can be daunting from a process and collaboration perspective. So, let me provide you with some context and explanation of how these different organizations (Capgemini MSI services, GETS PMO, outsourced service providers, and the State Agencies) work together in the delivery and Governance of the various infrastructure services.

GETS PMO Organization

As mentioned earlier in the strategic alignment section, Erica Keller is the PMO Officer at the Georgia Technology Authority. Keller has PMO responsibility in the GETS organization to develop and oversee all governance processes that support the GETS services and is ultimately responsible for implementing infrastructure projects.

The GETS PMO organization manages two types of projects.

The first type is Agency projects which originate from an agency business need. Agency projects can range from simple requests to add or upgrade circuits or as complex as implementing a new application that needs servers, storage, network connectivity, privileged access, disaster recovery, etc.

The second type is Enterprise projects that originate from GETS and require Agencies to participate. An example of this type of project is implementing a new Enterprise service management tool like ServiceNow. This was an actual project that Capgemini led, but that involved all of the agencies, GTA, and the service providers for requirements definition, testing, and training. "These types of projects range from small to very large projects, and our portfolio is typically represented by about 400 to 500 projects every month."[8]

The Capgemini Multisourcing Service Integration model provides "a comprehensive, collaborative way of working that enables multi-sourced IT services to operate together in the delivery of IT services that fully align with business objectives."[7]

Capgemini has a PMO that reports to the GETS PMO organization. "They manage the portfolio projects at a detail level. Some projects have multiple providers. For example, Unisys and AT&T may provide services on a specific project. Capgemini is responsible for preparing a fully functional integration plan, including multiple inter-dependencies."

Keller's PMO works closely with the Capgemini MSI organization. "My PMO team works closely and collaboratively with the Capgemini PMO team, and we meet regularly with service tower providers and Capgemini PMO team members. Our focus is to collaborate regularly to ensure the successful execution of all projects. and the service providers are providing the best possible service to our agencies effectively."[9]

The GETS PMO is responsible for aggregating all processes and is ultimately responsible for ensuring the successful implementation of Agency projects. Figure 8.10 represents the distribution of projects across the multi-sourced vendors.

As previously mentioned, Keller is responsible for managing all GETS projects, which average about 400–500 per month, and provides oversight to the Capgemini PMO team that manages the tactical aspects of agency projects. It's an interesting model and works as follows.

The GETS PMO function is unique due to the use of Capgemini as the Multi-Sourcing Integrator (MSI). As mentioned previously. Johnson wanted an independent vendor to oversee the various outsourced service providers. Capgemini filled the bill.

Capgemini MSI service is a "comprehensive, collaborative, way of working that enables multi-sourced IT services to operate together to deliver IT services that fully align with business objectives."[7]

IT organizations that outsource services need to focus on business outcomes. This may not be easy to do if a lot of energy focuses on managing the outsourced service providers. This is where the Capgemini Service Integration solution enables enterprises to focus on business outcomes instead of IT service management challenges.[Ibid]

Capgemini provides PMO portfolio management for all the agency projects and manages the integration for all agency projects that requires multiple towers of service. Capgemini is responsible for the following:

- Creating a fully operational integration plan that includes interdependencies from different service providers.
- Scheduling and running meetings, recording and publishing meeting minutes, updating and communicating project status communication plans.
- Managing day-to-day portfolio.

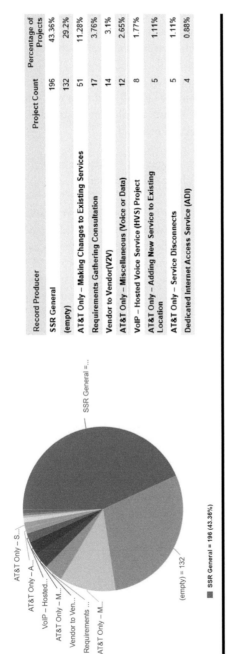

Record Producer	Project Count	Percentage of Projects
SSR General	196	43.36%
(empty)	132	29.2%
AT&T Only – Making Changes to Existing Services	51	11.28%
Requirements Gathering Consultation	17	3.76%
Vendor to Vendor(V2V)	14	3.1%
AT&T Only – Miscellaneous (Voice or Data)	12	2.65%
VoIP – Hosted Voice Service (HVS) Project	8	1.77%
AT&T Only – Adding New Service to Existing Location	5	1.11%
AT&T Only – Service Disconnects	5	1.11%
Dedicated Internet Access Service (ADI)	4	0.88%

Figure 8.10   Distribution of projects across multi-sourced vendors.

Managing Agency Requirements

The GETS PMO ensures that all Agency project requirements are documented, the design is complete, a project plan is in place, and a schedule is published. Keller has a team of Project Managers who govern and oversee this function.

> We have SLA's for projects to make sure we are meeting customer expectations. They sign off, and we sign off, and then we go to the solutioning phase where we create a Technical Solution Design, taking requirements and turning it into an actual solution.[8]

It's not uncommon for multiple agencies to request similar requirements. For services that they currently don't have, Keller explains:

> Here are two examples. The first is our disaster recovery program. We rebid our server solutions for disaster recovery, but agencies wanted additional options. As part of our resolution to this request, we developed a new service to meet our multiple agency customers' service level and recovery time objectives. The second example is from the Department of Revenue and Driver Services. Each has a unique application providing driver licenses, automobile tags, and vehicle titles. We worked with both agencies to develop DRIVES. This new cross-agency application provides a better interface and customer experience and incorporates all of these business functions into a single application.[Ibid]

Capgemini MSI

The Capgemini Multi-Service Integration Services is the hub that connects all the service providers

John Cardillo is Vice president for Cloud Infrastructure Services at Capgemini. The value of the MSI model is that it "enables enterprises to focus on business outcomes instead of IT service management challenges. It is a coherent end-to-end approach that allows companies to increase IT effectiveness and efficiency by overseeing the integration of Governance, Risk & Planning."[10,11]

- ■ Enterprise Planning & Programs
- ■ Service Management & Delivery
- ■ Service Performance Management
- ■ Relationship Management
- ■ Ecosystems
- ■ Contract & Compliance Optimization

Capgemini MIS Governance Process

Cardillo provides some insight into their governance process at GETS.

> We have a governance model that we use as oversight for vendors' services delivered to State Agencies. For example, Kathy Bailey is Senior Program Manager for Capgemini. We use the ITIL framework and have 26 discipline capability areas and integrate these to deliver the best process. As it relates to projects, we have a portfolio mode and PMs that deliver projects for individual agencies and transition teams that help us, onboard new vendors. Here's another example. Jana Wall is one of our Capgemini program delivery managers and works in our PMO organization. Her focus areas are processes, tools, agencies, and enterprise projects impacting GTA. Some enterprise projects have vendor projects that service providers between themselves.[10]

Governance Forums

Capgemini participates in all of the Governance forums. These forums meet either weekly or biweekly, or monthly. All key stakeholders participate in forum meetings. Capgemini PMO facilitates these meetings, records and publishes minutes, identifies any escalation issues, identifies issues, and communicates them if needed to other Forums. The goal is to minimize project risk. Unresolved issues are communicated via the GETS Escalation process and, if not resolved, are ultimately addressed at the GETS Executive Steering Committee. *(Author's note: more about the escalation process later in this chapter.)*

This Forum meets every two weeks. Attendees include Microsoft, Atos, who manage security services and mainframe, a GTA infrastructure consultant, and Keller, The GETS PMO Officer Janna Wall, the Capgemini Program Delivery Manager, who captures any issues that arise.

An example of collaboration and teamwork is when Unisys was to deliver servers in support of another initiative, and there were some constraints and interdependencies impacting delivery. Capgemini brought this issue up at a meeting. Unisys updated the team, a discussion ensued, and the resolution was to contact a senior manager from the vendor and expedite the delivery.

Another example is a software compliance issue that could impact a quarterly software license upgrade schedule. Unisys was having some difficulties with issuing its software licenses. It was a software issue, and the quarterly deadline for issuing software license updates was fast approaching. The issue was that additional tools had to be acquired to solve the issue. But for some reason, it wasn't getting resolved. At one of the Forum meetings, the unresolved issue was discussed. The team decided that this issue required escalation to the Executive Steering Committee (ESC) where a tiger team was formed to resolve the issue. It turned out that there were many moving parts to this software compliance issue, and collaboration and long hours were required to finally resolve the issue and the quarterly deadline for software compliance updates we met.

Continuous Improvement

Process optimization requires a continuous improvement plan. The reason is that focusing on enhancing and/or improving your processes will provide more value for your customers and improve the efficiency of process activities.

One of the GETS organization's processes continuously improved over time is the Issue Escalation Process. This was discussed earlier in the chapter (see Figure 8.7). I include the same graphic in the context of escalation, but it is numbered Figure 8.11. It represents the current three-level Governance Framework and Escalation process that improved over time. The first level is the Workstream "g" Governance level, where all the daily infrastructure activity occurs. Any escalation issue is elevated to the second level- the Enterprise "G" Governance. This level is represented by the various Forums/Committees that monitor infrastructure activities. If an issue cannot be resolved at this level, it is elevated to Executive Governance. The Executive Committee includes the GETS Management Committee and the MSI Governance Forum. Dean Johnson, as the COO, chairs the Executive Management Committee with John Cardillo of Capgemini as the co-chair. Sunil Aluri chairs the MSI Governance Forum with Sandra Robinson of Capgemini as the co-chair.

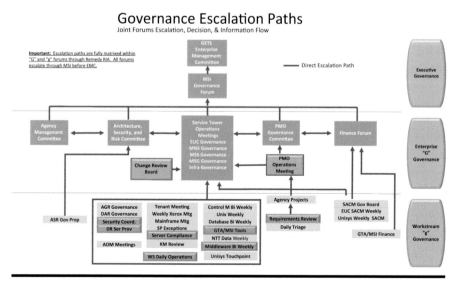

Figure 8.11   Governance escalation process – information flow.

Capgemini uses the Remedy tool to manage the issues, risks, and actions brought forward in any governance forums. And when escalation is needed, they have reassigned ownership in the tool. This automation allows for tracking and reporting for several issues, length an issue is open, and can even identify areas of continuous improvement in our processes.[9]

Keller explains how the escalation process improved.

We found that most of the escalated issues occurred at the Agency operations meeting where CIOs chair the meetings and the Capgemini Agency Relationship Manager is the co-chair. The resolution time for issues in these forums were lingering so we put more controls around the communication of Agency-specific issues and instituted escalation processes if standard timeframes for resolution were not met. Agency CIO made some recommendations to the very successful process. We then replicated the improved process as a standard for all Forums to follow.[Ibid]

There are other continuous improvement examples that Keller shared.

We continuously improve our governance management tools as well as Sharepoint, where we maintain all our forms and documents. And we have developers who improved our remedy ticket with automation resulting in an increase in efficiencies for our customers. Our developers worked hard to improve the functionality by creating a dashboard. We need to do more and will do so in the future. For example, we need to review the 300 standard reports we use to determine which to retire, improve, and/or revise.[Ibid]

Metrics

We've all heard various versions of the expression. You can't manage what you don't measure. It's true. So, if you're developing a governance solution for your organization, you need to include processes to measure how effectiveness and efficiency of your Governance strategy.

The GETS organization produces strategic, operational, and financial metrics to measure the effectiveness and efficiency of the infrastructure services delivered to State Agencies.

- Strategic metrics measure four key GETS Business priorities.
- Operational Metrics measure the PMO effectiveness and efficiency of project delivery.

Financial metrics measure the dollar costs and associated budget for delivering infrastructure services.

GETS Strategic Metric Reports

The GETS organization developed a standard set of Governance reporting metrics. At a strategic level, GETS publishes a monthly 50-page report titled "The GETS Program Measures" that includes detailed metrics for the four critical success factors, as shown in Figure 8.12.

1. Create a Secure, Reliable, and Recoverable GETS shared services delivery model: Figures 8.13–8.15 reflect an example of the reflect metrics on security, reliability, and recoverability. For each of these three reports, a dashboard of the current monthly rating provides a quick view of the status. In addition, the report provides the basis for each rating and a 9-month running average.
2. Continuously improve the quality and timeliness of GETS Services: As you can see, the format for each metric chart is similar. There are rating dashboard indicators (green, orange, and red) dashboard indicators, and a nine-month average rating bar and line graph (Figures 8.16 and 8.17).
3. Drive continuous improvement of Agency experiences: Again, the format for this metric is similar to the other charts.

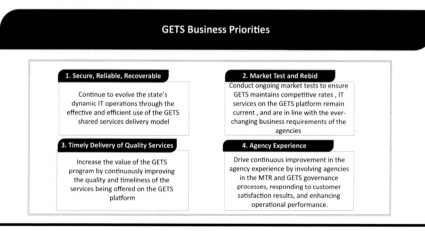

Figure 8.12   GETS business priorities.

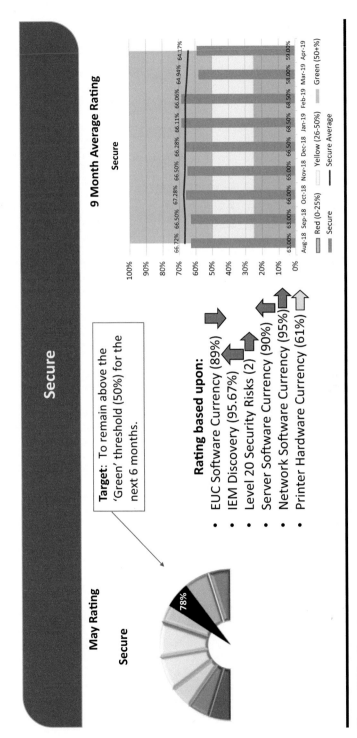

Figure 8.13   Secure.

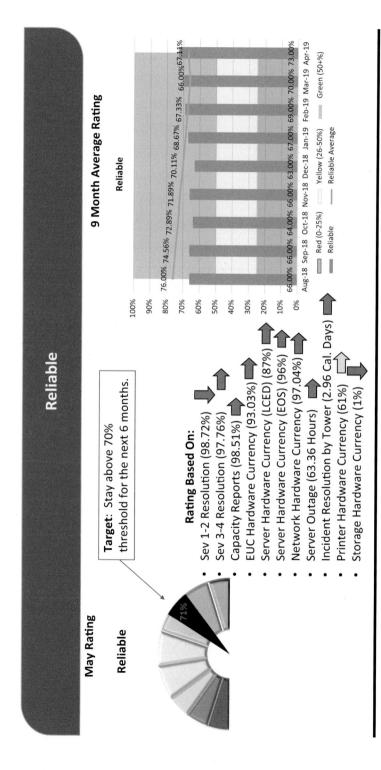

Figure 8.14 Reliable.

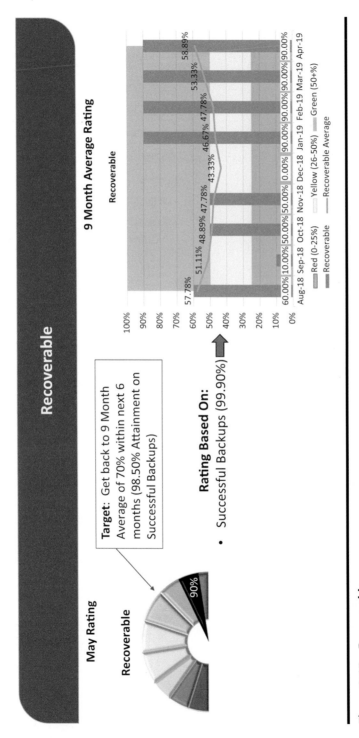

Figure 8.15 Recoverable.

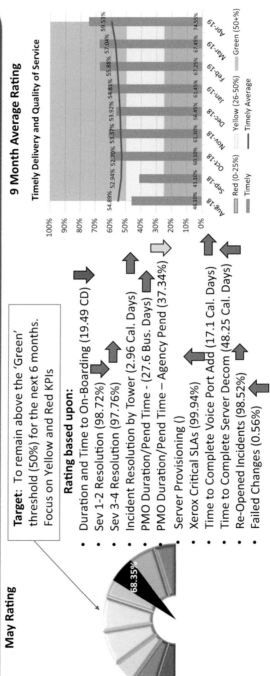

Figure 8.16 Timely delivery and quality of service.

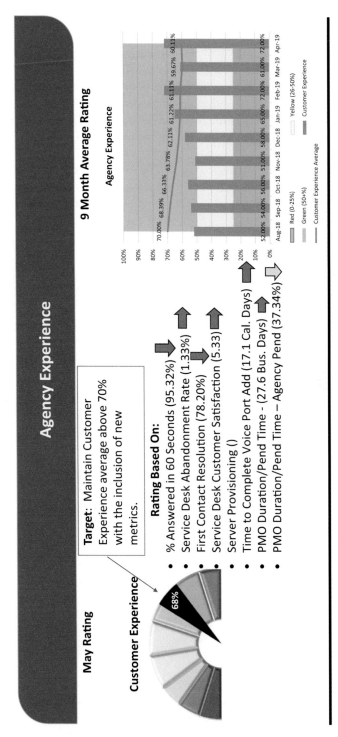

Figure 8.17 GETS agency experience.

Summary

Today, the GETS organization "gets" the job done. "We are a service organization and have over 1200 entities and 100,000 users utilizing our services", says Johnson.[4] But this was not the case back in 2007. Improving the delivery of infrastructure services to state agencies is part of the GTA strategic plan. As it turns out, Johnson's transformation of the delivery of infrastructure services by GTA and the GETS program to state agencies was perceptive. Let me summarize two of the key takeaways from this chapter.

The Georgia Enterprise Strategic Plan for 2025 identifies the five primary goals and associated timelines. Figure 8.18 is the graphic of the plan, previously referenced earlier in this chapter. As you can see, three of the significant goals directly

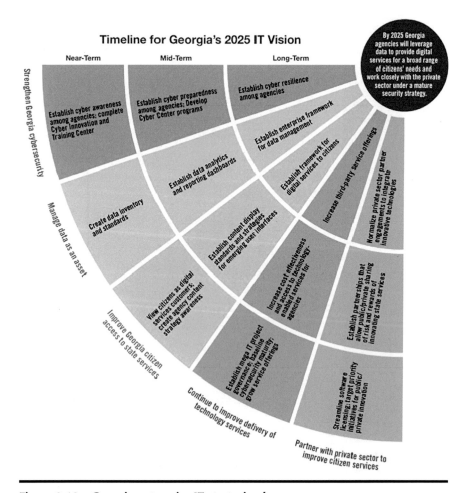

Figure 8.18 Georgia enterprise IT strategic plan.

A 10-year success story

*The Georgia Enterprise Technology Services (GETS)
program continues to meet the goals that originally
motivated centralization in 2009:*

- Consolidate IT infrastructure
- Secure state data
- Ensure a stable operating environment
- Ensure a well-governed IT enterprise
- Replace aging infrastructure
- Ensure robust disaster recovery
- Ensure adherence to industry standards

Figure 8.19   Georgia Enterprise IT Strategic Plan.

impact the services of the GETS organization. The five goals are listed below, and I've highlighted the three that affect the GETS organization

Strengthen Georgia Cybersecurity
Manage Data as an Asset
Improve Georgia Citizen Access to State Services
Continue to Improve Delivery of State Services
Partner with Private Sector to Improve Citizen Services

Figure 8.19 reflects the Delivery Savings achieved by the GETS organization over a ten-year period.

So when Johnson began GTA's transformation journey of the GETS infrastructure services in 2007, GTA leadership's vision directly aligned with the Georgia Enterprise IT Strategic Plan that defined the vision for 2025 technology services. And as you can see from Figure 8.19, Johnson, Keller, and the entire GETS team, the GETS organization "gets the job done."

Citings

1. https://gta.georgia.gov/calvin-c-rhodes
2. https://gta.georgia.gov/enterprise-governance-and-planning-main-page/it-strategic-plan
3. https://gta.georgia.gov/about-gta
4. Https://www.georgia.org/demographics#:~:text=Georgia%20remains%20one%20of%20the,in%20Georgia's%20population%20by%202030
5. Georgia Enterprise Technology Services (GETS) | Georgia Technology Authority.
6. https://gta.georgia.gov/dean-johnson

7. Dean Johnson/Phil Weinzimer interviews July November 19, 2019.
8. https://www.Capgemini.com/gb-en/service/technology-operations/infrastructure-services/service-integration/
9. Erica Keller/Phil Weinzimer interview August 8, 2019.
10. Cap video testimonial; https://www.youtube.com/watch?v=QrCwL3LGwsQ
11. Phil Weinzimer/John Cardillo interview, October 6, 2019.

Chapter 9

How the CIO of an Agriculture Conglomerate Reinvented Its Governance Competency to Improve Project Success

A business that institutionalizes a governance culture and focuses on process optimization, project alignment, and leadership excellence exemplifies the core tenets of Strategic IT Governance 2.0. The Andersons is such a company. Tony Lombardi – CIO and his IT team spearheaded the transformational change supporting the agriculture supply chain company growing to an $8 billion business.[1]

Harold and Margaret Anderson founded The Andersons Truck Terminal in 1947. The company started a grain terminal with nine truck bays along the Maumee River in Maumee, Ohio. They chose this location because of its logistical value for distribution since the Maumee river runs from northeastern Indiana into northwestern Ohio and Lake Erie. Today, this multibillion-dollar, 2,400-employee conglomerate provides grain, ethanol, plant nutrient, and rail service across North America and Canada. The company serves critical links across the North American Supply Chain through its four divisions – Trade, Ethanol, Plant Nutrient, Rail – at approximately 150 locations.[1]

DOI: 10.1201/9781003317531-9

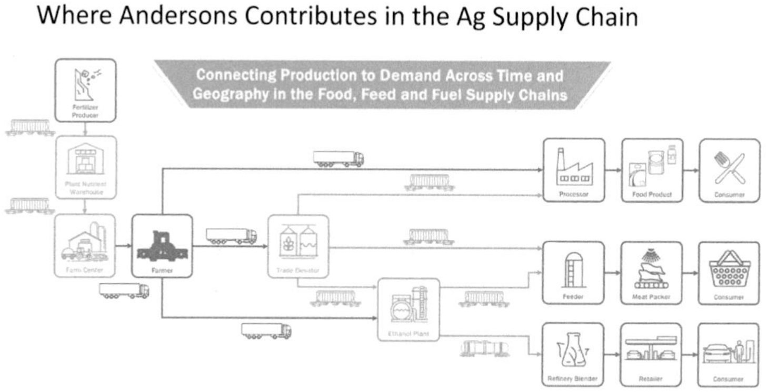

Where Andersons Contributes in the Ag Supply Chain

Figure 9.1 The AndersonsAG supply chain.[1]

The company buys, stores, and sells grain as a key value-added contributor within the agriculture supply chain. The Andersons supply chain is complex (see Figure 9.1). The company provides farmers services to help develop grain investment plans to determine how much grain to store in elevators, advise selling grain at future prices, and manage and minimize crop asset risk. On the crop input side of the supply chain, the company delivers numerous fertilizer products. The processing portion of the supply chain operates five ethanol plants and several fertilizer plants on the supply chain's crop input side. They own and lease rail car assets that transport grain, fertilizer, and ethanol logistics through lease service to other companies and rail operators. In effect, they manage the elements across the entire agriculture supply chain.[Ibid]

A few years ago, I learned about The Andersons when I presented Information Technology Strategy concepts to a large group of CIOs in Chicago on a beautiful October day. After my presentation, I mingled with the group and recognized Tony Lombardi. I walked over, re-introduced myself, and exchanged pleasantries. I met Lombardi a few years earlier when I spoke at another CIO event. Over the years, Tony and I communicated often. We shared our thoughts on the increasingly strategic role of the CIO and how technology today is one of the significant enablers of business strategy. Tony is smart, easy to talk with, and communicates well. We talked about how he and his team developed a governance process at The Andersons aligned very much with my presentation. I was eager to find out more about his process.

At the time of writing this chapter, Tony Lombardi was CIO at The Andersons. On September 30, 2020, he retired after a successful career. Fortunately for Lombardi, other companies were looking for interim CIOs, and Lombardi is still keeping busy and helping other IT organizations leverage technology in new and innovative ways.

While still CIO at The Andersons, Lombardi shared how his team developed and implemented a Governance process at The Andersons that changed the culture of the company's relationship with IT and provided significant business value. It is an amazing story but I'm getting ahead of myself. So let me take a step back and share with you his governance transformation journey.

Tony Lombardi – CIO

Lombardi received a bachelor of science degree from Moravian College in Bethlehem, Pennsylvania, and a master of science degree in computer science from Villanova University. His successful IT career spans 40 years in various technology disciplines, focusing over the last 19 years on IT strategy development and systems implementation and 10 years as a chief information officer. The Andersons appointed Lombardi CIO in September 2016, and Lombardi retired in 2020. At the time of this writing, Lombardi was still CIO at The Andersons. As I mentioned earlier, I've known Lombardi for a few years, and we've had numerous conversations about the changing role of the CIO and technology issues. I've spoken with some of his CIO colleagues and understand why they recognize him as an exceptional leader and team builder. He always works collaboratively across the organization, developing strong relationship building, technical and operational teams (Figure 9.2).

The Andersons IT organization was without a CIO for the three years before Lombardi joined the company. There was a big push for SAP, which involved numerous consultants and IT personnel working together in a siloed team. As the SAP implementation advanced beyond a difficult initial implementation, company executives decided it needed a professional IT executive to manage the technology organization and take it to the next level. Additionally, the executive team was feeling the effects of an underinvested IT capability that required experienced leadership.

During his first three years as CIO, Lombardi transformed IT by developing a Governance process that emphasizes business value through leadership excellence and IT efficiency, focusing on strategic project alignment and process optimization. Lombardi centralized IT, built an effective IT organization through process

Figure 9.2   Tony Lombardi, CIO-The Andersons, Inc.

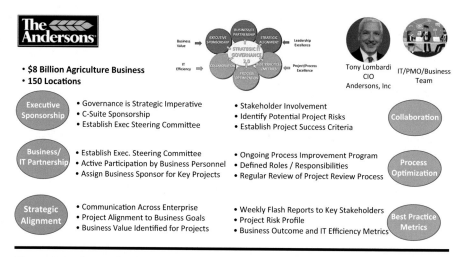

- **$8 Billion Agriculture Business**
- **150 Locations**

Tony Lombardi
CIO
Andersons, Inc

IT/PMO/Business
Team

Executive Sponsorship	• Governance is Strategic Imperative • C-Suite Sponsorship • Establish Exec Steering Committee	• Stakeholder Involvement • Identify Potential Project Risks • Establish Project Success Criteria	Collaboration
Business/ IT Partnership	• Establish Exec. Steering Committee • Active Participation by Business Personnel • Assign Business Sponsor for Key Projects	• Ongoing Process Improvement Program • Defined Roles / Responsibilities • Regular Review of Project Review Process	Process Optimization
Strategic Alignment	• Communication Across Enterprise • Project Alignment to Business Goals • Business Value Identified for Projects	• Weekly Flash Reports to Key Stakeholders • Project Risk Profile • Business Outcome and IT Efficiency Metrics	Best Practice Metrics

Figure 9.3   Strategic IT Governance 2.0 competencies – The Andersons.

improvement and controls, and implemented an enterprise governance process that has provided significant business value.

Over a few years, Lombardi created a Governance competency with The Andersons. Any transformation initiative such as this has its challenges and road-blocks. Below is a summary of Lombardi and his team's key competencies that align with the Strategic IT Governance 2.0 model (Figure 9.3).

The story of how Lombardi and his team were able to accomplish this is valuable for any executive wanting to improve their strategic governance competency within their company. Let me share how Lombardi and his team successfully implemented a Strategic IT Governance 2.0 model within The Andersons.

Developing a Vision and Reorganizing the IT Organization

Lombardi's early vision for the information technology team was "to provide services to the corporate functions as well as the other four other business units-Trade, Plant Nutrient, Rail, and Ethanol."[1] He realized that this first version of a vision missed a critical component. Lombardi understands that personnel in every company must work together to achieve the company's goals and objectives. Tony always focused on building coherent teams that cut across organizational boundaries and work together collaboratively. So, he – along with his team – improved his vision, "to be passionate about delivering high-quality IT-the right work done the rights way-that enables business growth, profitability, and user productivity while creating an energetic and enjoyable workplace for IT employees."[2]

To accomplish his revised vision, Lombardi recognized that he needed to reorganize the IT organization. Before Lombardi arrived at The Andersons, the company was on a multiyear SAP implementation journey. The main focus area for IT personnel was to support the SAP implementation consultants and maintain other systems and capabilities with staff across various business units using a cadre of IT personnel assigned to the central IT organization.

When Lombardi arrived at The Andersons, the initial SAP implementation was winding down while the subsequent phase was ramping up. He recognized that an essential element to the reorganization is to service corporate and the four business units. Over the next 18 months, he changed the reporting structure where all IT personnel reported into the central IT organization, regardless of location. IT personnel still performed the remaining SAP implementation tasks but now reported into a centralized IT structure. His next step was to evaluate his IT staff, determine which personnel could develop productive relationships with business leadership teams, and identify those that were very good technically and thrived in this role.

The early SAP projects relied on a large number of outside contractors. Tony believes,

> …for any implementation of 3rd party software to be successful long term, we need to develop self-sufficiency in how we build, use and enhance the software. Using contractors to create a train-the-trainer approach is fine, and I give credit my predecessor for insisting on "hand-in-glove" co-implementation as a training process. But to have contractors do all the work and then hand off the implemented solution to the users is almost a guarantee of user dissatisfaction when the software becomes operational.[3]

As the SAP projects shifted to other business groups, IT personnel developed the skills necessary to continue additional implementations and become trainers for the system users. This point is nontrivial. The IT team felt inhibited by the contractor staff-not that contractors were intentionally distancing, but in a quest to *get the job done.* When Lombardi decided to go all-in with insourcing, it was an opportunity to encourage and motivate the IT and business staff to take ownership. A highlight of the reorganization plan was the shift to insourcing and the ability for the team to step up and overcome the remaining SAP implementation challenges. The SAP implementation contractor played a valuable role in incorporating side-by-side training to Andersons' staff.

Executive Sponsorship on Value of Governance

Based on prior experiences, Tony knew that the only way to elicit executive support was to give them a level of transparency and input. IT started by demonstrating that transparency both one-on-one and in business team settings. They would ask: What projects is IT working on? Why and where are we improving our infrastructure? What are the exact cost details, and how are costs allocated? This transparency gave rise to credibility and trust as the IT organization transformed – which itself was also a transparent process.

Lombardi reported to Patrick E. Bowe, CEO of The Andersons. The executive management team consists of the CEO, the business group presidents, and the finance, HR, legal, and IT heads. Lombardi always believed that governance is an integral part of the IT organization and the business enterprise. As he developed his transformation plan, governance was a critical success factor. Lombardi has implemented transformations throughout his career and knows that the people component is critical for any transformation program. Lombardi recognized that changing the organization's culture to focus on project alignment, process optimization, and leadership excellence would be challenging. It took a while to create this awareness across the executive team, but ultimately they saw the business value in developing a robust governance process across the enterprise. The executive team recognized the business value of governance and supported the effort. Lombardi was now ready to move on to his other two initiatives.

Establish a Business/IT Partnership

One of the challenges for any CIO looking to create a strategic IT governance process that transcends the information technology organization's boundaries is to create information transparency. Lombardi recognized that business units traditionally consider IT organizations as a cost center where *technology stuff happens.* Lombardi wanted to change this perception to the business unit personnel regarding the information technology organization as a strategic partner. To accomplish this, he needed to create transparency of information for all information technology activities and create a governance culture where everyone worked together to achieve the company goals and objectives.

Lombardi established an Executive Steering Committee (ESC) for each of the four major business groups-Trade, Plant Nutrient (PN), Ethanol, and Rail-business to accomplish transparency. Each of the four committees consists of the business unit president and direct report business sponsors, CIO, IT directors, and key stakeholders. Over time, the attendees only included key decision-makers. The steering committee provides the necessary oversight for projects to mitigate potential risk areas and resolve any project issues that the project teams cannot resolve.

The Executive Steering Committee meets monthly, initially facilitated by Lombardi and eventually to the business relationship management teams. This committee reviews proposed, existing, and infrastructure projects that will impact the business and potential issues and challenges. The group also resolves any project issues that the project teams cannot resolve. The focus is on major projects over $100k, representing an important project to enable a strategic initiative or a technology infrastructure project, allowing the group to concentrate on those projects that impact the business group. The goal is to have transparency of information and include business unit leaders in the management of project oversight. After all, the IT organization executes projects identified by the business – other than internal infrastructure projects that provide the technology architecture and foundation for business systems. As Lombardi says, "we went from an organization not fully aligned with the business to be fully transparent in making decisions."[ibid]

Figure 9.4 represents an example of a slide used during one of the ESC meetings. The IT relationship manager presents the information to the meeting attendees and uses this slide to facilitate a discussion on these projects' status. You will note the information includes project name, priority ranking, current status, sponsor name, start and end date, and comments. I'll discuss how projects are prioritized further in this chapter.

Lombardi's team provides a listing of the major IT projects in the queue for implementation (see Figure 9.5). As Lombardi says, "I want the business to fully understand the project that impacts their business group directly when the projects start and the IT projects that provide an infrastructure foundation for enterprise business systems."[4]

The ESC includes the business sponsor for every significant project. Lombardi felt this is an essential component of business involvement, transparency, and communication.

> I needed to ensure that a business unit vice-president would step up to the plate and take ownership via a sponsorship role for every project. By having an executive sponsor, business unit leaders directly guide IT staff working on their projects. An executive sponsor is vital since every project that creates or enhances products or processes impacts the business enterprise. As business group vice-presidents became more comfortable in this role, they involved other leaders in their organization. The executive sponsorship role expanded within each business group as more leaders recognized the importance of the position.[ibid]

With the executive steering committee in place and business sponsors established for projects, Lombardi wanted to ensure that the executive committee was aware of all technology projects' status. The team worked on a cadence of weekly (became semi-monthly as the processes matured) project reviews and monthly transparency to the executive team. He accomplished this by publishing a Monthly Project Activities report. The business group presidents were interested in this report as it summarized all the visible and impactful projects. The one- to two-page report includes vital statistics for each project providing information such as investment information, business value, originating organization, project objectives, project status with a color-coded dashboard of red, yellow, green to indicate no issues, potential issues, and significant issues, as well as mitigation plans.

Business Group Project Priorities – Monthly Group review

Title	Rank	Status	Sponsor	Start Date	End Date	Comments
Location/plant to SAP	1	Active	[VP mfg]	2/20	9/2	See project flash slide
Business process to SAP	2	Active	[VP mfg]	TBD		See Lawn slide
Customer Portal Features	3	Active	[unit CEO]	Sprint Releases – 7/8 (next)		Customer data to be moved to production 7/8. Work is continuing on the invoice, BOL and contract documents for product A & product B
EDI for xyz suppliers	4	Completed	[vp ops]	1/20	7/8	ABC & XYZ go live scheduled for 7/8
Freight logistics automation	5	Planning	[vp ops]	TBD		Contracts/loads first, then logistics, then invoices plan will be for those. Same resources as SAP go lives (caution). Will need business resources to test.
Salesforce Features	6	Active	[vp sales]	Sprint Releases -7/30 (next)		See Salesforce slide
New freight hauler approvals	7	Assess	[vp ops]			Freight hauler onboarding process automation
[App] Hosted	8	Active	[vp channel]	7/15	9/8	Site A & Site B ready to be migrated to the [app] hosted environment
Plant shift worker posting app	9	Planning	[vp mfg, unit CEO]	TBD		Creation of online shift swap application. High level process/wire frame complete, working business case

On track against current baseline
Progress trending unfavorable

Figure 9.4 Division project priorities.

Major IT Project Summary – to CEO/Staff, All business groups
as of [date]

Project Name	BU	Investment $000	Value $000/yr	Status	PM/IT Lead	Comments	Go-Live Date
[Plant/location] to SAP				●		Good progress has been made on the fifteen development items with three completed and nine being tested. Data conversion updates are in process and development is continuing. The first mock data load starts in two weeks with the first FIT cycle following the load.	9/2
[group] plant-System				●		Working on C Design/Development. Wrapping up pass 1 of design for D	Site A & B complete Site C 10/1 Site D 3/25
Salesforce Features				●		Complete. Contracts and Orders for [products A & B] moved to production.	5/21 5/29
Salesforce Replace [legacy CRM]				●		Team currently working through interface specs for data sources A, B, C.	5/27 6/27
New – Business Activity/Position Report				●		Re-aligned the priority and timing for each deliverable at business request. Finalized development of forward looking views; focused on the ABC solution and enhancements to new views. Frequent changes requested.	8/10
[legacy system to existing customer portal]				●		Functional spec completed – starting review process. Working vendor set up.	10/6
SAP EHP8 Upgrade & Landscape Improvements				●		The upgrade is on schedule with testing in process. Scheduling all [product A] users to test their scripts in the QA environment.	7/1
Customer Portal Features				●		Team working through pdf invoices on Website; developing UI for [channel] Customers.	12/31

○ Project Scoping/Replanning
● Progress trending unfavorable or too early to tell
● On track against current baseline
● Progress off track & additional actions/re-planning required

Figure 9.5   Major IT project in queue.

Strategic Alignment

Strategic alignment has always been a critical challenge for any organization. The goal is to develop a process by which enterprise technology projects' selection aligns with the company's strategic goals and objectives and prioritize projects based upon a qualitative metric. One of the obstacles to an effective strategic alignment process is when individual business group executives request pet projects that improve their business unit performance even though they do not align with the enterprise business strategy. Doing so creates a subset of projects that inhibit the effective use of IT resources to support the enterprise business strategy and associated goals and objectives.

Creating a Project Prioritization Process

A president leads each of The Andersons four business groups. When Lombardi started the monthly steering committee meetings, his goal was to create a transparent communication path. To accomplish this, he and his team developed an objective process for prioritizing projects that would replace the subjective discussions that inevitably create conflict amongst the attendees. Lombardi created a Prioritization Framework template used for every new project and reviewed it at the monthly meetings with the group vice presidents. The objective of the Prioritization Framework was to "Develop a transparent model, adopted across all groups/functions, for prioritizing – therefore resourcing – IT investments in the most optimal sequence for value capture."[ibid]

Before the development of the prioritization process, subjective discussions took place, resulting in non-value-based discussions. Lombardi created a single database of projects and used an objective process for prioritization to resolve the subjective discussions. The factors included alignment to business strategy, customer impact, internal user impact, financial return, the likelihood of success, alignment to IT architecture, and a few other factors – initially equally weighted – more to have the conversation than insisting on a calculated project sequence. While helping to recommend project sequence, the framework enabled the business teams to consider other factors (customer impacts, timing with other initiatives) in determining an ordered list of projects. IT had a few guidelines as well – once started, a project finished (unless it was so "off the rails" that success was unlikely); IT owned "how" and business owned "what"; and a few others. Ultimately, the model was simplified and weighted for more transparent communications, but the essential factors and outcomes remained consistent.

> This proved to be a very difficult process to maintain & we frequently encouraged the business groups to sequence their priorities – given various factors legitimately at play at any given time. The process did allow IT and the business leaders to objectively reject potential projects

(minimally back-burner) that couldn't meet the prioritization criteria. We were also able to compare across groups for the best values for the enterprise.[Ibid,2]

The business sponsor and IT business relationship manager score each criterion as high, medium, or low Impact and document any appropriate comments. The PMO consolidates each project's scores and reviews them within IT leadership and business unit leaders. What happens when there are competing priorities? Lombardi told me,

> We work hard to recommend a sequence for our projects - and therefore resource assignments - for the good of the enterprise, all scoring and benefits considered. We've never had a challenge we couldn't resolve. We can collaboratively agree that we can do these two projects but not all three. It's a collaborative process, and the business units trust our opinion, and IT frequently has to accommodate the more pressing business need or opportunities. There is no perfect process. There is always an element of subjectivity on the part of each business unit group. We try to balance the perspectives, resolve any conflicts, and stay transparent regarding overall value.[Ibid]

Lombardi said that the process works well.

> We have a pretty effective process due to the collaborative nature of our organization. In our monthly meetings with the business leaders, the project team provides a status update for all projects, what we are working on now, project issues, pipeline projects, etc. We have a conversation about reprioritizing based upon competing priorities and current market needs. Everyone understands resource constraints, budget issues, and a host of other challenges in project execution. We have always been able to resolve any issues that come up; that is the positive nature of our collaborative culture. The key to success is in the transparency of the prioritization process and open and honest communication.[ibid]

After Lombardi retired in September 2020, he took some time off to relax. Still, he quickly got back in the CIO role as an interim CIO for a chemical company, and one of the areas needing improvement was project prioritization. Figure 9.6 is an IT Project Prioritization ToolTemplate Lombardi developed with his IT team in collaboration with the business leaders. Figure 9.7 is the Scoring Guide used to identify the project value across five categories the following categories

IT Project Prioritization Tool – Template

As of Date:

Weighting Factors Low to High (1,2,3) — Above: Scoring Guide Factors with 0,1,3

Business Area	Project Title	Sponsor	Value Reason	Charter? (Y/N)	Strategic Fit	Customer/user Impact	Financial Impact	Technology Fit	Project Score	Likelihood of Success (Y/N)	Bus Case & Plan (Y/N)	Phase	Prioritization Notes / Comments
					3	2	3	2	3				
Operations	[vendor] Renewal - Simplify Architecture		Revenue Maintaining	Y	1	3	1	6	42	Y		Complete	Same scope as prior; Teams added
Distribution	[abc] Automation		Effic./Productvty - Soft $	Y	6	3	3	6	57	Y		Execution	Kickoff scheduled; [tool] upgrade in process
Quality	Analytics for [abc] utilizing Power BI		Revenue Generating	Y	6	3	3	6	51	Y		Execution	[source] data complete; waiting to tie sales data
Customer Service	[web app] - Enhance usability		Customer Demand	Y	1	1	3	6	29	Y		Execution	In process by [vendor]; waiting completion date
Operations	Implement new SOP process for quality		Effic./Productvty - Soft $						0			Planning	SOPs now in the tool; workflow vendor issue open
Customer Service	Automate [specialized] inspection audit		Effic./Productvty - Soft $						0			Planning	Programming done; waiting user accept.
Operations	Automate [specialized] audit		Effic./Productvty - Soft $						0			Planning	Programming done; waiting user accept.
Marketing	EDI - [new partner]		Customer Demand						0			Planning	Slow progress - long periods of [partner] silence
Cust Service	[app] Rewrite/Reposition		Revenue Generating	Y	6	1	3	6	57	Y		Initiation	(Holding) Deciding on features lists/focus groups
Operations	[automate procurement proces]		Effic./Productvty - Soft $	Y	3	3	3	6	44	Y		Initiation	IT working on a functional spec
IT	[finance item] - Compliance *(new!)*		Legal/Compliance	Y	0	1	6	6	35	Y		Initiation	Mandatory - evaluating vendors
Finance	[abc] Automation *(new!)*		Effic./Productvty - Soft $	Y	3	1	3	6	42	Y		Next	Wait until [project] complete
Operations	Improve Supply Chain [process]		Revenue Generating						0			Next	Discovery - Evaluate tool options
Operations	Automate [customer] Business Models (APIs)		Revenue Generating						0			Next	Business Process documentation in progress

Figure 9.6 IT project prioritization tool – template.

SCORE CRITERIA	Score	6	3	1	0
Strategic Fit		- Critical to achieve strategy	- Clear line-of-sight to achieve strategy	- Indirect visibility to achieve strategy	- No impact on achieving strategy
Customer/User Impact		- External customer game changer	- Internal process game changer - External customer process/data improvement	- Internal process improvement - No external customer impact	- No internal user impact
Financial Impact (3 year ROI)		- >xx% IRR, <xxx payback, <xxx duration	xx% – xx% IRR, xxx payback, xxx duration	<xx% IRR, >xxx payback, >xxx duration	No return; no payback, >24 month project
Technology Fit – Architecture, Skills, Capabilities		- Well known/understood technology - Clean architectural fit - Existing in-house skills/capabilities - No customization	- Some technology risk - Some architectural challenges; resolvable - May need skill training or short term consulting/contracting - Minimal customization	- Significant technology risk - Significant architectural challenges; resolutions could be risky - Need significant skill training or longer-term consulting/contracting	- New/unknown technology; high degree of architectural challenge - Need to hire skills or longer-term consulting/contracting - Significant customization
Likelihood of Success – Clear sponsorship, Business team readiness, anticipated adoption		- Sponsorship clear - Degree of change well understood - Business process change	- Sponsorship shared - Uncertain degree of change or changed may not be welcomed	- Sponsorship uncertain - Significant business change; users may not be ready	- No sponsorship - Business changes would have significant negative impact to users

Discretionary Project Value Reasons:

Revenue Generating

Revenue Maintaining

Cost Savings (Hard $)

Efficiency (Soft $)

Customer Demand

Non Discretionary Project Reasons: (Scored/resourced separately)

Maintenance (no new functionality implemented)

Legal/Compliance

Figure 9.7 IT project prioritization tool– scoring guide.

Strategic Fit
Customer/User Impact
Financial Impact (3-year ROI)
Technology Fit – Architecture, Skills, Capabilities
Likelihood of Success – Clear sponsorship, Business team readiness, anticipated
adoption.

You can see from the Scoring Guide in Figure 9.7 the scoring ranges are based upon a scoring characteristic that ranges from 6,3,1,0, with 6 representing a high score and 0 representing a low score. The IT Prioritization Tool and accompanying Scoring Guide is an example of a tool you can use. Modify it as necessary for your organization to prioritize and score your projects. IT will help take some of the subjectivity out of the process.

Collaboration

A true believer in collaboration is Richard Gonzalez, CEO of the global pharmaceutics company AbbVie, Inc. He believes that "a critical part of AbbVie's success is face-to-face interaction and cross-functional collaboration and is a cornerstone of AbbVie's high performance." He also believes that it is essential to "preserve and nurture our culture so we can continue to accelerate, to climb higher and to help the next generation of patients."[5]

Lombardi is also a fervent believer in using collaboration to instill a teaming culture enabled by active and transparent communication. Earlier in this chapter, I identified the numerous ways Lombardi developed collaboration as part of the governance process's Business/IT Partnership competency. There are other examples, as well, and let us explore a few.

Establishing a Collaborative Environment

Establishing the Executive Steering Committees was a cornerstone of building a collaborative IT-Business collaborative model at The Andersons. During the early stages of the governance transformation, Lombardi recognized that IT personnel felt disconnected from the business, and he had to do something to correct this.

To facilitate a business-IT collaborative culture, Lombardi transferred some business personnel into the IT organization. Business analysts, project leaders, and other skills came over to IT in the consolidation. This allowed an opportunity to cross-train and enabled IT to use resources where best needed for the enterprise. Further, it encouraged staff to branch out to work on other business groups' technologies to improve their skills and enhance their potential career path.

Another example is in fully opening IT financials to the business leadership and finance teams. Providing financial data to business leaders offered a sense of where they can control costs and where prior decisions dictate current cost commitments (such as a software maintenance agreement or amortization of a capital project). "We were also very transparent about the root causes and resolutions of business-impacting interruptions/outages, along with the resulting process changes that improved the results."[2]

Business Relationship Managers

Lombardi needed a bridge between IT and business to facilitate conversations and maintain the pulse and needs of business units. Lombardi established the role of Business Relationship Manager (BRM) as that *bridge*. "I assigned IT Staff to the BRM role with specific responsibilities for delivering IT services to their assigned business unit."[Ibid] One of the requirements of the BRM role was a solid background in business. Lombardi felt that BRMs would

> Excel at providing the necessary interface between IT and the business units with this background. *They would listen to business needs, provide transparency, improve communication, drive change and strategy as collaborative partners, and bring a team-based approach to connect IT with the business.*[ibid]

As Lombardi describes it, "we went from an organization that sometimes told the business what we did to one that is now fully aligned in terms of what they need – and occasionally and with growing frequency what we think they need."[4]

Information Transparency

Lombardi also recognized that business unit management's perception was that they were not well informed about the status of projects. They felt that they were basically in the dark, and this lack of transparency led to the inaccurate belief that

> IT was doing their own stuff, and we did not understand why. By providing transparency of information through the BRM, weekly/monthly status reports, and including business stakeholders in IT meetings, they were now able to be fully informed of which projects were in play, which was in backlog, resources utilization status, the status of issues, etc. We were also very transparent of project costs and how each business was contributing business value through the execution of these projects.[Ibid]

As a result of these changes, Business Unit management engaged in a collaborative partnership with IT.

Collaboration is one of the six competencies of a Strategic IT Governance 2.0 model. It is a critical component of the strategy and incorporated within each of the other five competencies. At The Andersons, collaboration is a critical success factor in the governance process, and it is key to the success of the Executive Steering Committee. Business Relationship Managers cannot collaborate with their business peers, and the PMO cannot achieve success unless personnel collaborate with business stakeholders. Strategic alignment of project requests to business strategy requires business and IT personnel to collaborate effectively. So, you can see that creating a collaborative culture in The Andersons enabled IT and business teams to work together to create new and enhanced products and services that improve the competitive positioning of The Andersons in the Agriculture market.

Process Optimization

Lombardi realized from his management experience that developing a governance competency requires effective processes. As discussed earlier in this chapter, Lombardi established executive sponsorship and a business and IT partnership as a foundation layer for the new governance model. In parallel with these efforts, Lombardi established a Project Management Organization with the IT organization. He recognized that as the company grew and provided additional products and services to its customers, the portfolio of projects in size, complexity, and breadth would increase. Lombardi and his team have made numerous process improvements along the way. The following are four examples.

Improving Product Management Techniques

Lombardi and his team improved Product management techniques for those solutions and services that benefit from a different governance methodology. These solutions include customer portals and apps that are both internally facing and externally facing (think transportation service collaboration). The notion is that a team – development, operations, sponsor – dedicated to a regular cadence of feature delivery highly responsive to user feedback is both productive and efficient. Lombardi provides a good *example*.

> A good example is our customer portal – the business group and IT engaged a vendor to facilitate a customer journey map that highlighted the capabilities that our customers would most value. This led to a prioritized features list well-served through agile/sprint-based releases, which generated feedback influencing the future features list. Customer

adoption was excellent, and the content & capabilities of the portal led to meaningful growth.[3]

Enhanced Use of Agile Techniques

As technology increases in complexity, it is often difficult to truly understand all the end-state product features. Using Agile techniques allows us to identify bundles of features that can be delivered quickly, provides for systematic development, review, update, and adaption based on potentially evolving value criteria. Using Agile techniques enables business and IT teams to collaborate through an iterative build process.

> The team has also begun to move in the direction of products versus projects – where we treat a given application as if it were a real software product for sale. Feature lists are agreed in collaboration with the business teams and Agile methods to cycle through development, testing and release phases.[ibid]

Lombardi and his team incorporate a variety of product management techniques where processes are best used.

> We've incorporated techniques for those solutions that benefit from a different governance methodology. These solutions include customer portals and apps that are accessible internally and externally, such as transportation service collaboration. The notion is that including operations, development personnel, and sponsors working together produces a regular cadence of feature delivery that is highly responsive to user feedback is both productive and efficient.[Ibid]

Lombardi and his team incorporate Agile techniques. "We use agile techniques to help identify features that can be delivered quickly, where the end-state product features may not be well-understood upfront and where the business teams and IT prefer to collaborate through an iterative build process."[ibid]

Establish a PMO

Lombardi recognized that one of his challenges in managing projects was the lack of an effective PMO organization. Lombardi knew that he had to develop an effective PMO process to ensure project oversight and governance success. "We had project management talent, made a few hires, set up some "lite" standard processes. Over time we built refinements such as a home-grown time entry system linked to a project attribute database and generated metrics for use by our managers."[Ibid]

Develop a Project Life Cycle Process

Lombardi and his team developed a Project Life Cycle process that provides a framework for managing projects. This framework provides a common understanding across the company of the phases and associated activities for projects. As you can see in Figure 9.8, the project life cycle starts with the ideation phase, moves onto assessing the value of the project, then planning the project, executing the implementation, and finally closing the project. This common framework helps the executive team, business group management, and IT personnel understand the project's lifecycle journey and actively participate in project reviews.

Each life cycle phase comprises a set of activities. For each of these activities, Lombardi and his team developed a set of processes that defined the specific actions, templates, roles, and responsibilities for personnel involved. Business group and IT personnel worked collaboratively to develop these processes, another critical success factor in engaging business personnel in project management activities.

Best Practice Metrics

As mentioned previously, a successful strategic IT governance process incorporates two types of metrics. The first is business outcome metrics, and the second is IT efficiency metrics. Although each represents a success measurement, they are different. Let me explain.

Business Outcome Metrics measures specific business results that impact revenue, improve business process efficiencies, increase customer value, and other business outcomes. The focus is to identify the business outcomes you want to achieve due to the project and measure its success.

IT efficiency metrics relate to project execution. The focus is to identify the metrics that measure the execution status of a project. These metrics usually provide the project schedule status, financials, resource utilization, risk, issues, quality, etc. And Lombardi and his team incorporated business outcome and IT efficiency metrics into their governance process in various ways.

Weekly Flash Reports for the most significant and visible projects provide an overview of the project and incorporate key metrics. Lombardi issued weekly flash reports depending on the various project attributes, "We would collectively agree that an individual project required less frequent flash reporting."[Ibid]

The Project Prioritization Model changed over time and included at different points categories of business outcome metrics. These are Business Strategy Alignment, Customer Impact, Financial Impact, and Likelihood of Success. For each requested project, the sponsor identifies the desired business outcome category the project would achieve.

For the most part, these value attributes were understood at project initiation without necessarily delving into the specific business metrics or dollar figures.

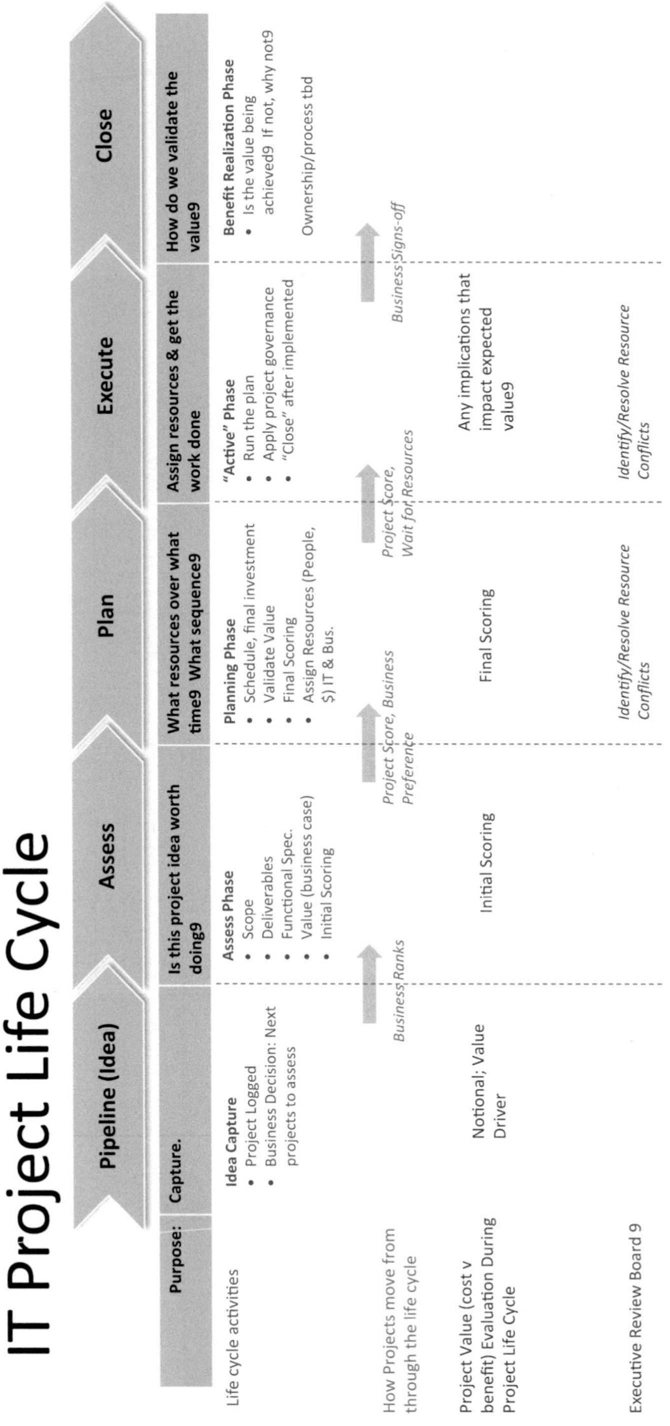

IT Project Life Cycle

	Pipeline (Idea)	Assess	Plan	Execute	Close
Purpose:	Capture.	Is this project idea worth doing9	What resources over what time9 What sequence9	Assign resources & get the work done	How do we validate the value9
Life cycle activities	**Idea Capture** • Project Logged • Business Decision: Next projects to assess	**Assess Phase** • Scope • Deliverables • Functional Spec. • Value (business case) • Initial Scoring	**Planning Phase** • Schedule, final investment • Validate Value • Final Scoring • Assign Resources (People, $) IT & Bus.	**"Active" Phase** • Run the plan • Apply project governance • "Close" after implemented	**Benefit Realization Phase** • Is the value being achieved9 If not, why not9 Ownership/process tbd
How Projects move from through the life cycle	*Business Ranks*	*Project Score, Business Preference*	*Project Score, Business*	*Project Score, Wait for Resources*	*Business Signs-off*
Project Value (cost v benefit) Evaluation During Project Life Cycle	Notional; Value Driver	Initial Scoring	Final Scoring	Any implications that impact expected value9	
Executive Review Board 9			*Identify/Resolve Resource Conflicts*	*Identify/Resolve Resource Conflicts*	

Figure 9.8 IT project life cycle.

SAP EHP8 Upgrade & Landscape Improvements

Project Manager/IT Lead:	Jane Doe
Phase:	Execution

Executive Summary Narrative

The upgrade is on schedule with testing in process. Reaching out to all [product] users to test their scripts in the QA environment.

Go Live Date	7/13/20	Status Date:	6/1/20
Overall % Complete	78%	Overall Health:	⬆

Issues/Risks

I/R	Brief Description – Action Plan/Mitigation	Owner	Target
R	Screen differences and other items caused by the upgrade might impact the running of [product] scripts. Mitigation: Reach out to all individuals with production [product] licenses and request testing be performed in QA.	Jane	6/8/20

Key Milestones

RAG	%	Task Name	Baseline	Revised	Actual
C	100%	ECB Upgrade	11/15/19		11/15/19
C	100%	ECT Upgrade	12/18/19		12/18/19
C	100%	ECD Upgrade	4/30/20		4/30/20
C	100%	BWD Upgrade	5/29/20		5/29/20
G	35%	[Tax sw] Non-Prod Upgrade & Testing	6/29/20		
C	100%	ECQ Upgrade	6/3/20		5/22/20
C	100%	BWQ Upgrade	6/3/20		5/22/20
G	10%	ECQ\BWQ Testing	6/29/20		
NS	0%	ECP\BWP Production Upgrade	7/13/20		
NS	0%	[Tax sw] Upgrade *	TBD		
NS	0%	ECR Creation**	TBD		

Accomplishments

- ECQ and BWQ are upgraded
- Vertex non-prod is created and being tested in ECE, so it won't impact other testing and the

Plans

- Complete QA and [Tax sw] testing with priority on the QA testing.
- Plan Go Live communications, including end user notifications on screen differences and system down time.
- Work with end users on testing [product] scripts.

* -The [Tax sw] upgrade might not go live the same time as the prod. upgrade. Decision will be made based on testing progress.
** -The ECR creation can occur anytime after the production upgrade is completed. Timing will depend on available resources.

Figure 9.9 SAP EHP8 upgrade and landscape improvements.

Sponsors knew what they were on the hook for, and the business leaders kept the sponsors focused on the desired outcomes and held them accountable. While this doesn't make for a clean "metrics" story, it points to the level of collaboration and mutual understanding of value. "Sponsors and business leaders knew when the juice was worth the squeeze and didn't rely solely on metrics."[Ibid] Not to discount good measurement, there were undoubtedly clear outcomes achieved and attributed to an IT project that included good business change management practices. There were specific wins for IT, and these included cost, cycle time improvements, staff reduction, productivity gains, and others.

Figure 9.9 is another example of a status report that reflects an example of a project status summary report for an SAP release upgrade. As you can see, the overall health of the project is green and is 78 percent complete.

Summary

Developing a governance culture within The Andersons involved much patience, guidance, and leadership. Most importantly, executive management, middle management, and personnel across the business are committed to recognizing that governance is a strategic initiative that requires project alignment, process, optimization, and leadership excellence. But the journey is not over. There is still more work to be done. "The collaborative culture among IT and business personnel was and still is a driving force that enables us to develop a governance culture that drives customer value, achieving our business goals and objectives that ultimately improves shareholder value."[6]

At the time of this writing, Tony is preparing to retire from a very successful IT career. He is leaving The Andersons with a governance competency that will bear fruit for many years to come. More importantly, Lombardi developed a company culture that focuses on project alignment, process optimization, and leadership excellence.

Citings

1. https://andersonsinc.com/history
2. Tony Lombardi and Phil Weinzimer telecon October 22, 2019.
3. Tony Lombardi and Phil Weinzimer telecon November 14, 2019.
4. Tony Lombardi and Phil Weinzimer telecon August 4, 2020.
5. https://www.cnbc.com/2020/09/11/pharmacabbvie-employees-raise-safety-concerns-with-return-to-work-plans.html
6. Tony Lombardi and Phil Weinzimer telecon July, 20, 2021.

Chapter 10

How the State of New Jersey Applied an Innovative Governance Model to Create a Transparency Website to Track COVID-19 CARES Act Funding

During the COVID-19 Pandemic, Congress passed CARES (The Coronavirus Aid, Relief, and Economic Security act) that provided funds for States to utilize emergency programs that would provide relief to individuals, businesses, and government operations. The Governor of New Jersey wanted to provide Transparency for how these funds would be utilized and mandated the IT organization to develop a public website that reflected how the State spends the COVID-19 relief money. The Governor's challenge to the IT organization was to create the website within 90 days. The governance process used by the State IT organization utilized the six competencies of The Strategic IT Governance 2.0 model. More details on the governance process used to develop the website follow.

DOI: 10.1201/9781003317531-10

Background

The Coronavirus Aid, Relief, and Economic Security (CARES) Act, signed into law on March 27, 2020, allotted $2.2 trillion, mandatory spending provisions, and emergency discretionary appropriation to provide relief to individuals and businesses, and government organizations.[1] The CARES Act comprises two main parts: Division A, authorizing language for several programs and mandatory spending provisions, and Division B, which includes emergency, discretionary appropriations. The State of New Jersey received $10.3 billion of the $350 billion provided to State and Local governments. In October, New Jersey governor Phil Murphy announced, "New Jerseyans deserve to know how the State is addressing the COVID-19 crisis and how their taxpayer dollars are being spent."[2] To accomplish this, Governor Murphy issued an Executive Order to develop a Transparency site within 90 days. The goal of the website is to provide

> Oversight and public confidence in the expenditure of federal recovery funds. And it will centralize information for the public on federal funding data and federally funded contracts to ensure New Jerseyans that the State is properly stewarding coronavirus recovery funds.[3]

The Governor, the New Jersey Office of Information Technology (NJOIT), the Office of the State Comptroller (OSC), and the Governor's Disaster Recovery Office (GDRO) worked as a team to develop the transparency site within 90 days of the date of the executive order. The website would track the State's eligible and planned use of any funds disbursed by the federal or State government to help New Jersey residents, businesses, non-profit organizations, government agencies, and other entities respond to or recover from the COVID-19 pandemic. It would provide a list of the contracts involving the allocation and expenditure of recovery funds and provide information on the various disaster recovery resources available to residents, businesses, and government entities.

Following is a deeper dive into how the governance model that creates the COVID-19 Transparency website maps to the Strategic IT Governance 2.0 model (Figure 10.1).

Executive Sponsorship/Agency IT Partnership

Obtaining Executive sponsorship for IT projects can sometimes be challenging. This was not the case for the COVID-19 Transparency project. As mentioned earlier, Governor Phil Murphy was the executive sponsor and champion for the project. "I knew I had Executive buy-in from the Governor when he issued Executive Order 166 on July 17, 2020."[4]

Strategic IT Governance 2.0 Model

Figure 10.1   Strategic IT Governance 2.0 model.

The Executive Order mandated the development of a transparency site within 90 days to track the State's eligible and planned use of any COVID-19 funds disbursed by the federal or State government. Poonam Soans, Chief Data Officer & Director of Application Development at the State of New Jersey, was assigned to develop the website. Soans has been with the State of New Jersey's IT organization for over 19 years and is highly skilled in the technology and business functions of the State. Soans was excited to take on this project as she knew it was strategically important for the State and would also benefit its citizens. Poonam realized that even though the Governor's Executive Order provided the sponsorship for the Transparency website, she needed to partner with key subject matter experts who would be instrumental in developing and capturing the required data. "Implementing the development of the Website would require a partnership between the IT organization and other State departments."[4] Poonam scheduled a meeting with her CTO (Chief Technology Officer), Christopher Rein, at the NJ Office of Information Technology. She mentioned to Rein that she needed to research potential commercial off-the-shelf solutions, which Rein agreed to. Poonam also knew that her team couldn't do this alone. "We need to partner with some of the key stakeholders."[ibid] The stakeholders Poonam referred to were Daniel J. Kelly, Executive Director of GDRO, and Kevin D. Walsh, the Acting State Comptroller from the Office of the State Comptroller (OSC). Rein agreed, and Poonam scheduled a meeting with Kelly, Walsh, Rein, and herself to discuss the project, some potential COTS solutions that are low-code, high-impact and the need for this team to oversee the project. The group agreed, and their first task was to develop a process for keeping the State's data current so the website would reflect accurate and current data. With Executive buy-in now in place, Poonam's next task was to develop an Agency/IT Partnership to develop and implement the website.

When Poonam's team began planning to populate the website, they realized that the primary data would be extracted from the New Jersey Comprehensive Financial System (CFS) that is hosted by the Enterprise Data Warehouse at NJOIT. But there are other required data stored in various other State Agency databases. Poonam knew that "It was very important for us to have accurate and current data."[4] Poonam communicated with the various agency heads to describe the project and identify the need for current and accurate data as a critical factor for a successful website. Her recommended solution was for each agency to appoint a senior-level official as the "COVID-19 Accountability Officer who is ultimately responsible for the proper disbursement of COVID-19 recovery funds by their respective agency."[4] Poonam's team developed a process for the COVID-19 Accountability Officers to provide the necessary data relative to the awards and expenditures that are NOT tracked via the CFS to her COVID-19 Transparency website team (Figure 10.2).

Collaborating with the State Agencies by identifying COVID-19 Accountability Officers helped identify current and accurate data and created an expanded team of subject matter experts who were key in developing the COVID-19 Transparency website. As described previously, Poonam and her team received an extract from the New Jersey CFS. Additionally, her team collaborated with GDRO to review and account for all required data from the State Agency COVID-19 Accountability

State Agencies With COVID-19 Accountability Officers

- Department of Agriculture
- Board of Public Utilities
- Casino Reinvestment Development Authority
- Department of Children and Families
- Department of Community Affairs
- Department of Corrections
- Department of Education
- Department of Environmental Protection
- Department of Health
- Department of Human Services
- Judiciary -Administrative Office of the Courts
- Department of Labor
- Department of Military and Veteran Affairs
- Department of State

- Department of Transportation
- Department of Treasury
- Housing and Mortgage Finance Agency
- New Jersey Office of Emergency Management
- NJ Economic Development Authority
- NJ Public Broadcasting Authority
- NJ Redevelopment Authority
- NJ Transit
- Office of Homeland Security and Preparedness
- Office of Information Technology
- Office of Innovation
- Office of the Attorney General
- Office of the Secretary of Higher Education
- South Jersey Transportation Authority

Figure 10.2 State agency with COVID-19 Accountability Officers.

Officers. As Poonam said, "Collaboration is key to ensuring that the quarterly process we have set in place works."[ibid]

Cooperation by stakeholders, especially the Accountability Officers, is achieved by sending each a reminder before the due date. "If there are any stragglers on the due date, we seek the assistance of the Executive Director of the GDRO (Kelly) and his team to work with the Accountability Officers to secure the necessary data."[ibid]

Strategic Alignment

One of the challenges for Poonam's team was how to manage the other projects for the State.

> Meeting the 90-day timeline was going to be a challenge. In addition to the regular operational and coordination challenges, the State was budget and resource-constrained, as we had to cut costs due to the ongoing Pandemic. The COVID-19 Transparency website was our top priority, and we had to place other ongoing projects on hold while working on this.[4]

The Agencies appreciated *that* Poonam's team continuously informed them of the status of their projects. "It was a truly collaborative process," said Poonam.[ibid]

Process Optimization

Poonam knew that to achieve the 90-day target to build the COVID-19 Transparency website would require some changes in processes. As mentioned earlier, her team developed several processes to update the project team, stakeholders, and agencies on the project's status. Following are some of the key process changes.

One of the key challenges in developing the website was collecting data within the 90-day deadline. Poonam knew from her experience that it could take months to build such a site. Poonam researched several COTS solutions and chose the Open Budget and Open Finance solutions from Socrata.

> Also, we knew our Data Warehouse already housed the bulk of the data that we needed – it was just a matter of getting them the business requirements for the data we needed. We also decided on leveraging Microsoft Forms to build and send reporting templates to the Accountability Officers. Each of these effects ensured process optimization/successful completion of the project.[Ibid]

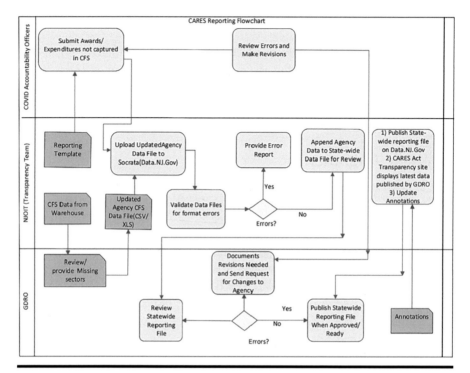

Figure 10.3 CARES Act reporting flowchart.

Another key process improvement was updating the process flow diagram for capturing data cumulatively to the current quarter versus the initial current quarter only requirement. Figure 10.3: CARES Act describes the flow of data through the reporting process

Overview of the CARES reporting process
1. The Transparency team receives CFS file extracts for both Awards and Expenditures from the Data Warehouse.
2. The team also sends Microsoft forms to COVID-19 Accountability Officers to collect NON-CFS Awards and Expenditures data.
3. Transparency team tracks submissions on the forms.
4. New programs are added to the forms as/when requested by AO'S.
5. An additional reminder is sent and followed up with GDRO if needed.
6. The team checks for any missing sector and emails GDRO for information on it.
7. Once submissions are received from AO'S – the dataset file that also includes duplicate files is sent to GDRO for validation. (Governor's Disaster Recovery Office and Poonam's Transparency team are the two teams doing the work.)

8. After receiving information from GDRO, the dataset is uploaded to a staging site for review by GDRO.
9. After receipt of the approval, the dataset is published to the public by the Transparency team.

During the website development process, Poonam and her team frequently met to review status and optimize the processes and associated tasks in the development process. No steering committee was established. "We held weekly and bi-weekly meetings to determine if any new processes needed refinement and reviewed the data requirements to determine if any process changes were necessary. It was a very iterative process and enabled us to react quickly."[ibid]

Best Practice Metrics

A key metric for the project was the ability for citizens to drill down into the complex financial data set used. "We developed a standardized list of terms used for our performance dashboards and rolled up the results."[ibid] Following are two snapshots from the COVID-19 Transparency website that provide such drill-down access for State personnel and the New Jersey citizens. Figure 10.4 is the New Jersey COVID-19 Oversight webpage.[5] Figure 10.5 reflects the expenditures broken down by State Sector,[6] and Figure 10.6 reflects the awards broken down by federal agency.[7]

Figure 10.4   State of New Jersey – COVID-19 oversight and funds tracker website.

Figure 10.5 State of New Jersey: COVID-19 funds tracker – expenditures by state sector.

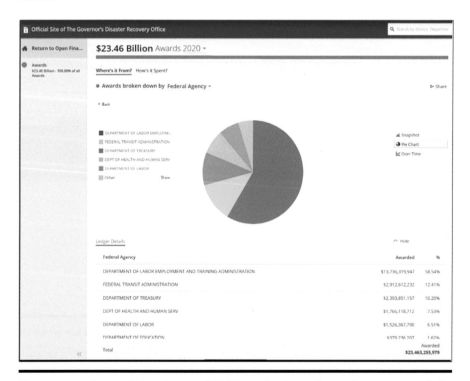

Figure 10.6 State of New Jersey: COVID-19 funds tracker webpage – awards by federal agency.

Summary

Poonam's success is rooted in the way she leads and her work ethic. She is expected to make big decisions, and that is not always easy, especially when there is a lot of money on the line. This is why it is so important for her to spend time doing her research, listening to the concerns of client agencies, and then using that information to reach a decision. "We are a team, and we all represent the State of New Jersey. As a leader, one needs to have the foresight and the gumption to take risks." Learning from her example can help anyone become a leader people are excited to emulate.

> I will do all it takes, everything I can within my power, and with the assistance of my teams to serve New Jersey. It may be a cliché, but if you love what you do, then it isn't work, and if we all share that belief, then we will be successful for the people of New Jersey.[2]

As much as Poonam is driving this data-led initiative, she will be the first to admit that it is by no means a one-woman show. She is surrounded by incredibly dedicated people who are as committed as she is and goes as far as to say that without them, the task at hand would be immensely difficult. "It all starts with having a great team," she enthuses.

> I'm very fortunate that I have great people working with me who understand my enthusiasm and my get-it-done attitude. I set priorities for my team based on the deliverables, and I also have a lot of support from other IT teams and management.
>
> I make sure that everyone on the team plays a different role, according to their strengths. Knowing your team, their personalities, what they can do, their strengths and their weaknesses. In other words, you know who to approach when you are in a rush, and you know which team member to go to when you want it done right and you have the luxury of time. For example, one may not be the best goal scorer, but they are great at moving the ball forward. You know that if you pass that ball to the person who can score, the team has a better chance of winning. I really think that makes a lot of difference.[7]

Using a cloud-based solution that is low-code, high-impact, placing data visualizations and dashboards for data analysis, and utilizing Agile techniques in the weekly and biweekly team meeting cut the project cost by at least half.

The new CARES Act transparency site is a testament to Poonam, her stakeholders, and team members, who instituted a governance process and launched the website on time and under budget. More importantly, it provides the citizens of New Jersey the Transparency the Governor wanted for how CARES Act funds are distributed.

Citings

1 https://www.kff.org/global-health-policy/issue-brief/the-coronavirus-aid-relief-and-economic-security-act-summary-of-key-health-provisions/?gclid=Cj0KCQjw5au GBhDEARIsAFyNm9GdTjCwG6BYSDe-F3Py47ne4XrOEQyMQTqQbGM_ zonGapUXQSnNSXwaAiN0EALw_wcB
2 https://www.nj.com/coronavirus/2021/05/nj-getting-105b-in-stimulus-aid-heres-how-much-each-county-and-4-dozen-towns-will-get.html
3 https://nj.gov/governor/news/news/562020/approved/20201016c.shtml
4 Poonam Soans / Phil Weinzimer Interview June 21, 2021, October 13, 2021.
5 https://covid19reports.nj.gov/#!/dashboard
6 https://covid19funds.nj.gov/#!/year/2021/operating/0/sector?x-return-url=https: %2F%2Fcovid19reports.nj.gov%2F%23!%2Fdashboard&x-return-description= Return%20to%20Open%20Finance,
7 https://covid19funds.nj.gov/#!/year/2021/operating/0/sector?x-return-url=https: %2F%2Fcovid19reports.nj.gov%2F%23!%2Fdashboard&x-return-description= Return%20to%20Open%20Finance,
8 https://www.b2e-media.com/magazines/state-of-new-jersey

Chapter 11

How a Raytheon Team Collaborated with Stakeholders to Improve Project Success

The Federal Aviation Administration (FAA) embarked on an ambitious multiyear, $1 billion program to modernize the aging equipment air traffic controllers utilize in 331 airports across the United States. Raytheon Company (now known as Raytheon Technologies) received the award.[1] During the first few years of the program, everything was progressing on schedule. One of the project milestones was to conduct a user meeting with a team of air traffic controllers to view and evaluate the Raytheon engineers' prototype design. The air traffic controllers were critical stakeholders of the new system but were not consulted during the requirements or design phases, per FAA direction. As you can imagine, the user meeting did not go well, and the project suffered the consequences. The FAA controllers identified numerous changes and improvements required for the new system and wouldn't accept or use it until implemented. As a result, the FAA changed their policy, allowing the controllers to collaborate with the Raytheon team in implementing the identified changes. Raytheon expanded the management team, bringing in additional senior experienced managers to direct and coordinate the expanded project. The project scope and schedule were restructured, impacting cost and ultimately extending the program over two decades, with the final system installed in May 2021 at the Grand Canyon National Park Airport. Participation by air traffic controllers, who were the key stakeholders, improved the system design and resulted in the users' wholehearted

DOI: 10.1201/9781003317531-11

acceptance of the new system. As one of the air traffic controllers said, "STARS is head and shoulders above what we had before. I can't imagine going back to the old system."[4] The program was recognized by the Air Traffic Controller Association (ATCA) for exceeding customer expectations and improving flight safety across the United States, receiving ATCA's Annual Industry Award in 2018. *Aviation Week* magazine recognized the program for its long-term program success and nominated it for the Aviation Week Quality Center Program Excellence Award.[5]

Who are your stakeholders? They are your management team or sponsor (approving your project and funding it), your internal organization that benefits from the initiative, and your external users, typically your customers or business partners. Collaborating with all your stakeholders is critical when developing and introducing new products, services, or enterprise tools for your organization. Why is this important, and what is the resulting fallout? Ignoring your stakeholders puts your endeavor at risk, and failing to involve them at every level of the development process reduces the likelihood of a successful outcome. Schedule delays, budget overruns, user non-acceptance, unreliable products, and ultimately project cancellation are some of the possible consequences.

This case study provides an overview of the project, and why including stakeholders in project design is a critical component of any project Governance model. Collaboration is a key component of the Strategic IT Governance 2.0 model. This case study is an excellent example of effectively including key stakeholders in every project to improve collaboration and project success.

Raytheon

Raytheon Technologies is a technology and innovation leader specializing in defense, civil government, and cybersecurity, and other government markets throughout the world. The company develops technologically advanced and integrated products, services, and solutions. They are among the world's leading aircraft engine suppliers for commercial, military, business jet, and general aviation customers. Their core business includes integrated air and missile defense; electronic warfare; command, control, communications, computers, cyber, intelligence, surveillance and reconnaissance; and space systems.

Best known for its Patriot Air and Missile Defense System, Raytheon has a broad portfolio of defense and related programs for government customers. More recently, Collins Aerospace, a division of Raytheon Technologies, developed the optical systems for the Mars Rover Robotic vehicle, one of the more publicly recognized Raytheon Technologies products.

Air Traffic Management (ATM) is one of Raytheon's business areas. ATM provides systems and solutions to government aviation agencies throughout the world. These systems, currently in use in over fifty (50) countries, include Automation, Communication, Navigation, Surveillance, and Air Traffic Management products supplied to civil and military markets.

The FAA is the world's premier aviation authority and provides overall air traffic management within the United States, controlling over 5 million square miles of air space. Air Traffic Controllers, located at Airports and the 22 En-Route Traffic Control Centers (ARTCC) throughout the United States, provide overall traffic control of aircraft on the ground and in the air at all times.

The controllers utilize radar systems, automation displays, and communication systems to monitor aircraft positions and ensure safe separation between aircraft and direct takeoffs and landings.

The STARS Program

The FAA embarked on an ambitious program to modernize aging equipment utilized by air traffic controllers. Dim black-and-white displays and obsolete computers were in use and needed replacement. The Standard Terminal Automation Replacement System (STARS) program was a competitive procurement, and Raytheon was awarded the contract beating out incumbent contractor Lockheed Martin. The FAA established system requirements without input from the air traffic controllers. Why did they exclude the users? Previous FAA programs where controllers participated in defining requirements were never completed due to constant changes imposed by the controllers. The FAA was determined to keep the controllers at arm's length this time to ensure program completion and success.

Excluding the user community – the air traffic controllers and equipment maintainers – turned out to be a serious mistake, critically impacting the program. How the program evolved is best told by Mel Weinzimer, Raytheon's Deputy Program Manager. Before you read on, I need to inform you that Mel's last name is no coincidence. He is my fraternal twin brother.

Mel Weinzimer holds a bachelor's degree in electrical engineering from Brooklyn Polytechnic Institute (now Tandon School of Engineering, New York University) and a master's degree in Engineering from the University of Pennsylvania. His career at Raytheon Technologies Company spans 38 years, holding positions of increased responsibility from design engineer, lead engineer, Program Manager to Director.

Weinzimer has held positions as Software Lead, SM-2 Block IV Missile Development Program, Program Manager, SM-3 Missile Program, Deputy Program Manager STARS program, Director, FAA Automation Programs, and Director, Surveillance Radar Programs, for the Airspace Management and Homeland Security business segment. Weinzimer served on several special assignments, including Site Manager for the Fore River Power Plant project, a 750 MW co-generation power plant constructed by Raytheon Company in Weymouth, Massachusetts, which was having difficulty and needed a program manager with special skills.

Following his retirement, he continued as a consultant to Raytheon for the next 12 years serving on the faculty of Raytheon's in-house education program, assisting in curriculum development and teaching program management courses to prospective Program Managers. Weinzimer was also a guest lecturer at the Defense

Acquisition University (DAU) and has taught program management to Department of Defense civilians and military personnel at the Huntsville, San Diego, and Ft. Belvoir campuses.

Weinzimer describes how he became involved in the FAA project.

> I had just completed my current assignment as Program Manager for the Standard Missile-3 program and met with my business Vice President. I asked him to assign me to a program that was in trouble. He immediately identified the recently restructured STARS program that was behind schedule and could use some management help. Little did I know what challenges awaited me.[2]

One of Weinzimer's first tasks was meeting with the current STARS program manager and being briefed on the program's history, accomplishments to date, and finding out why the program was recently restructured. During the briefing, Weinzimer thought to himself, "It was clear to me that the program was entering a new and complex phase where much could go wrong."[Ibid]

The project objectives were developing and deploying new computers with state-of-the-art software and color display systems for civilian and military air traffic controllers. The program would replace the existing 40-year-old black and white display screens and aging computers currently in use. Figure 11.1 shows the new display system, STARS, and the older black-and-white system, side by side.

Figure 11.1 The New STARS display, on the left, replacing the 25-year-old black-and-white display.

The new system featured high-resolution, bright color displays, modern computers, up-to-date user interfaces (keyboard, mouse, pull-down menus), and employed multiple hardware and software backup systems. These new systems would be installed at all 331 Terminal Air Traffic Control Centers (TRACONS and RAPCONS) and towers at civilian and military airports throughout the country and overseas (see Figure 11.2), including the top 5 busiest airports in the world.

What Went Wrong

As previously mentioned, the FAA did not include air traffic controllers and equipment maintenance technicians, the users, when establishing requirements for this new system. When the Raytheon team presented their prototype system to a group of air traffic controllers, it was wholeheartedly rejected. Users raised the following concerns citing safety and user difficulties in operating and maintaining the equipment. Among their objections are the following:

- Use of the QWERTY keyboard – The legacy system used a custom square keyboard for data entry where the keys were in alphabetical and numerical order (see Figure 11.1). They insisted that the QWERTY Keyboard system recommended by the Raytheon project team was insufficient and the legacy keyboard configuration should be retained, citing safety concerns.
- Pull-down menus – The pull-down menus with their solid background blocked the screen. They wanted transparent menus so that they could view the screen when using menus.
- Font size and color – They also wanted larger fonts and unique colors for other data types such as aircraft position, velocity, and flight numbers.
- Screen control – The keyboard controlled display screen parameters such as brightness, contrast, map orientation, and scale. The legacy system had switches and knobs surrounding the screen that controlled these functions. (see Figure 11.1) The controllers insisted that similar manual controls be implemented in the new system.
- Computer fan noise – The fans inside the computer chassis were noisy. Each controller workstation had multiple computers, and the controllers objected to the high background noise.
- Equipment repair and replacement – Equipment maintainers found it challenging to remove system components from the equipment racks.

The Air Traffic Controllers and Equipment Maintainers were members of powerful unions (NATCA and PASS) and insisted that the changes they identified needed to be made. Otherwise, they would reject the new system. At that point, the FAA had no choice but to listen to the users and engage with the Raytheon design team.

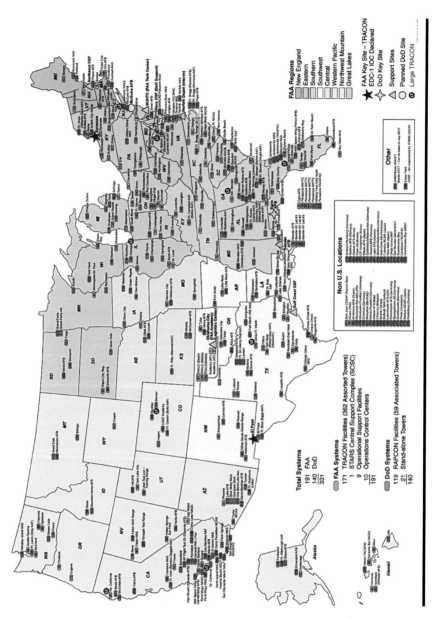

Figure 11.2   Planned 331 STARS air traffic control sites.

A joint evaluation committee was formed and included members from the FAA, air traffic controllers, equipment maintainers, and Raytheon. Throughout many months, user events were conducted at Raytheon laboratories. The users sat at the prototype display terminals along with Raytheon engineers, evaluating the system in detail and proposing changes that the joint committee reviewed (see Figure 11.3).

The joint committee chaired by the FAA reviewed the changes and was authorized to approve or reject proposed changes. They had configuration control authority. The approved changes were added to the system requirements documents, implemented in the design, and subsequently reevaluated by the users. Figure 11.4 reflects the controller workstation with implemented changes.

Allowing the end-users to be involved and engaged was a turning point in the program. It was now their program, not just the FAA's!

This process had several beneficial effects, both short- and long-term. First, it allowed the users to be part of the design process, and they were now involved in the requirements definition, implementation, system test, and key site evaluation.

Second, they now "owned" the design and had a stake in the program's success. The users who were part of the review process became advocates, promoting the system to fellow controllers and maintainers across the country. Per the National Air Traffic Controllers Association: "STARS works, and there is no reason why every terminal facility in the country shouldn't have it. Controllers are clamoring for it."

Figure 11.3 Air traffic controller working with Raytheon engineers at user involvement events.

Figure 11.4   STARS controller workstation with implemented changes.

Finally, the collaborative process also engendered trust between the Raytheon team and the controllers, which would be long-lasting and beneficial when needed for future changes. As one of the air traffic controllers at the El Paso airport said:

> We feel that STARS hardware is far superior to the previous version and the STARS software gives so much more capability.... STARS is head and shoulders above what we had before. I can't imagine going back to the old system.[4]

Project Impact

The hardware and software changes recommended by Air Traffic Controllers in the middle of the program significantly impacted cost and schedule. "If all the needed changes were incorporated, we anticipated at least a two-year delay in the delivery of the first system. So the program required restructuring."[2] With Air Traffic Controllers concurrence, the FAA and Raytheon agreed to an initial configuration containing only a subset of the required changes that could be delivered sooner to selected airports. It would then be followed by more complete configurations, each with more of the changes implemented. Ultimately five system configurations, introduced in phases, would be implemented, with each successive configuration incorporating more of the newly imposed requirements. This "spiral development" approach allowed for early systems deployment at smaller airports while developing the full set of features desired by larger airport sites.

The first configuration, designated EDC-1 (Early Development Configuration 1), was completed and installed at the El Paso, Texas airport in December 1999 and Syracuse, NY, airport in January 2000, within a year of the initial schedule. Subsequent configurations (EDC-2, FS-1, FS-2) followed and were installed at selected airports. The last configuration (all changes implemented) was installed at the Philadelphia, PA, airport in July 2002, three years later than the initial program plan. The FAA declared the STARS system fully functional and operational in May 2003 and planned future installations at other airports could now proceed. Overall program costs up to this point had more than doubled.

The next phase of the program, delivery, and installation of the remaining 300+ STARS systems around the country also became a challenge. FAA budget constraints limited the number of STARS systems that could be ordered and installed annually. Lockheed, the incumbent contractor, was constantly lobbying the FAA and Congress to stop the installations and allow Lockheed to install their systems. As a result, the annual installations varied from 10 to 40 systems, with the last of the 331 STARS systems completed and installed in May 2021.

An interesting footnote involved the military version of the system. In addition to civilian airports, the system was also planned to be deployed at army, air force, and navy airport installations throughout the United States. The military air traffic controllers loved the system during their evaluation of the prototype system, and, unlike the civilian Air Traffic Controllers, accepted it without any needed changes. They were all young men and women familiar with modern computers and accepted the system as designed. As a result, the STARS system as originally designed (see Figure 11.5) with

Figure 11.5   STARS display for military air traffic controllers.

Figure 11.6   STARS installation at Eglin air force base.

full functionality (no changes needed) was successfully installed at Eglin Air Force Base, Florida, in December 1999. The installation was on time per the original program schedule, two years ahead of the civilian Philadelphia installation (see Figure 11.6).

Award-Winning Program

Despite the rocky start, the STARS program successfully continued once users were brought on board and participated. The 110th system was delivered in October 2004. *Aviation Week* magazine recognized the program for its long-term program success and nominated it for the Aviation Week Quality Center Program Excellence Award.[5] The Raytheon Team also received the Air Traffic Controllers Association (ATCA) Industry Award for setting deployment records and exceeding customer expectations[6] (Citation: ATCA Awards Presentations, Oct. 2, 2018).

Celebrations are an important part of any major program. Figure 11.7 is a picture of the Raytheon project team celebrating the 110th installation. Mel Weinzimer is the third person from the left. Figure 11.7 is the project team celebrating with the FAA Administrator Jane Garvey (Figure 11.8).

Figure 11.7 **Mel Weinzimer celebrating the 100th STAR system install with the project team.**

Figure 11.8 **Raytheon project team with FAA administrator Jane Garvey.**

Summary

Did Raytheon learn from this experience? You bet they did. End-user collaboration is an integral part of the operational process employed by Raytheon's Missiles & Defense unit. A January 2022 article by Raytheon discusses how they integrate end-user collaboration they call *Soldier Touchpoint*, where members of the U.S. Army embed in the radar's technical and production teams. Soldiers see and touch the radar and share feedback with engineers to ensure the system meets user expectations (Figure 11.9).[7]

Figure 11.9 Raytheon user involvement.

Citings

1. https://www.rtx.com/
2. Mel Weinzimer/Phil Weinzimer interview September 15, 2021.
3. National Air Traffic Controllers Association, June 9, 2003.
4. Henry Munoz, El Paso Air Traffic Controller at from Users Group meeting at El Paso, *El Paso Times*, January 2020.
5. Letter to Raytheon, September 22, 2004.
6. ATCA Awards Presentations, October 2, 2018.
7. http://www.raytheonmissilesanddefense.com/news/feature/soldiers-see-and-touch-full-scale-ltamds

Chapter 12

How a Candy Confectionery Mastered a New Governance Model to Improve Business Performance

---

The purpose of this chapter is to demonstrate how an effective Strategy Realization Office (SRO) can greatly enhance Governance around strategy execution and monitoring. The strategic elements included in this chapter have been sanitized for proprietary reasons. The processes, tools, and techniques utilized by the SRO, as described in this chapter, are factual and reflect the great work of the SRO team and executive management.

If you are a candy aficionado, then you must be familiar with Mike and Ike° fruit-flavored candy, or Hot Tamales°, the very popular, spicy, cinnamon-flavored chewy candies, or Peeps°, the three-dimensional marshmallows shaped like chicks and bunnies at Easter. And then there's Goldenberg's° Peanut Chews°, first made as a WWI ration for the U.S. military. And to top it off, the famous Teenee Beanee° gourmet jelly bean. These products and other sugar confectionery products are manufactured and distributed by Just Born Inc., the nearly 100-year-old Bethlehem, PA-based privately held company founded by Sam Born and his two brothers-in-law, Irv and Jack Shaffer, succeeded by his son, Bob, and then, grandson Ross Born and nephew David Shaffer.

Candy making is as much an art as a skill. As Just Born matured in its candy-making, it has evolved its governance processes, both in the manufacturing and

DOI: 10.1201/9781003317531-12

in project governance processes. Most companies succeed in developing a strategy but fall short in executing the realization of these strategies into tangible business outcomes. In 2016, Just Born embarked on developing a Strategic Governance framework that would support the realization of business benefits for four primary business objectives. The governance framework, supporting processes, and associated metrics became the lynchpins in the Just Born Strategic Governance framework, which aligns with the six competencies of the Strategic IT Governance 2.0 model. Following is more detail on how the Just Born Governance framework evolved and its alignment to the Strategic IT Governance 2.0 model.

Background

In late 2016, Ron Arnold, then Sr. VP -Human Resources, led a company-wide restructuring effort and saw the opportunity and need for creating a Strategy Realization Office (SRO) for Just Born. Arnold previously worked for Merck, where he was a member of a well-established SRO office, which produced tangible results in enabling the realization of business strategy by developing a governance process for all enterprise projects. Arnold presented the SRO concept to the Just Born Executive Team in January 2017 and explained how it helped Merck realize business strategy and could do the same at Just Born. The Executive Team recognized the link between strategy and execution success and approved the creation of the Just Born Strategy Realization Office (SRO). Given Arnold's prior SRO experience he was asked to form and lead the SRO and was appointed as Sr. VP & Chief Strategy Officer for the Company. At about the same time, Just Born was expanding its Board of Directors from just Ross Born and David Shaffer as the owners to including five independent directors. This new Board fully embraced the SRO concept and continued to support it after Arnold retired in late 2019. With Ron Arnold's retirement Ed Broczkowski, who worked with Ron Arnold in building out and operating the SRO, took over as leader and was promoted to Vice President, Strategy Realization Office.

Executive Sponsorship

The Just Born Executive Team approved the SRO initiative sending a clear message to the organization that this initiative has the blessing of the most senior leadership, including the owners of the Company.

The Executive Team worked with the SRO to create a new, more robust strategic plan that includes its strategic Purpose, Vision, and four primary business objectives, as shown in Figure 12.1.

- ■ Strategic Purpose: Bringing sweetness to people's lives
- ■ Vision: To be a highly respected confectioner with beloved brands and enthusiastic fans

Purpose: Bringing sweetness to people's lives

Vision: To be a highly respected confectioner with beloved brands and enthusiastic fans

Objectives

| Establish Organizational Effectiveness | Gain Consumers | Focus on Customers | Drive Results |

Figure 12.1 Strategic plan – example.

- Business Objectives (actual wording is different than shown in the example):
  - Establish Organizational Effectiveness
  - Gain Consumers
  - Focus on Customers
  - Drive Results

The four primary business objectives provide a clear path forward for Just Born. The challenge for the SRO was to develop a governance roadmap that linked these four business objectives to the various strategic projects and ensure that projects align with the four business objectives and realize the identified business benefits. How did they do this? Read on to find out.

The Strategy Realization Office

Ron Arnold is credited with successfully bringing the SRO concept to Just Born to more effectively support the company's strategic planning and strategy execution efforts. Arnold's background includes over 35 years of engineering, human resources, organizational effectiveness, and strategy office experience across multiple industries. He joined Just Born in 2011 as the VP of Human Resources.

Arnold saw the potential benefits to having an SRO at Just Born and first convinced the Company's president and then the owners that those benefits would greatly outweigh the cost of the small SRO team he proposed. As a final approval step, he presented his SRO proposal to the Executive Team. Arnold explains that his proposal included three primary roles for the SRO:

1) *Leading and enhancing the Company's strategic planning process. Strengthening organizational alignment with the strategic plan, including building associate (employee) understanding and buy-in. And educating associates on business matters, the competitive landscape, etc., to provide them context for strategy, goals, objectives, etc.*

2) *Providing effective portfolio and project management execution techniques and tracking. Facilitating initiative prioritization, sequencing, and resource allocation across and within the portfolio.*

3) *Supporting the translation of strategies into actionable, functional, and cross-functional goals and objectives. Monitoring organizational performance and helping address barriers to goal achievement, performance acceleration, and sustainability.*

The SRO was approved and established as an enterprise organization since numerous non-technology projects also need governance. Consistent with the roles stated above, the objective of the SRO is to facilitate the strategic planning process as well as the organizational communication and commitment to the strategic plan. It is also responsible for monitoring the execution of the strategic initiatives and projects to ensure the realization of identified benefits. In addition, the SRO is responsible for highlighting any activity or event that brings risk to strategic execution and collaborates with other executives to mitigate those risks.

Within the SRO, a Project Realization Office oversees project execution and portfolio management. It is also responsible for developing and facilitating the organizational stage-gate process and commercialization readiness teams.

Arnold decided to retire from Just Born in late 2019 after seeing that the SRO was well established in fulfilling the above roles, that the strategic plan was being successfully executed, and that he had sufficiently trained and mentored his successor to take over leadership of the SRO. Following his retirement, Arnold started Ironclad Management Consulting to help other organizations improve their strategic planning and strategy execution.

Ed Broczkowski now leads the SRO, including the PRO. He is a 25-year veteran at Just Born. His previous roles at Just Born included Director, Business Advisory Services, Director, ERP Implementation, and Associate Vice President of Corporate Performance Acceleration (which was his initial role in the SRO).

Broczkowski describes why the SRO is an integral component of the Just Born strategy.

> It was essential for us to develop an SRO strategy and implement an SRO. Previously, we were undisciplined, didn't have a good framework, and chased shiny objects. We just didn't have the strategies, discipline, or processes to ensure that our projects supported our business strategy. We used some best practices in creating the strategic plan and developed deliverables that the executive team agreed to. Implementing an SRO is a major change initiative and no small task. The organization has embraced the concept; it is the right thing to do, it's attainable, and it focuses our organization on making the Company operate better and position Just Born for future growth.[1]

Strategic Alignment

The SRO team worked closely with the Executive Team to create a Strategic Plan Governance Map that aligns the four primary business goals with its associated strategies, initiatives, and projects. *(Author's Note: The map has been sanitized for proprietary reasons but includes three strategies for the first business objective.)*

Figure 12.2 represents an example of the Just Born Strategic Plan-Example drilled down to a lower level of detail. The Strategic Plan aims to provide the framework for the business objective and its associated strategies, initiatives, and projects for each business objective. This framework drives all the activities of the SRO and operating business units at Just Born in identifying and managing the associated strategic projects for the company. In essence, this is the roadmap that ensures proper alignment for all project-related activities.

Look at the first business objective, "Establish Organizational Effectiveness." You will notice three strategies (1A, 1B, 1C) to support the business objective,

- *Associate Development*
- *Create an engaging organization*
- *Refine Processes*

Figure 12.2   Strategic plan-example of next level.

Each of these strategies aligns to specific initiatives and their associated projects. Broczkowski provides some context:

> The Executive Team identified twelve strategies and twenty-three Initiatives to support the four primary business objectives, and we have over 100 projects to support these Initiatives. The Strategic Plan Governance Map provides clarity and alignment. It starts at the top with a vision and identifies the goals and underlying strategies and associated projects to achieve the business outcomes that drive our business success.[1]

The SRO team also created a strategic alignment tool that reflects the initiatives and each of the associated projects for each of the four primary business strategies, as shown in Figure 12.3. This provides a clear roadmap the SRO uses to govern the 12 strategies and 23 initiatives and associated projects of the Just Born strategic plan.

**Strategic Alignment
Objectives, Strategies, Initiatives & Projects**

Strategic Objective #1 Organization	Strategic Objective #2 Consumer	Strategic Objective #3 Customer	Strategic Objective #4 Efficiency
Strategy 1 Initiative 1: - Project - Project	**Strategy 4** Initiative 7: - Project - Project	**Strategy 7** Initiative 12: - Project - Project	**Strategy 10** Initiative 18: - Project - Project
Initiative 2: - Project - Project	Initiative 8: - Project - Project	Initiative 13: - Project - Project	Initiative 19: - Project - Project
Initiative 3: - Project	Initiative 9: - Project	Initiative 14: - Project	Initiative 20: - Project
Strategy 2 Initiative 4: - Project - Project	**Strategy 5** Initiative 10: - Project - Project	**Strategy 8** Initiative 15: - Project - Project	**Strategy 11** Initiative 21: - Project - Project
Initiative 5: - Project - Project	Initiative 11: - Project - Project	Initiative 16: - Project - Project	Initiative 22: - Project - Project
Strategy 3 Initiative 6: - Project - Project	**Strategy 6** Initiative 11: - Project - Project	**Strategy 9** Initiative 17: - Project - Project	**Strategy 12** Initiative 23: - Project - Project

Figure 12.3 Strategic alignment – objectives, strategies, initiatives, and projects framework.

Collaboration

As the SRO evolved, it became apparent to the operating managers that this initiative provided real value for Just Born. There were no pushback issues at the operational level.

"The Executive Team and managers see us as a liberating force, consider us internal consultants, and are very comfortable working with us," says Broczkowski.[1] The SRO is an enterprise business unit since many of the strategic projects impact many of the Just Born business units. And the SRO is supported by the IT organization. Rachel Hayden, who was Vice President and CIO, said, "it was essential for us to put together a strategy. I supported this initiative and the team used some of the best practices in creating the strategic plan that the Executive Team agreed to."[2]

Collaboration is part of an ongoing process within Just Born. The Just Born Strategic Plan (Figure 12.1) shows that the four primary businesses objectives. These four objectives are constantly communicated across the Just Born business units. They become part of the Just Born culture that defines the behaviors and activities of all business associates. And further, the strategic alignment tool that represents all the objectives, initiatives, and associated projects for each of the four primary strategic business objectives is constantly reviewed and updated as it impacts almost every single associate in Just Born.

Broczkowski believes that the SRO fosters collaboration across all the Just Born functional areas.

> With an effective SRO in place, we facilitate governance by providing process, metrics, and sponsorship. We've created charters and project teams and rely on each functional leader (HR, IT, Finance, etc.) to work together to apply appropriate governance for each of our projects. We have 23 strategic initiatives currently in place that impact IT, Finance, H.R, Supply Chain, Sales, and Marketing and support our four-pillar framework.[ibid]

Process Optimization

The SRO team developed many new tools and processes to optimize strategy execution at Just Born. Following is a list of some of them followed by more detail.

- Initiative Charter
- Situational Summary Report
- Project Status Summary
- Strategic Project Completion Checklist
- Strategy Realization Scorecard-Strategic Portfolio Dashboard
- Strategy Realization Scorecard-Strategic Execution Tracker

Initiative Charter

As mentioned earlier, Just Born identified 12 strategies and 23 initiatives to support the four key strategies (Organization, Consumer, Customer, Results). The executive team represented each of the 23 initiatives as short statements. For example, identifying new products, growing store distribution, improving operating efficiency. The challenge for the SRO organization was to flesh out each initiative statement into a template that reflected the critical components of the initiative. To accomplish this, the SRO team developed an Initiative Charter (see Figure 12.4). The charter is a comprehensive overview since it provides pertinent information about the specific initiative, its team members, scope information, key objectives, deliverables, dependencies, and the associated projects.

Broczkowski describes the process of completing the data for the Initiative Charter. "The first thing we did was assemble a few Subject Matter Experts for each initiative to identify who we should add to the team that can add value in completing the Initiative Charter template."[1]

Initiative Charter - Example

Number	Initiative Name	Initiative Start (Year/Qtr)	Initiative End (Year/Qtr)
1A-1	Build Strategic Plan buy-in and track execution	2019/Q1	2022/Q4

Strategic Alignment (Strategy/Objective):	E-Team Sponsor	Initiative Lead
Strategy 1A: Associate Development Objective 1: Establish Effective Organizational Effectiveness	Joe C	Ed D

Initiative Team Members:

#	Name	Knowledge/Expertise	Effort (High, Medium or Low)
1	Ed D - Lead	HR, Strategy, Finance	Med
2	Kathy K	HR, Communications	Med
3	Frank C	Operations	Low
4	Chris T	Project Mgt. Office	Med
5			
6			

In-Scope	Out-of-Scope
1 All locations, all levels, all associates	1 The work covered by other related initiatives
2 Identifying/recommending potential items related to strategic plan communication and buy-in	2 Communicating directly with external stakeholders
3 Monitor strategic execution	3
4	4

Key Objectives (What are we trying to achieve?)	Deliverables (What does success look like?)	KPIs
Associates have a solid understanding of our Strategic Plan (as appropriate for their role), with sufficient associates bought-in/committed.	Well executed communication & enrollment plans. Associates move up the commitment curve.	Most (>50%) at 'Positive Perception' by 9/30/19, and at 'Buy-in' by 7/31/20.
Associates effectively working together towards realizing our strategies]	Demonstrated improvements/strong business results	Strategic milestones achieved and >80%

Dependencies/Precursors Needed	Key Assumptions/Enablers
Need strategic plan finalized and approved	Resources required for surveys and communication tools will be available

#	Project Name	Lead	Description/Key Activities	Start	End
1	Building Commitment to the Plan	Ed D	Develop and execute a robust communication, enrollment and engagement plan	2019/Q1	2021/Q3
2	Strategic Plan Execution Management	Chris T	Initiatives/Projects Portfolio Management, KPI Tracking, Progress Reporting, Success Stories, etc.	2019/Q1	2022/Q4

Additional Considerations:

Figure 12.4 Initiative Charter – examples.

The Initiative Charter team identified the appropriate business champion for the initiative who would act as an initiative sponsor. The team then identified some critical data to include in the Charter and what is in and out of scope. This helps determine the boundaries of the initiative effort. Also included was a list of dependencies required for the initiative. What does the team need to complete this initiative? This could be funding issues, specific personnel, or other required items for the initiative to be successful. The Initiative Charter also included a list of projects that would achieve the goals of the initiative. For large projects, a Project Charter also is used, and the project manager provided it to the initiative team for review and approval.

Situational Summary Report

Status reports at the operational level are a necessary tactical activity for those on initiative and project teams and for business stakeholders. The SRO team wanted to update the Executive Team regularly and developed the Situational Summary Report (see Figure 12.5).

> Every month, we require the initiative leader to prepare a situational summary explaining the project and providing visibility into the project details. Is the project on schedule? Are the deliverables on track? Are there scope or other issues?. Every quarter I prepare a summary and present it to the Executive Team.[ibid]

The Situational Summary Report provides the status for each initiative and its associated projects. Figure 12.5 is an example. The report contains three sections. The first section provides a green, yellow, and red dashboard status on the project's overall status, deliverables, and charter/scope, followed by a comments section on major accomplishments. The second section addresses the risk status of the project with information on risks, mitigations strategy, and status and identifies action for the next reporting period. The final section provides status information on the projects that are part of the initiative.

The example report for an initiative titled Drive Strategic Plan buy-in. Following are key highlights.

- The overall status on schedule, deliverables, and scope are green.
- There are no risks. The KPI, Strategic Plan Commitment Level is "positive."
- There are three actions identified for the next reporting period. One of the two projects for this initiative is completed, and the second is on track.

SITUATIONAL SUMMARY REPORT

JUST BORN
QUALITY CONFECTIONS

Initiative Name: 1A-1 Drive Strategic Plan buy-in and Track Execution
Initiative Leader: Ed D

Reporting Period: June, 2021

Initiative Sponsor: Joe C

STATUS/RISKS/ACTIONS:

	Green (Controlled)	Yellow (Caution)	Red (Critical)	Reason for Deviation
Overall Status	☒	☐	☐	
Schedule	☒	☐	☐	
Deliverables	☒	☐	☐	
Charter Scope	☒	☐	☐	

Comments/Major Accomplishments:

- Continued to coordinate and support strategic execution tracking

Risk Status:

- **Risk: None**
  - **Mitigation Strategy:**

KPI	Original Target/ Date	Revised Target/ Date	Status (On-Track, At-Risk, Complete)
Strategic Plan Commitment Level	• 'Positive Perception' by 6/30/19 • 'Buy-in' by 3/30/20	Bus Associates: • 'Positive Perception' by 9/30/19 • 'Buy-in' by 12/30/21	On-track • Critical mass of Associates appears to be at 'Understanding'/'Positive Perception' level

Actions for Next Reporting Period:

- Monitor communications of 2021 strategic projects and any resulting changes
- Continue to drive awareness through new associate orientation sessions
- Schedule update meeting with the Initiative Team

Project Status Summary

Project Name	Project Lead	Green (Controlled)	Yellow (Caution)	Red (Critical)	Comments
Building Commitment to the Strategic Plan	Ed D	☐	☐	☐	**Completed** 2021/Q3
Strategic Plan Execution Management	Chris T	☒	☐	☐	On track Members are Ed D and Frank C

Figure 12.5 Situational summary reports.

The initiative leader completes the Situational Summary and forwards the document to the SRO for review. The SRO reviews for completeness and identifies any potential areas that need to be addressed. Broczkowski explains.

There was one project where the initiative leader identified the need for additional research, and he was having difficulty getting this approved. I went to see the executive sponsor who informed me that they were busy on another initiative and were very apologetic for not addressing this. They immediately contacted the initiative leader to approve the funding.[ibid]

Strategic Project Completion Checklist

Broczkowski meets with Just Born's CEO Ross Born regularly to review specific project and initiative progress. During one of these meetings, Ross said, "didn't we do something like this before? He asked me if we capture lessons learned that could be applied as part of an ongoing continuous improvement program to improve our processes?" "I told Ross I would look into this." '

When Broczkowski returned to his office, he gathered his team to discuss Ross's comment. Sure enough, the team confirmed what Ross had thought. The one project included an item that was similar to another project completed earlier in the year. Broczkowski explains, "The previous project recommended that manufacturing change some of the Peeps® chick assembly line parameters to improve product quality. The team realized that this improvement would also apply to other marshmallow items as well." *So the SRO team decided to institute a Strategic Project Completion Checklist* that would capture lessons learned as part of an ongoing and regular project completion activity (see Figure 12.6).

The example checklist is for a project titled *Building Commitment to the Strategic Plan*. Here are key highlights from the example checklist.

- Project completion date is projected for Q3 2021, and Ed D is the project and initiative leader.
- The Project Deliverables/Accomplishment section provides a recap of the project.
- A key KPI is identified.
- Two key processes are identified of which one is complete, and the second is targeted for a December 2021 completion.
- The comments section identifies the "need to review survey results to determine if any follow-up actions are required."

The Project Leader, Initiative Leader, and Executive Sponsor complete the Strategic Project Completion Checklist. This ensures that each of these project owners is in sync with the completion activities. The SRO team reviews each checklist to ensure it is complete and whether some recommendations can apply to future projects as part of an ongoing continuous improvement process.

Strategic Project Completion Checklist - Example

Project Info Section

JUST BORN
QUALITY CONFECTIONS

Project Name: Building Commitment to the Strategic Plan

Completion Date (Yr./Qtr.): 2021/Q3

Initiative Name: 1A-1

Major Project Deliverables/ Accomplishments:

Project Leader: Ed D

Initiative Leader: Ed D

Exec Sponsor: Joe C

| PROJECT RECAP SECTION | MET OBJECTIVES (CHECK IF COMPLETE): ☒ |

Develop and execute a robust communication, enrollment and engagement plan. These started with initial awareness meetings with all associates and then were extended as part of a new associate orientations.

-In addition, regular meetings were established with key stakeholders like Initiative Leads to ensure continued engagement during strategic execution.
-Lastly a survey is planned for later in 2021 to make sure we remain on track

On-Going KPIs from Project (if applicable):

- Associate Strategic Alignment / Buy-in Survey in December of 2021

Required Process Transfers:

PROCESSES	AREA or PROJECT RESPONSIBLE	STATUS (Complete, At-Risk)
• Continue New Associate Orientation in Strategic Plan	• SRO	• Complete
• Follow-up Activity as determined by December 2021 survey	• SRO	• After Dec. 2021

Comments (additional risks, opportunities, etc...):

Need to review survey results and determine if any follow-up actions are required for the current or future Strategic Plans.

Figure 12.6   Strategic project completion checklist.

Metrics

Metrics are an important component of any governance strategy, and the SRO provides a dashboard report and bar graphs reports on the portfolio of initiatives and associated projects.

Strategy Realization Scorecard – Strategic Realization Scorecard

The Just Born strategy identified 23 initiatives that drive projects for each of the initiatives. The SRO created a dashboard report that provides status on the initiatives.

As you can see in Figure 12.7 Strategic Portfolio Dashboard, the first row of data reflects the status of the 23 initiatives, where 21 are in process, and 2 are completed. Of the 166 projects that support the 23 initiatives, 70 are in process, 66 are complete, and 30 have not started. Another important data point is the number of Just Born personnel involved in the initiatives. As you can see, 49 percent of the associates are engaged in these initiatives, which support the strategic importance of the initiatives. If the percentage was low, one would wonder if the initiatives have real business value.

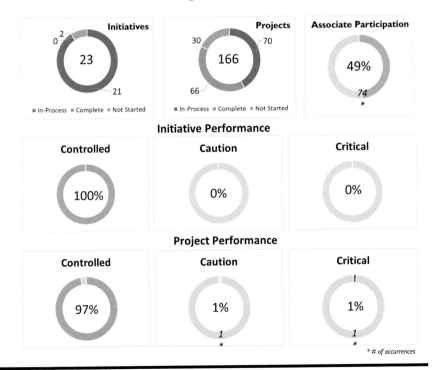

Figure 12.7   Strategy realization scorecard example – portfolio dashboard.

The second section of the dashboard provides data on the performance of the initiatives. As you can see, each of the 23 initiatives is in control, meaning that everything is on course and is expected to remain on course. The third section provides status on the performance of the projects, where you can see that 97 percent of the 166 projects are on course, and there are no issues. One percent of the projects are in the caution or critical category. Of the 166 projects, only 3–4 projects fall in the caution or critical category. Caution indicates when the project is not on course, but a plan is in place to mitigate any issues. A project marked "critical" demonstrates that there are issues, and there is no plan to mitigate the issue.

Strategy Realization Scorecard – Strategic Execution Tracker

Accompanying the Strategic Portfolio Dashboard is a Strategic Execution Tracker thermometer style dashboard report that provides more insight into the 166 projects that support the 23 initiatives by reflecting which projects are aligned to each of the four key business objectives.

As you can see in Figure 12.8, the first part of the bar graphs on the left reflects the number of complete, in-process, or not yet started projects. On the right side, one can see the number of projects aligned to the four business goals (organization, Consumer, customer, efficiency). An in each business goal category, the data are further divided to show how many projects are complete, in-process, or not yet started.

If you take a step back, you will notice more completed projects in the Organization goal than in Consumer. And more in the Consumer goal that Customer. And more in Customer than Efficiency. This is by design, and this is part of the overall strategy. The first goal around the organization was to create an effective organization before focusing on *gaining consumers*.

The Strategic Execution Tracker provides a great example of a thought-out strategy that is executed very efficiently.

Summary

- How has the Strategy Realization Office helped to achieve the business strategy at Just Born? The SRO drives business value and improves organizational culture. Retired CEO Ross Born explains:
- The SRO drives business value by making sure we align at all business levels in terms of what we are looking to achieve strategically. It also ensures we provide the correct resources at the correct times to execute those activities. The SRO also tracks the execution and acts in a consultative role to help mitigate any issues. Without the SRO, our most important strategic objectives are too often not completed or completed without realizing the intended benefits to the organization.

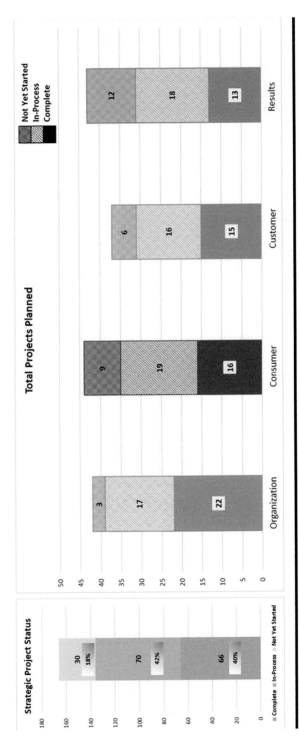

Figure 12.8   Strategy execution tracker – example.

The SRO has provided cultural benefits in alignment, empowerment, and collaboration. With half of our business associates working on elements of strategic execution, they have a strong sense of how they align with our plan and support its execution. The use of Initiative Teams to oversee strategic execution has created 23 empowered teams that are resourced and tracked but otherwise responsible for delivering the agreed-upon deliverables. Lastly, the teams are nearly all cross-functional, resulting in a very collaborative organization.

If your organization is serious about developing a strategy development and execution governance process, the executive team must consider establishing a Strategy Realization Office.

Citings

1. Ed Broczkowski/Ron Arnold/ Phil Weinzimer interview, August 2019.
2. Rachel Hayden / Phil Weinzimer interview, September 9, 2019.

Chapter 13

How the CIO at Carestream Reinvented Its Strategic IT Governance Competency to Improve Project Success

Carestream is an innovator in the health care industry. The company is a worldwide provider of medical imaging systems, X-ray imaging systems for non-destructive testing, and precision contract coating services for various industrial, medical, electronic, and other applications, all backed by a global service and support network.[1]

With 4,500 employees servicing customers in 150 countries around the globe, the information technology organization requires a strategic and innovative leader that focuses on building a team of IT professionals that support the company's products and services. Fortunately for Carestream, its Chief Information Officer, Bruce Leidal, fits the bill perfectly. Leidal has a track record of building effective and efficient IT organizations, streamlining processes, reducing costs, and transforming IT organizations. Leidal has an impressive resume. He was CIO at Hayes Lemmerz International, the largest manufacturer of automobile wheels globally, Director of Global IT Strategic Planning at General Motors, and Director of Advanced Technology at Federal-Mogul corporation. He was also a management consultant

DOI: 10.1201/9781003317531-13

for AT Kearney and Systems Thinking, gaining managerial experience at EDS and technical expertise at Texas Instruments.

When Leidal arrived as CIO at Carestream in 2008, he inherited a project governance methodology that was approximately 11 years old and difficult for project managers to use due to continual activities over time. During Leidal's first couple of years at Carestream, he developed an entirely new organizational operating model and project governance model that dramatically improved project performance and aligns with the Strategic IT Governance 2.0 model. Figure 13.1 reflects the Carestream governance model and its alignment with the Strategic IT Governance 2.0 model and Figure 13.2 reflects the team structure to support the Carestream governance model.

Roles and Responsibilities of the Key Players

Executive Leadership Team (ELT) Sponsor
- Responsible for the business outcome and the expected Business Benefits
- Remove roadblocks to mitigate risks that are not under the control of the project
- Final approver at Project Executive Board meetings
- Chairs the Project Executive Board

Steering Team
- Participants are the key managers impacted by the change
- Approves recommendations to the Executive Board on changes to scope, timing, and cost
- Responsible for change management to ensure project acceptance
- Responsible for validating and committing expected business benefits plan and baseline

Project Manager
- Manages schedule, resources, cost, communications, risks, and issues of the project
- Coordinates the activities of the Business Project Leader and IT Technical Leader
- Leads the Project Executive Review meetings

Business Project Leader
- Accountable to ELT Sponsor for business outcome
- Shared with Project Manager – Responsible for the status, critical issues, key risks, and action plans for the business readiness activities
- Owns the project scope
- Manages and communicates Benefit Plan/Register
- Responsible for change management, process design, user acceptance testing, and training

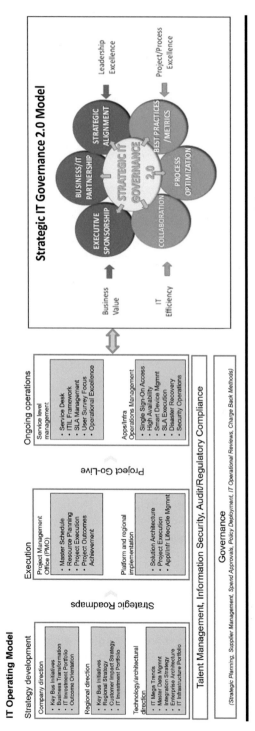

Figure 13.1   Carestream governance model alignment with Strategic IT Governance 2.0 model.

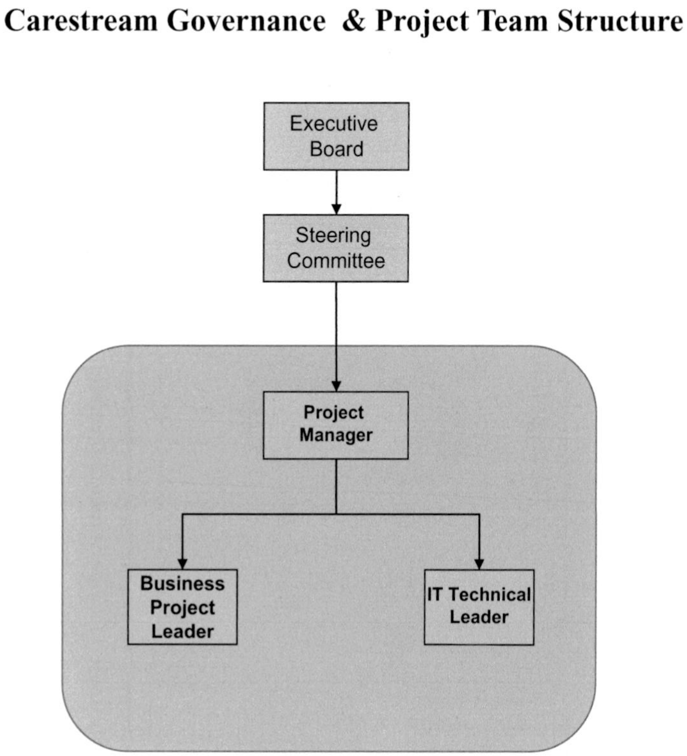

Carestream Governance & Project Team Structure

Figure 13.2   Carestream governance and project team structure.

IT Technical Leader
- Owns the technical solution to meet the project scope
- Provide work direction to the technical team that is implementing the solution
- Shared with Project Manager – Responsible for the status, critical issues, key risks, and action plans for the technical solution activities
- Responsible for the completion of all technical project deliverables

Executive Sponsorship/IT Business Partnership/Collaboration

Executive sponsorship is a critical component of any project governance strategy. Even though governance had been in effect for a few years, a CEO change led to an opportunity to focus the execution. In a meeting with his CEO, Dave Westgate. Leidal explains. "In one of my very early meetings with the new CEO, he said, "I'm getting mixed reviews of project delivery performance that impact budgets and schedules. I think you should look into it." Leidal met with his team to review past projects that had both schedule and or budget overruns. What he found out was disturbing. His team told him the following. "Every time we have a strong project sponsor, projects are on time, on budget, and to expectation. But when we don't have a strong project sponsor, we continuously have scope changes that negatively impact schedules, budgets, and satisfaction."[2]

When Leidal next met with the CEO for a regular update meeting, he mentioned the CEO's comment about him receiving 'mixed reviews' on project performance and updated the CEO on his analysis of past projects where schedule and cost overruns occurred. What the CEO said next was music to Leidal's ears. "Well, Bruce, if you don't have a strong executive sponsorship and ownership, don't do the work."[ibid] At Leidal's next meeting with his direct reports, he shared the CEO's comments. He began an education process to help his staff understand why strong executive sponsorship is critical to project success. He told his team that strong executive sponsorship was a must-have for any project in the future.

Over the next few months, his team diligently made sure that projects included strong executive sponsorship. Over time, the team was able to identify the strong executive sponsors from those that lacked commitment. The strong executive sponsors were actively involved in projects, whereas those that lacked commitment just took on the role without active involvement. Over time, Leidal's team figured out how to ensure only projects with strong executive sponsors would move forward.

On the business side, Leidal focused on relationships with his business peers.

> I spend a lot of time with my business peers (Regional Presidents, CFO, COO, CTO, etc.), with whom I meet regularly and participate in executive project reviews. Clear roles & responsibilities ensure IT teams understand how to work with our business, and business teams understand how IT executes projects. Clear roles and responsibilities build a Business/IT partnership that results in collaborative Business/IT teams that work well together in addressing business problems.[2]

We have provided the Project Managers a safe place to raise escalations via a 30-minute stand-up session every other week for all projects. The Project Managers do not provide status, and they only indicate confidence level and escalations. This has significantly reduced the time needed to resolve issues and remove roadblocks.

Strategic Alignment

Every new CIO assesses the current state of the IT organization. One of the areas that Leidal felt needed improvement was selecting projects for the upcoming fiscal year. Figure 13.3 represents the Global Portfolio Process Overview. Leidal said he went through what he called "host the debate" scenarios, where he tried to facilitate the discussion on selecting forthcoming projects. The CFO would determine the maximum spending for all projects included in the Operational Expense and Capital budget.

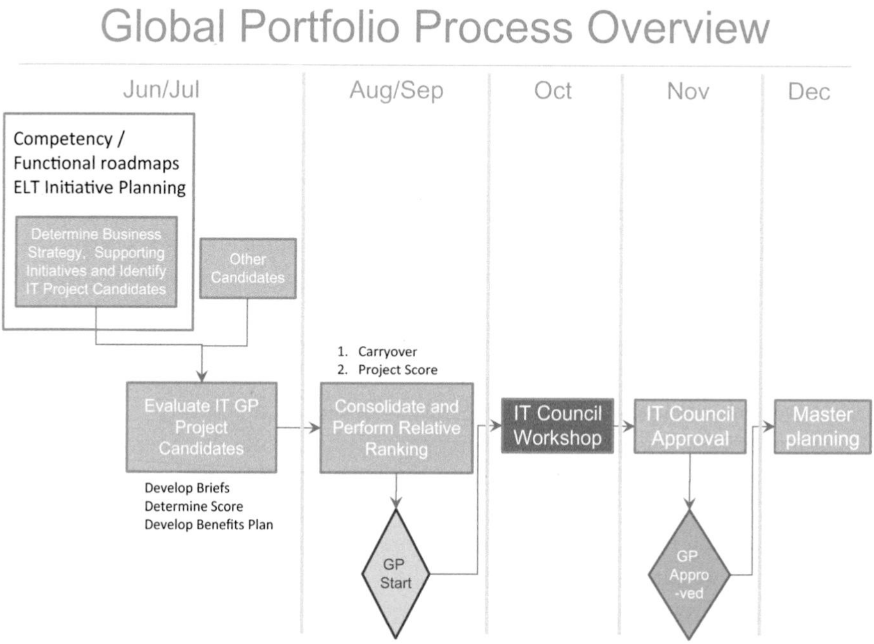

Global Portfolio Process Overview

Figure 13.3 Carestream global process overview.

But the challenge was how to identify which projects would be selected. What he found was that there was no scoring mechanism for this process. Leidal is a strong believer in using scoring mechanisms to determine strategic alignment. "Scoring is the way to drive consensus as a first step in having a debate about proposed projects," says Leidal.[2]

Leidal identified project type, risk tolerance, project cost, and ROI as the four elements every project request requires. A score is assigned to each element, and this process enabled the selection committee to agree on the proposed project list. Figure 13.4 represents an example of the Project Scoring Matrix and is followed by additional info on the components of the matrix.

1. Strategic Alignment: Identify the alignment of the proposed project to the approved roadmap. Is it strategic, productivity improvement, risk mitigation, regulatory, etc.?
2. Risk Mitigation: Identify project risk as low, medium, or high and assign an appropriate score.
3. Net Present Value: Identify the appropriate NPV for the selected project
4. Financial Payback Period: Identify the payback period for the selected project
5. Project Risk: Identify the project risk for the selected project
6. Risk Mitigation Score: Identifies the Risk of the project based upon the Project Scoring Matrix by category.

Project Scoring Matrix Example

	Category	0	2	4	Score 6	8	10	Enter Score	Weight	Weighted Score
Business Value										
Strategy	Strategy Alignment (Roadmap)	Not on Roadmap	On Competency or Function Roadmap	NA	Third Ranked Program on Competency or Function Roadmap	Second Ranked Program on Competency or Function Roadmap	Top Ranked Program on Competency or Function Roadmap	0	30	0
Operations	Risk Mitigation - Operational (Obsolescence/End of Life, Vendor Support, Operations Reliability) - Compliance (Legal, External Regulatory, Internal Controls)	Select Risk Mitigation Score (Likelihood & Impact)	Select Risk Mitigation Score (Likelihood & Impact)	Select Risk Mitigation Score (Likelihood & Impact)	Select Risk Mitigation Score (Likelihood & Impact)	Select Risk Mitigation Score (Likelihood & Impact)	Select Risk Mitigation Score (Likelihood & Impact)	0	30	0
Financials	Net Present Value	No NPV calculated	>$0.5M	>$2M	>$6M	>$10M	>$15M	0	20	0
	Financial Payback Period	No payback period calculated	Greater than 3 Years	3 years or Less	2 Years or Less	1 Year or Less	Less than 6 Months	0	10	0
Project Risk										
Delivery	Project Execution Risk	Very High	NA	High	Moderate	Low	Very Low / None	0	10	0
	Risk Criteria: Benefits Realization, Business Governance/ Readiness/ Change Mgmt, Technology Maturity, Resources, Schedule, Cost									
Total Score (max score 1000)										**0**

Comments:
1
2
3
4
5

Risk Mitigation Score

Likelihood	Very High (>75-100%)	4	8	10	10
	High (>50-75%)	4	6	8	10
	Moderate (>25-50%)	2	4	6	8
	Low (0-25%)	2	2	4	4
		>$500K-$1M	>$1M-$10M	>$10M-$20M	>$20M
			$ Impact (Annual)		

Figure 13.4   Project scoring matrix – example.

After completing the Project Scoring Matrix, the next step is for the project sponsor to develop a business case, develop financial models on the ROI, and agree on the soundness of the financials.

Process Optimization

Leidal implemented several process improvements to improve operational efficiency. Below are some of the key process changes made, followed by more detail for each.

- Project Management Methodology
- Changing IT Culture
- Training Material
- Vendor Management Office
- Project Status Meetings
- Escalation Process

Project Management Methodology

One of the initial assessments conducted by Leidal was the Project Management Methodology. The previous project management methodology was purchased from a big six firm before the establishment of the Project Management Institute (PMI). The methodology was 10 to 12 years old when Leidal arrived at Carestream. As Leidal explains,

> my observations were that a project manager wouldn't have time to do all the work and make the project successful. I didn't see any PMI methodologies included (PMBOK, PMI certification, etc.) or ITIL standards incorporated. When the IT team presented the methodology to me, it appeared to be very bureaucratic and unique. It appeared difficult to execute and would also be difficult for people to use who weren't experienced in using it.[ibid]

Leidal is very process-oriented and wanted to leverage the product development methodology used by the company to gain rapid acceptance. "Every executive in Carestream knows what every Gate in the product development process represents," says Leidal. Stage Gates are a technique that divides projects into distinct phases where there is a decision point to determine if the deliverables of the phase are complete and the project should continue to the next phase. Leidal incorporated Stage Gates into the Carestream project management methodology as it is a fairly standard practice across the medical device industry. He also aligned the State Gates to the PMI body of knowledge and incorporated it into the current methodology. Figure 13.5 represents this alignment.

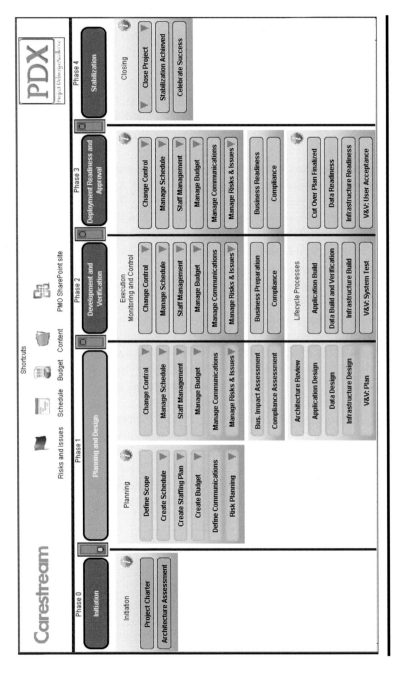

Figure 13.5 Carestream stage-gate alignment to PMI methodology.

Changing IT Culture

During his first few weeks on the job, Leidal assessed the personnel in the IT organization and made several changes that impacted how the IT organization would be perceived in the future.

> I exited an IT executive, and it had a huge ripple effect across the broader organization. The then CFO called me and wanted to know why I needed to replace this individual he thought was the #1 ranked person in my organization, and I told him I ranked him last. That was a big surprise.
>
> Next, I asked my team why the PMO organization was two levels down from the CIO on the organization chart13 At this level, it had no teeth. I didn't receive a reasonable response. So, the next step was to elevate the PMO manager and have her report directly to me.[ibid]

These two changes significantly impacted the IT organization, and, as Leidal explains, "…a few people saw the 'writing on the wall' and left, yet others began to realize that my overall objective was to build a highly effective and efficient IT organization."[ibid]

Figure 13.6 IT Organizational Design represents the current structure of the IT organization. The previous organizational model had each IT executive responsible for similar and overlapping responsibilities. Leidal used a straightforward IT organizational design to ensure single individuals were responsible and accountable for clearly defined areas. Each part of the organization knows what they are responsible for and how their role fits the broader IT organization.

One of the major project-related changes implemented by Leidal was what he called "The 3-Pack of project governance." The project manager can't do it all. A Business Project Leader needs to be in place to focus on the scope, change management, and user acceptance, and this is the Business Project Leader. Likewise and there needs to be a Technical Leader responsible for the technical solution. Every project has a 3-pack team composed of the project manager, business project leader, and technical leader.

Training Material

Early in Leidal's career, he was a management consultant at AT Kearney.

> I learned a lot about change management and have brought my learning into the Carestream organization. If I can provide our teams with the right tools and processes, we can build an effective organization that can solve any business problem[ibid]

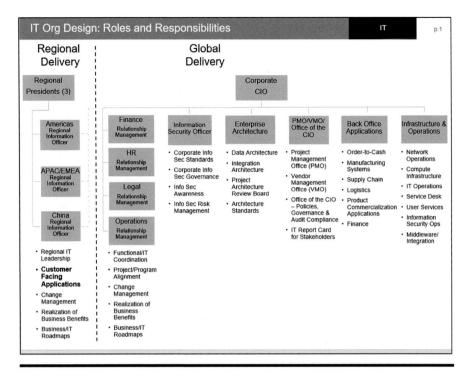

Figure 13.6   IT organization design: roles and responsibilities.

Leidal and his team developed extensive training material for managing projects.

> We had to do this. Project Managers execute projects every day, doing from a few too many a year. Technology leaders may be involved in only a few projects a year to many, and business project leaders may only do one project in their career.[Ibid]

So, to help these individuals perform well in their roles, Leidal and his team developed a robust set of training materials.

Vendor Management Office

Leidal outsources both applications and operations with multiple outsources. Managing outsourcers is not easy and requires expertise in-house. To accomplish this, Leidal implemented a Vendor Management Office. His management team, who previously worked for Deloitte, EDS, and IBM Global Services, completed the design. Leidal explains why. "When I built the team, I wanted personnel with outsourcing experience from either side of the table with consulting experience."[2]

Project Status Meetings

As part of the project status meeting, the 3-pack prepares and presents the data. The Project Manager prepares for the meeting by ensuring that the business case is still valid, the change management process is followed, and any user acceptance testing data is up-to-date. The Technology leader responsible for delivering the project needs to be up-to-date that the technology solution used for the project is still valid. The business project leader represents the key stakeholders and provides input on how the stakeholders view the project's status. As Leidal explains, "When we separate the roles, as we do in the 3-Pack, we get a level of collaboration that results in improved project execution."[ibid]

There are different types of project meetings. Following are some examples.

- Steering committees are scheduled weekly or biweekly, and executive board meetings are scheduled once per month. The steering committee is made up of the managers that the change will impact. The project executive board is made up of the executive sponsor and executives impacted by the change.
- Phase Gates are determined by gatekeepers from the business and IT who review project evidence and determine if the phase gate passes or fails. The project plan determines the Phase Gates and gatekeepers are active members of the project team.
- Communication needs to be consistent as it forces teams to prepare and not delay project schedules. The rule is to hold stage-gate reviews based upon the project schedule. Leidal shared that teams sometimes delay stage-gate reviews, which slows down the project, impacting schedule and cost.

One process Leidal dramatically improved was the project closure, one of the key project deliverables. "Projects that go well provide us lessons learned that could help us keep projects successful. Projects that fail will help us to prevent future project failures. It's a win-win process".[Ibid] Leidal is a 30-year competitive sailor and used his experience in helping his teams understand the importance of lessons learned. It can improve the systems development life cycle, methodology, roles and responsibilities, architectural decisions, project schedules, etc. Leidal explains how lessons learned to relate to his sailing experience.

> A the end of every sailboat race, we either celebrate our victory or drown our sorrows, but we celebrate either way. We talk about lessons learned during the celebration process, what went well, what didn't go well, and what we would do differently. Every race is different. So if you're racing in a mixed fleet, where boat designs are different, you look at the competitors and develop a race strategy, what boat I want

to stay close to, or which boats I should keep my distance. I start with a plan for every race, knowing that events impact your tactical decisions, which have to be made during the race, forcing you to revise your overall plan.

Escalation Process

Every project experiences risks. The challenge is managing risks and developing an efficient escalation process for risks that aren't appropriately addressed. Leidal and his team developed the escalation process that holds the project manager responsible for maintaining the risk register and reviewing its status at every project executive board review. The steering committee can escalate an issue to the project executive board if it deems appropriate.

Best Practices/Metrics

4-Up Report

Leidal knew from experience that project status meetings are not the easiest to manage. Without a formal framework and process, things can get out of hand. To enable project status meetings to focus on the key project metrics, Leidal developed the 4-Up Report. Figure 13.7 represents the 4-Up Report that focuses on the key metrics and answers many of the questions one would want to ask for any project. As Leidal explains,

> A project manager cannot anticipate all of the questions that may arise in a project executive board meeting. The project manager needs a mechanism to answer many of the questions on a single slide. This report provides the project manager with a tool for focus the conversation on the area(s) they would like to address.[ibid]

The 4-Up Report provides a high-level overview of the four key areas of a project.

The Scope/Status is presented in the upper-left section and provides a description and status for the project. The lower-left section presents project financials. The upper-right section provides a schedule overview with key milestones. And the lower-right section provides risk/issues. Presenting key data this way avoids unnecessary questions upfront and helps to focus the conversation on the key elements of the project.

4-Up: A Format That Answers the Typical Questions

Project Name	Schedule	Cost	Risk	Status Date: Feb. 11, 2009	Project Manager
OTD Time Improvement	⇨	⇦	⇕	Go-live Sep 10, 2009	I.R. Write

Scope / Status

Project description

Implement a new process and system to significantly improve Order-to-Delivery timing.

Project status update

- Scope is unchanged.
- Requirements workshop completed.
- System stabilization testing is underway.
- Daily reporting of user issues are declining.
- All previously reported, very high, and high issues are fixed.
- Continuous-Improvement Team established to increase error-proofing.

Cost CPI 1.01

	2009	2010	Total
Approved Budget	$ 11.7	$ 0.5	$ 12.2
Actual Spend	$ 11.5	$ -	$ 11.5
Forecast	$ -	$ 0.5	$ 0.5
Total	$ 11.5	$ 0.5	$ 12.0
Variance	$ 0.2	$ -	$ 0.2
Percent variance	2%	0%	2%

Carestream

Schedule SPI 0.85

Phase	Date
Strategic Planning	18-Jun-08
Assessment and Planning	18-Dec-08
Design on plan	18-Feb-09
Design completed	1-Apr-09
System Test Readiness	3-Jun-09
Start production conversions	29-Jun-09
Systems Readiness	1-Aug-09
User Readiness Testing	5-Aug-09
Finance Go/No-Go	20-Aug-09
User Cutover Go / No Go	26-Aug-09
Delivery Date	**10-Sep-09**
Systems Stabilization	27-Jan-10
Business Stabilization	27-Jan-10

2009/2010: J F M A M J J A S O N D J

Risks/Issues

Risk & Issue Mitigation Dashboard

ID	Risk / Issue Description	Mitigation	Change from Last Review	Criticality	Probability	G/Y/R
2	New stabilization issues continued to be raised	Focus on fixing of what is broken and manage enhancements via Governance process.	New	H	H	
3	Financials	Provide users with additional training and hotline support to clear billing deferrals and confirmations.	New	H	H	

Figure 13.7 Carestream 4-p framework.

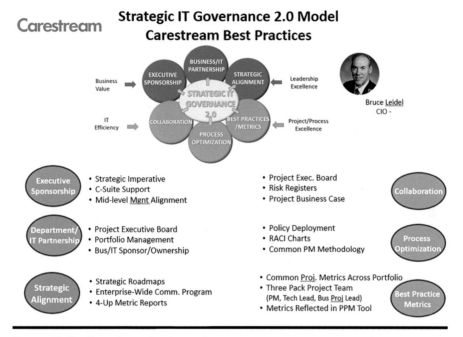

Figure 13.8   Carestream best practices.

Summary

The overall IT governance model, organizational design, and project execution methodology have led to a high-performing IT organization that has delivered millions of dollars of project investments over many years. More importantly, the governance model has helped Carestream's top-line growth, continuous improvement of business processes, and reduction of business risk.

Leidal reinvented the governance model at Carestream and incorporated a set of best practices that align with the Strategic IT Governance 2.0 Model. Figure 13.8 reflects these best practices for each of the six Strategic IT Governance 2.0 competencies.

Citings

1. https://www.carestream.com/en/us/company
2. Bruce Leidal/Phil Weinzimer interview, December 6, 2019.

Chapter 14

How Miratech Implemented a Governance Methodology to Rescue a Failing Project

Following is a case study of a company that used a governance methodology that aligns with the Strategic IT Governance 2.0 Model. The Miratech team completed the 80,000-hour two-year tax assessment project on time and within budget, a feat any organization would be proud to achieve. Miratech accounts for its 99 percent on-time and within budget success through a relentless desire to apply best-in-class principles. Hire the brightest and most intelligent people, develop world-class methodologies and tools, and build proprietary technologies that enable collaborative teams to excel in project design, software development, and project execution.

As you will conclude from reading this case, Miratech has a robust collaboration, process, and metrics-based methodology and toolset-Agile Portfolio System™ that aligns with The Strategic IT Governance 2.0 model.

This case study aims to help companies understand the complexities of delivering complex software development projects and applying a best-in-class methodology and associated tools to successfully implement technology projects to achieve a company's strategic goals and objectives. Hopefully, this case study has accomplished

DOI: 10.1201/9781003317531-14

this goal, and your next strategic technology/business challenge will leverage some of the lessons learned.

Following is the case overview, followed by more information on The Miratech Agile Portfolio System™ methodology.

Case Overview

The Western European Principality of Liechtenstein needed a significant redesign of their tax revenue process and supporting application. After difficulties with a vendor, they partnered with the Miratech Group to *rescue* the project. And indeed, Miratech succeeded in implementing the project on time and within the budget that consumed 80,000 person-hours. The Miratech Governance process utilizes their Agile Portfolio System™ methodology that aligns closely with the Collaboration, Process Optimization, and Best Practice Metrics competencies of The Strategic IT Governance 2.0 Model. The following case study provides details on the background, planning, and execution of the project (Figure 14.1).

Liechtenstein is one of the smaller, yet wealthy, countries in Western Europe and required an updated tax assessment application to manage its tax revenue process. It awarded the contract to Abraxas Informatik AG. Unfortunately, Abraxas experienced some resource challenges during its two attempts to develop an updated tax assessment application. Abraxas needed help to *rescue* this project and contracted with the Miratech Group, based on its previous successful experience utilizing Miratech in development projects and its 99 percent delivery success rate.

The results speak for themselves. Miratech Group successfully developed an innovative tax assessment application. It delivered the two-year 80,000 person-hours project on time and within budget, a hallmark achievement for any company but typical for Miratech. They have a 99 percent success rate at delivering complex strategic projects. Miratech received the 2020 CIO 100 Award recipient for their

> …unique way of delivering IT projects of any complexity on time and on budget using the Miratech Agile Portfolio System, a set of proprietary methodologies and tools developed and perfected over decades of operation. Miratech covers the entire software development cycle, bringing their clients the most agile, efficient, and effective delivery approach.[1,2]

Following is a case study that includes project background, pre-contract activities, estimating project hours, project organization, Miratech Agile Portfolio System, project execution, and a summary section.

The objective of this case study is to help companies understand how to successfully leverage a global technology company's competency to deliver software development projects on time and within budget.

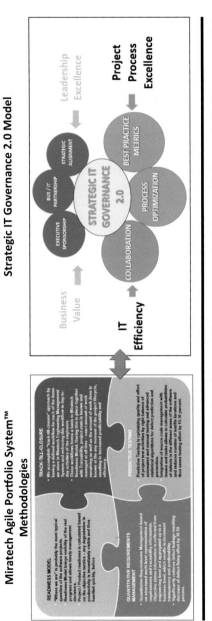

Figure 14.1 **The alignment of Miratech Agile Portfolio system methodology with Strategic IT Governance 2.0 competencies.**

Background

Liechtenstein is Europe's fourth-smallest country located in central Europe, bordered by Switzerland on the west and south and Austria to the east and north. It has a $6 billion economy that relies heavily on its tax revenue system to support government services. Although only the size of Rhode Island, Liechtenstein has one of the world's highest GDP per capita. So, tax revenue is a huge deal.

As you can imagine, a key strategic objective is to optimize tax revenue. The tax assessment system assesses all taxation types for legal entities, natural persons, and partnerships.

A few years ago, the Liechtenstein finance organization recognized that the tax assessment system was built on an outdated and no longer supported and maintained technology. The risk to the government was immense. If the system experienced a failure, the tax authority would not obtain the necessary support or perform the required maintenance to restore the system and make it operational again, potentially resulting in a stoppage of the taxation process and impacting tax revenues.

The Liechtenstein finance organization contracted with Abraxas Informatik AG since they developed the original application. Abraxas notified the finance organization that the original system, built on a legacy platform, would no longer provide application support services. So, the finance organization decided to contract with Abraxas to design a new, modern, and updated tax assessment system.[3]

The objective of the tax assessment system is to support the tax declaration and calculation process. Individuals enter pertinent tax declaration information into the system, which calculates and invoices the individual's appropriate tax. Abraxas faced some resource challenges during its two attempts to modernize the application and needed help.

Abraxas contacted the Miratech Group to help *rescue* this critical project. They knew Miratech could help since they had very positive experiences working with Miratech on past projects, which gave them confidence that the Liechtenstein tax assessment modernization project would succeed.

Valeriy Kutsyy, CEO at Miratech, articulates the value Miratech provides its customers.

> Miratech is a technology company that helps visionaries to change the world. We are a global IT services and consulting company that brings together global enterprise innovation and start-up innovation. Today we support digital transformation for the largest enterprises on the planet. By partnering with both large and small players, we stay at the leading edge of technology, remain nimble even as a global leader, and create technology that helps our clients further enhance their business. Our culture of Relentless Performance enables over 99% of Miratech's engagements to succeed by meeting or exceeding scope, schedule, and or budget objectives since our inception in 1989.[1]

Miratech has a 99 percent project success rate, innovative technology, management personnel – 90 percent with master's degrees, high-performance teams that deliver, a robust award-winning methodology, and a proactive project management process. Each of these competencies represents the six faces of a Rubik's Cube. Anyone who has attempted the Rubik's knows how difficult it is to master the cube's alignment for each of the six faces. Many technology companies have varying degrees of maturity in each of the six areas. However, Miratech has mastered and integrated all six into a set of solution offerings that provide companies, regardless of industry and the ability to transform their IT organizations from cost centers into strategic partners and revenue producers.

The tax assessment project exemplifies how Miratech's mastery of these six competencies delivered a two-year complex 80,000 person-hours project on time and budget utilizing a highly motivated collaborative team approach and award-winning Agile Portfolio System™ methodology.[4]

Pre-Contract Activities

The Liechtenstein finance organization realized it needed to upgrade INES-the current tax assessment application, based upon two critical drivers. The first was Abraxas notified the finance organization that it would no longer provide support for INES. The second was the need to add functionality to improve the efficiency of the tax assessment process; based on recent changes to the tax laws. The finance organization awarded Abraxas the contract to develop and modernize a new tax assessment application since they developed the original system.[4]

Abraxas experienced several challenges in developing the new tax assessment application and failed at two attempts. Abraxas management recognized that they were in trouble and needed a strategic partner to *rescue* the project. Personal relationships between executives at Miratech and Abraxas formed the strategic partnership for the tax assessment project. The business relationship started in 2017 when Abraxas contracted with Miratech to provide a Near Shore Development project that enabled Abraxas to experience Miratech's world-class development and delivery capability.[5]

Miratech provides strategic technology services across the globe. Management concluded that local sales agents, who understood the economics, competitive environment, and technology needs of the local geography, are a much better sales model than having sales personnel travel around the world sales calls in unfamiliar geographies. One of these sales agents is Markus Waser, an internationally experienced senior business and technology executive with over 30 years of experience in the services industry and a solid track record in business development, strategic planning, complex global project execution, agile software development, outsourcing, and nearshoring. He specializes in business process and technology innovation and transformation, digital omni-channel banking platforms for retail banking, wealth

Figure 14.2   Alexander Maximenko – application services director at Miratech.

management, and corporate banking. Waser operates out of Zurich, Switzerland, and is very familiar with Switzerland's business environment and surrounding countries (Figure 14.2).

Waser reacquainted Miratech with Abraxas, who was eager to have Miratech provide a cost estimate to help rescue the tax assessment project. In late summer 2017, Abraxas provided documentation to Miratech with a request to prepare a cost estimate for the new tax assessment application. The documentation included the rationale for replacing the current application and a gap analysis that identifies how the new system would differ from the existing application. Under time pressure from the Liechtenstein finance organization, Abraxas requested Miratech to provide a quote within one week. Alexander Maximenko is the Director of the Application Development Services at Miratech. He wanted to ensure that the cost estimate was as accurate as possible. "To make sure that the cost estimate is as precise as possible, I used five different cost-estimating techniques that resulted in similar cost estimates, and, as a result, I was confident that our cost estimate was reasonable."[5]

Abraxas reviewed the estimate, and the feedback to Miratech was that it was too high. Miratech suggested that a Discovery session to review the project requirements would help Miratech and Abraxas validate the scope and enable Miratech to review its estimate.

In August 2017, Maximenko conducted a two-day Discovery Workshop in Switzerland with the architect and chief developer from Abraxas. As mentioned previously, Miratech's on-time and on-budget success rate for projects is 99 percent. A critical factor in achieving this metric is identifying the project scope, timelines, technical requirements, budget constraints, key milestones for the design, development, and project management activities. Maximenko's goal of the Discovery session was to confirm or modify the project requirements and, if necessary, adjust the Miratech cost estimate.

The Discovery Workshop was a success.[Ibid] The two-day session resulted in the following conclusions.

1. The current system consists of an Oracle Data Base and GUPTA, an SQL relational database management system
2. The Oracle database and GUPTA are current technology and maintainable. As a result, we decided to keep the Oracle database intact, significantly reducing the scope and cost.
3. The second major decision was to divide the project into two phases.
   a. Phase one would include developing the technology to support the tax assessment application processes in a time-frame that would meet the finance organization's April 2019 deadline based upon tax law legislation.
4. With a planned completion date of April 2020, the second phase would add an administrative tool allowing users to configure parameter settings and the tax assessment system's business rules. The administrative tool was a crucial part of the solution because of frequent tax legislation changes in Liechtenstein. Maximenko explains the importance of the administrative tool as follows. "The administrative tool allows the user to quickly integrate tax law changes into the system without expensive rework of the system every time the tax law changes. Upon completion of phase one, users accessed the new Tax Assessment system combined with the legacy version of the Administrative Tool until phase 2 completion." Miratech refined their cost proposal after the Discovery Workshop session and met with Abraxas to discuss the revised pricing. Abraxas still found the quote too high as compared to another competitor's quote. Maximenko met with Abraxas and utilized "…a technique similar to the one used in his initial estimate. "I shared with Abraxas a few different methods of how we developed the final pricing. My goal was to ensure that Abraxas concluded Miratech is confident in our approach and pricing methodology." Maximenko convinced Abraxas that their cost proposal was reasonable and supportable and awarded Miratech the contract to develop and implement a modernized tax assessment system for Liechtenstein's finance organization.[Ibid]

Project Implementation Methodology – Estimating Development Hours

Project managers request developers to provide information on their specific tasks; is it ready or not, and how much time is required to complete the task, using a bottoms-up approach.

Miratech addressed this issue by creating the Agile Portfolio System™ Managing software development projects is a skill developed with years of experience and insight. Maximenko understands all the pitfalls that can occur during these types of projects. "A frequent reason software projects fail is the inability to correctly estimate and identify the real size of the project and assign the right resources." And even if the estimates and resource assignments are correct, Maximenko points out that "… project challenges and associated hiccups always occur, and when this happens, project teams go into reactive mode, which disrupts the natural cadence of the project and chaos erupts. The ability to properly manage project risk stems from a lack of an approach to measure progress using proactive project management techniques."[Ibid]

Correctly estimating project hours and associated costs for system development projects is a critical step and must consider each of the related activities involved in the following major phases of a system development project.

- Initiation Phase – project Initiation, project definition, and problem statements
- Planning Phase – requirements definition, detail planning, estimation, and scheduling
- Execution Phase – project team organization, code development, test, production release, quality assurance, and program management
- Project Closure – monitoring, controlling, closure, and review.

The estimating process usually involves project team members (IT and business stakeholders) developing hourly estimates for project activities based upon the type of requirement using qualitative techniques, such as experience on similar work or project history estimates. Unfortunately, we are all aware of the 75 percent project failure statistics due to inaccurate estimates that lead to scope changes, quality issues, rework, etc. These poorly developed estimates result in lengthy project delays, increased cost, and a lack of trust in IT organizations.

Miratech Group has a 99 percent on-time and within-budget success rate. One of the significant factors that account for this success is how Miratech estimates hours for each of the detailed developmental tasks required for the project. Rather than using qualitative techniques, Miratech utilizes a quantitative method called Function Point Analysis (FPA). FPA is a technique used to measure software requirements based on breaking down the project requirements into specific functions and assigning quantitative metrics for each function point identified. The function points are translated into associated hours of effort, key milestones, and risk scale. This quantitative technique takes the guesswork from the estimating process and results in an accurate estimate of development hours and, ultimately, overall project costs. Additionally, it is independent of technology/programming language, provides clarity in contract negotiations, and facilitates more accessible communication with business groups.

Miratech has honed its Function Point process over the years and, as a result, confidently estimates fixed-price contracts that it delivers successfully 99 percent of the time.

Project Implementation Methodology – Project Organization

Miratech considered the tax assessment project a very high-risk project due to Abraxas's tight timeline for project completion. Miratech team included an experienced Project Manager and 15–20 developers, dependent on the workload. A Steering Committee from Miratech included Markus Waser and Alexander Maximenko. Abraxas's executives included the Head of Tax Solutions, Tax Assessment Project Manager, Head of Sales. The Steering Committee met regularly to review the project status and assess if the team included the right mix of system analysis, designers, and developers and reviewed any significant issues and potential risks.

Project Implementation Methodology – Miratech Agile Portfolio System

Project execution is where the rubber meets the road. Every technology professional involved in technology projects is aware of the many hurdles project teams need to overcome to deliver complex projects on time and within budget. The reality is that every project has challenges, and some companies overcome this by mastering their *reactive* capability in responding to project issues. But this is not the desired skill set. To truly excel consistently at delivering complex projects on time and within budget requires management, the PMO, and the delivery team to work together in a collaborative environment to *proactively* identify and mitigate potential project risk. And Miratech is a company that masters this competency with their Agile Portfolio System™. Here's how they do it.

Companies around the globe have different maturity levels for the governance processes that manage their project portfolios. Miratech management realized several years ago it needed to have a near-perfect on-time and on-schedule track record in project design, development, and execution, to succeed as a strategic partner in reinventing IT for its customers. As previously mentioned, companies that master project execution do so *proactive* and not *reactively*. Miratech developed an Agile Portfolio System that embraces world-class methodologies and tools.

The Miratech Agile Portfolio AI system comprises integrated proprietary tools and methodologies based upon accepted industry standards. The system covers the full software development cycle, including business requirements, architecture, coding, peer reviews, testing and production maintenance, and support to enable the efficient use of an agile approach for delivery. The system automatically collects data needed for real-time project status monitoring and potential project defect prediction. The system is designed to increase the software product development process's visibility and project management purposes. Data and associated analysis are visible on the Live Dashboard via mobile phone, desktop, and laptop, making the project state accessible to the managers at every level (from CxO to Team Leads).

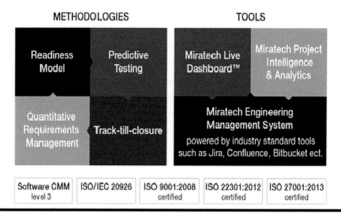

Figure 14.3   Miratech Agile Portfolio System™.

This geographically distributed, cloud-based AI system allows for 30–40 percent higher productivity in software engineering than industry averages (Figure 14.3).[6]

Tax Assessment System Modernization – Project Execution

Managing project status for large software development projects is a daunting task. As mentioned previously, Miratech uniquely addresses this. Miratech assigns function points for each software development activity and estimates an upper and lower limit of the project's expected results. When actual results occur outside of these boundaries, real-time alerts notify the project manager to take appropriate action. Miratech developed the Product Readiness Analysis technique as part of their Agile Portfolio System™ methodology. "This method includes some of the principles from the Statistical Process Control techniques (SPC). It is used successfully by manufacturing companies for decades. In 1988, the Software Engineering Institute suggested that SPC could apply to non-manufacturing processes, such as software engineering processes. Levels 4 and 5 of the Capability Maturity Integration Model (CMMI) use this concept."[5]

Figure 14.4 represents the cumulative function points for the tax assessment project for each week. Following is a description for each line.

- Line 1 – The top line (green line) represents the cumulative optimal number of planned function points for each project month.
- Line 2 – The second line from the top (light green) represents the cumulative number of monthly function points in the project plan.

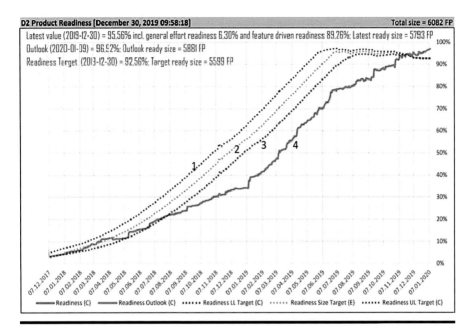

Figure 14.4 Miratech readiness analysis – tax assessment project.

■ Line 3 – The third line from the top (red line) represents the minimum cumulative number of completed function points for each project month.
■ Line 4 – The bottom line (green line) represents the cumulative number of actual function points completed for each project month.

Maximenko understands the challenges of managing complex software development projects. "If you want your project to be on time and within budget, you need to identify issues early and develop mitigation strategies that counter the potential risk."[Ibid]

Maximenko realized that the Miratech had an aggressive timeline to complete the project. The project started in October 2017 and progressed according to plan until May 2018, when the cumulative number of completed function points deteriorated from planned projections. As Maximenko describes it, "we were not progressing fast enough to deliver on time, and we realized that something had to change. We identified a tiger team to assess the project and develop recommendations." Yuri Kramar is a senior program manager at Miratech and is experienced in managing software development teams, process improvement, and team collaboration. Following are the observations and recommendations identified by Kramar (Table 14.1).[Ibid]

Maximenko and other Miratech executives agreed with the Tiger Team Assessment and implemented the recommendations.

Maximenko realized that changing the teams' behavior and translating these into actions would not occur quickly. It took a few weeks to help the team understand

Table 14.1 Miratech Tiger team assessment summary

Category	Observation	Recommendation
Team Personnel	A few team members are not performing to plan due to insufficient skill maturity and need replacement, and additional team members with appropriate skills are required.	Replace identified team members and add team members with mature software development skills.
Process Improvement	Tasks are not assigned appropriately—tasks are based upon what developers want to work on and not upon project *need*.	Task assignment processes require improvement based on need and developer skill level. Assign higher complexity tasks to senior developers and lower complex tasks to junior developers.
Team Cohesion	Team members not working with each other optimally	Train team on collaboration techniques, improving communications, status reporting, etc.
Team Commitment	Team members not displaying a commitment to overall project goals and working on short-term activities	Train team on visualizing overall project goals and end state and translate into work activities, assign tasks to developers that align to overall project objectives.
Liechtenstein Task Assessment SME Availability	Availability of one Subject Matter Expert (SME) to respond to Miratech questions requiring quick decisions to keep the project timeline on schedule	Identify categories (low, medium, high) for SME decisions, and delegate low and medium ones to Miratech, improving productivity. In addition, scheduled face-to-face meetings between Miratech business analysts and Abraxas SME should occur monthly to address any outstanding questions.

the performance gaps that hindered their performance and a few months working with the team to improve their teaming and decision-making skills.

Kramar mentored both the project manager and team members during a three- to four-week period. Kramar attended every team meeting and provided his insights to the project manager and team members. His goal was not to make the decisions but help the team be more collaborative and make the right decisions. Kramer describes how he mentored and coached the team.

> During one of the team meetings, a developer was reviewing his work, and Kramar said, "Stop. Why are you doing this? The developer explained his rationale, and Kramer asked a series of questions to help the developer and team realize that the decision was incorrect. I worked with the team to help them understand what the right decision should be."

These were the types of interactions that helped the team improve their performance over time.[Ibid]

After a few months of coaching and mentoring, the team improved its performance. Kramar and Maximenko continued to provide regular oversight and mentoring, and coaching as necessary. But the team continued its improvement, and as seen from the Product Readiness Analysis chart, the team completed all the deliverables and met the planned targets.

Summary

As you can see from this case study, Miratech has a very strong collaboration, process, and metrics-based methodology and tool set. And it strongly aligns with The Strategic IT Governance 2.0 Model. Following is a summary of the case followed by more information on the Miratech Agile Portfolio System™ methodologies.

The Miratech team completed the 80,000-hour two-year tax assessment project on-time and within budget, a feat any organization would be proud to achieve. Miratech accounts for its 99 percent on-time and within budget success through a relentless desire to apply best-in-class principles. Hire the brightest and most intelligent people, develop world-class methodologies and tools, and build proprietary technologies that enable collaborative teams to excel in project design, software development, and project execution.

Today, companies leverage technologies to a greater degree than ever before, focusing on creating customer value, optimizing business processes, and even reinventing business models. As a result, companies now recognize that technology strategy needs to be part of the corporate strategic plan. And given the complexity of technology today and its impact across the entire value chain, company executives need to be more strategic in selecting technology partners to assist its technology and business units in implementing complex technology solutions.

Following are four key best practices your organization can apply in the selection of a technology partner.

1. Define your business problem: Make sure you adequately define the business problem you want to solve and its associated impact on your business. Too many organizations define underlying issues instead of focusing on the strategic business challenges that impact revenue, cost, or business processes.
2. Chose a partner that understands the strategic use of technology: Strategic technology vendors must understand how to leverage technology appropriately to address your business challenges. Today's business environment is complex, and technology alone will not solve the problem. It's about developing a solution that involves the right technology, optimized business process, and personnel working in collaborative teams
3. Select technology partners with consistent on-time and on budget performance history. Don't be a statistic of failed project implementation. Make sure the technology partner you chose has a constant on-time, on-budget track record. Otherwise, your project could be delayed, cost more money, and, even worse, negatively impact your business.
4. Focus on the business solution: Many companies are enamored with the latest technology and choose to implement it without impacting the business. Successful strategic technology solution providers focus on solving the business problem and choosing the right technology that addresses your company's business needs, challenges, and strategic objectives.

This case study aims to help companies understand the complexities of delivering complex software development projects and applying a best-in-class methodology and associated tools to successfully implement technology projects to achieve a company's strategic goals and objectives. Hopefully, this case study has accomplished this goal, and your next strategic technology/business challenge will leverage some of the lessons learned in this case study.

The Agile portfolio System Tools include the following four categories: Miratech Live Dashboard, Miratech Project Intelligence & Analytics, and Miratech Engineering Management System.

Miratech Live Dashboard – visualizes actual and historical data, including metrics, risks, status information, and traceability, and provides up-to-date information about the project through the Miratech Live Dashboard, available from both web and mobile devices.

Miratech Project Intelligence & Analytics – *captures actual and historical data, and applies statistical methods to analyze them*

> Miratech Engineering Management System – a set of powerful industry-standard tools used by agile teams to create and organize documents, manage test requirements and store and manage software code.

Jira is a workflow tool to manage work. Miratech developers use this tool to record time and manage their workday tasks, including function point activities. Data from Jira enables the project manager and other key stakeholders to analyze developer productivity and work efficiency.

Confluence is a collaborative tool used to organize team documentation. Miratech uses Confluence to store team documents and structure project documents. It also links Jira tasks and helps improve the efficiency of team activities.

Bitbucket is a repository management tool. Miratech uses Bitbucket to store source code and links to Jira workflow activities.

Following is more information on the Miratech Agile Portfolio System™ methodologies (Figures 14.5–14.9):

Miratech Agile Portfolio System™: Methodologies

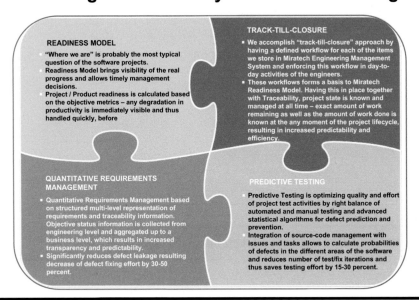

Figure 14.5 Miratech Agile Portfolio System™ methodologies.

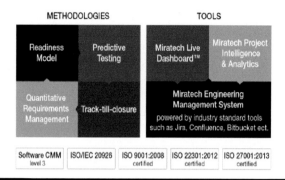

Figure 14.6 Miratech Agile Portfolio System™.

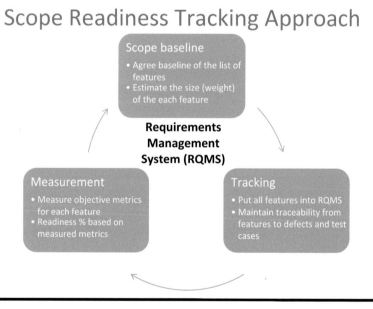

Figure 14.7 Scope readiness tracking approach process.

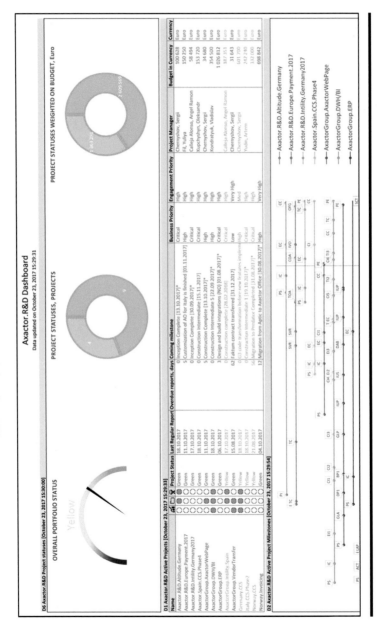

Figure 14.8   Axactor R&D dashboard.

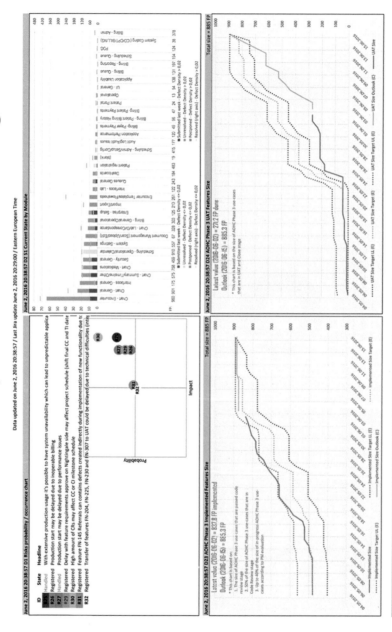

Figure 14.9 Dashboard example-test execution progress.

Citings

1. https://miratechgroup.com/
2. Miratech Named a 2020 CIO 100 Award Winner – miratechgroup.com
3. www.abraxas.ch
4. https://miratechgroup.com/99_percent_success/miratech_agile_portfolio_system/
5. Alexander Maximenko/Phil Weinzimer interviews October 2,9,16, 2020.
6. Markus Waser/Phil Weinzimer interviews; October 13, 2020; November 26, 2020.
7. https://miratechgroup.com/solutions/

Chapter 15

How the State of Georgia Implemented a Governance Solution Saving Millions of Dollars Each Year

Case Overview

The State of Georgia has over 100 state agencies that design, develop, and implement hundreds of projects each year that impact the services provided to its citizens. I have had the opportunity to spend time with executives and management personnel to understand and write about the governance process in managing and providing oversight for state agency projects.

This case study provides the background, development, and implementation of a governance solution that saved millions of dollars in project costs each year.[1] The methodology used aligns with the Collaboration, Process Optimization, and Best Practice Metrics competencies of the Strategic IT Governance 2.0 Model, as shown in Figure 15.1.

The following case study provides details on the background, planning, and execution of the project

DOI: 10.1201/9781003317531-15   **241**

Alignment

Strategic IT Governance 2.0

Advanced Management **Insight**

BUSINESS VALUE

BUSINESS VALUE

- Strategic Imperative
- C-Suite Sponsorship
- VP/Director/Manager Sponsorship

- Sr. Executive Sponsorship
- Division Mgmnt / PMO Sponsorship
- PMO/ Project Team Alignment

- Business Governance Board
- Business Partnership Collaboration
- Business Sponsor Ownership

- Best Practice Project Methodology
- Collaborative Project Input
- Project Sponsor Engagement

- Enterprise Communication Program
- Business / Technology Plan
- Project Selection/Alignment Process
- Business Outcome Metrics

- Project Portfolio Tracking
- Stakeholder Input to Ensure Strategic Alignment
- Corrective Recommendations to Align Project Success

PROCESS EFFICIENCY

PROCESS EFFICIENCY

- Stakeholder Involvement
- Predictive Project Risk Indicators
- Defined Project Success Criteria

- Best Practice Assessments
- Continuous Stakeholder Input
- Team Input Linked to KPI's / EWS

- Project Implementation Review Panel
- Defined Process, Roles, Resp. Matrix
- Real-Time Project Monitoring
- Continuous Improvement Process

- Issue Logging/Tracking
- Project Methodology & Process Compliance
- PM Best Practices

- Proactive Project Management /Status
- Predictors for Project Success
- Collaborative Project Status Process
- Efficiency Metrics to Measure Success

- Dynamic Project Dashboards
- Phase Gate Measurement
- Metrics, KPIs and EWS Selection

Figure 15.1 The alignment of Strategic IT Governance 2.0 with GTA GEMS/ TrueProject PM application.

State of Georgia – Project Governance

I am sure you have read about the 25–35% failure rate for IT projects. Yet, these statistics have become the standard and acceptable norm for project management organizations. One could logically ask: How can this be when there are dozens of project management solutions in the marketplace, used by thousands of companies that focus on achieving project success? As a CIO or PMO Director, are you ready to write off millions of dollars of inefficiencies and waste?

This is not the case for the Georgia Technology Authority (GTA), which manages information technology (IT) for the State of Georgia with an annual IT budget of more than $1.2 billion. Tom Fruman, Director of Enterprise Management, was the GEMS program sponsor, and Calvin Rhodes was the State CIO who supported Fruman's initiative and signed off on the project. Fruman retired on June 30, 2018. Calvin Rhodes retired on June 30, 2021, after ten years of service at the State and was the longest-serving active state CIO in the nation

Rhodes understands the implications of project risk. "We are the stewards of taxpayer dollars and need to manage project risk," says Rhodes.[2] While at the State of Georgia, Fruman was responsible for the organization that provides governance for the $400–900 million of critical projects executed each year by the 119 state agencies. Fruman believes "project success requires applying a discipline of process and insight to the management of project portfolios… It's all about reducing risk and uncovering what's going on behind the numbers that Project Managers typically report."[3] Fruman knew from experience that process trumps tools. So, his first step was to reinvent the governance processes on project oversight. The next step was to find a tool to support the governance process. After several failed project portfolio solution implementations, he found the perfect governance tool to support the reinvented governance process. Fruman "chose The CAI TrueProject Suite because the solution provides a governance layer of process discipline, best practices, and predictive analysis to reduce risk and improve project success, regardless of the PPM tool used by agency project teams."[Ibid,.4]

We need to look at how the State of Georgia manages its IT organization, the project governance process, and its challenges, the implementation process, and the value of the CAI TrueProject Suite to clearly understand how Fruman and his team implemented the GEMS programs to reinvent its governance processes and a supporting tool that provided dramatically improve project performance and saved millions of dollars each year.

The Office of the CIO at the State of Georgia

Calvin Rhodes was appointed to the role of Chief Information Officer in January 2011 for the GTA. His team of 165 IT professionals (plus another 1000 IT members from its two primary service providers) delivers information technology solutions and services across the State's 119 agencies. Rhodes has extensive business and technology experience. He established Paladin, a private investment firm, and was Executive Vice President at Fulton Paper Company, where he held several executive positions in operations and IT. With a technology and business background, his mission for the State of Georgia is to "connect Georgians to their Government by leveraging technology. It's all about enabling citizens to access government services more easily."[2] One quickly learns after speaking with Rhodes that he views the State of Georgia Information Technology Organization as a business by providing value to its customers. Rhodes has three main strategies for the GTA.

- Consolidate state agency IT infrastructure and network services into an enterprise shared services model to improve efficiencies.
- Implement a full IT governance structure, providing transparency across state agencies so everyone can see anything relative to spend.
- Enable agencies to provide online services which improve the value and empower the citizen.

As you would imagine from an executive with a strong business background, Rhodes is all about improving processes. "We are aligning IT with business processes and goals and providing technology innovation through leadership and collaboration with our strategic agency customers, vendor partners, and key stakeholders," says Rhodes.[2]

The Project Governance Process

As previously mentioned, Tom Fruman was the Director of Enterprise Governance and Planning (EGAP) before his retirement in 2018 and reported to the state CIO. He leads the organization that works with the state agencies to promote an enterprise approach to technology. "We provide policies and standards, education and awareness, and advisory services to these agencies. These services enable them to plan, manage, and deliver technology to their constituents."[3] Fruman's team operates as an oversight group across several disciplines, including security, strategy, planning, data governance, and portfolio management. "Our goal is to leverage IT dollars that provide the best value while managing risks. His team accomplishes this through a governance philosophy that "brings the good process to ensure the success of IT investments."[Ibid]

Each of the 119 state agencies operates as an independent division, similar to a federated model. A commissioner leads each state agency, and a management team executes the agency's mission. IT projects are identified, developed, and implemented within the agency. Each agency has a CIO.

To help state agencies achieve success for their IT projects, Teresa Reilly-Director of the Enterprise Portfolio Management Office (EPMO) – the organization within The Enterprise Governance and Planning (EGAP) – provides oversight, training, and consulting. When asked about the objective of the EPMO, Reilly responded with, "Our objective is to ensure IT project success and improve project management maturity practices through portfolio management, project assurance, and the development of policies, standards, guidelines. We also provide consulting, education, and training in support of our core mission."[5]

A few of her significant points can summarize Reilly's philosophy on project assurance:

- Project management is a defined discipline, but you need a balanced view of how the project is progressing.
- We need to provide a level of discipline in managing projects to reduce project risk.
- We need to help project managers become more proactive in responding to risks.
- Capturing views of the project from key stakeholders provides a more realistic view of potential project risks.

The EPMO is important in the governance of state agency projects because "we can help improve the State's capabilities to deliver business benefits through the successful deployment of information technology projects," says Reilly.[Ibid]

Reilly's team focuses on state agency projects that are the most critical and complex with implementation costs of greater than $1 million or have a significant business impact on the State and citizens. For example, a project that provides driver license renewal may not exceed $1 million but could be a disaster if implementation issues arise and create driver license renewal problems.

To achieve their goal, the EPMO employs the following four-step process to provide governance for state agency projects:

1. CAPTURE HIGH-LEVEL DATA for the portfolio of projects that agencies identify as projects for investments.
   - Agencies provide information on projects they are considering for investment (Project Name, Objective, Investment Summary, Benefit, Business Case, etc.).
2. EVALUATE AND IDENTIFY the subsets of projects and associated data reviewed monthly by the Critical Project Review (CPR) Panel.
   - The CPR provides oversight for complex and/or critical projects, i.e., projects greater than $1 million or significant business risk that would impact the State's citizens, regardless of the project cost.
   - The GTA CIO (Calvin Rhodes) is the chair for the monthly CPR.
   - Attendees include GTA Personnel (Calvin Rhodes (Chair) – CIO, Jeff Strane – Director EGAP, Teresa Reilly – Director EPMO); State Agency Personnel (state agency Project Manager, state agency business owner, and the vendor project manager, if there is one); the Independent Verification & Validation (IV&V) vendor (the GTA contracts with independent consultants/vendors to conduct project reviews and recommend specific actions to improve project success); and a representative from the Governor's office.

- Teresa Reilly's team (EPMO) prepares a projects review book that includes key information for the projects reviewed by the CPR.
- Each project team (Project Manager, Business Owner) presents the project status to the CPR (approximately 20-minute sessions).
- Projects identified with significant risk are forwarded for a CPR review by the Governor's office.

3. PROVIDE EDUCATION AND TRAINING to state agency personnel to improve their skills in managing information technology projects.
   - Teresa Reilly's organization (EPMO) includes highly experienced project management personnel who provide training to state agency project teams on the art of project management.

4. ADVISE STATE AGENCIES of industry frameworks and best practices to ensure successful project execution.
   - EPMO personnel have extensive project management experience and provide project teams with various templates and best practices to minimize project risk and improve skills.
   - Conduct project audits via the IV&V Program.

Challenges with Enterprise Governance

Governing hundreds of projects executed by 119 different state agencies has its challenges. To better understand the challenges faced by Fruman's team in governing projects, let's examine the following two areas:

A. Fruman's philosophy on governance, how each agency manages projects, and previous attempts at implementing project management systems

Fruman's governance philosophy is based on his project management and IT experience. "I believe people want to do the right thing, but sometimes need guidelines, training, and oversight to help them improve their skills, reduce project risk, and ensure a successful project outcome."[3]

The state agencies do not use an enterprise project management tool, and most use Microsoft Project and the tools provided by the vendor performing the project implementation work. Each agency is responsible for project execution and chooses the project management tool to use.

Fruman's team tried on two previous occasions to implement an enterprise project management tool for use by all the state agencies. Unfortunately, these implementations failed. Fruman believes that "These robust tools are great, they capture a lot of information, but at the end of the day, you are a slave to the tool. They are so rigorous; you spend a lot of time making the tool work, as opposed to making it work for managing the portfolio of projects."[Ibid] Fruman summarizes that the three main reasons for the failed implementations were that the tools "Were too complex, required a lot of training, and required *a lot of effort to maintain*".[Ibid]

B. Major governance challenges faced by the Enterprise Governance and Planning team (EGAP)

The process for collecting and analyzing project data is critical for the EGAP team in effectively performing their governance role. There are four significant barriers for any organization to overcome in completing this process:

- Include key stakeholders in project review meetings.
- Make sure you are collecting the correct data.
- Minimize data gathering time.
- Make sure you properly analyze the data.

The EGAP team incurred a lot of time gathering data and wasn't capturing the correct data to apply proper governance. As a result, there were many challenges that Teresa Reilly's team experienced in performing governance for the state agency projects. The six significant challenges prior to the implementation of the CAI TrueProject Suite are summarized below.

1. INCLUDING KEY STAKEHOLDERS AND MANAGEMENT IN PROJECT MEETINGS is a must for project review meetings. Reilly review meetings didn't include all the key stakeholders and management from the Agencies when their projects were reviewed. This led to the inaccurate status of projects and the ability to make key decisions on project issues.

2. GATHERING PROJECT DATA from agency project managers is cumbersome and preparing monthly dashboard reports using Excel is time-consuming.
   - Every month, project managers complete a manually generated Excel spreadsheet with numerous tabs, which provides status for each project indicator (schedule, budget, business objectives, risk, issues, organizational readiness, etc.) and project financials.
   - It takes about 80 person-hours of effort to collect project managers' data and consolidate it into a presentation package.
   - Comments provided by the project manager are subjective and represent the Program Manager's view of the project without real supporting data
   - The project data is imported into a GTA spreadsheet that drives green, yellow, or red status.
   - The GTA spreadsheets are consolidated into a comprehensive document used by each Critical Panel Review (CPR) panel member during the monthly CPR reviews.

3. PROJECT DATA IS PREPARED by the project manager and doesn't represent input from key stakeholders.
   - Data provided by each project manager and represents best efforts as to project status. However, it is only the view of the project manager. Lack of input from key stakeholders masks potential issues and increases the potential for project risk.

4. ACCESS TO DATA IS LIMITED – It's a push, not a pull, limiting access only to those involved in preparing and reviewing the monthly data. It is not shared across the agencies to foster learning and continuous improvement.
   ■ Data is captured in Excel spreadsheets and therefore is static.
   ■ Data is not available to everyone.
   ■ Data is pushed to users rather than pulled from a web-based application.

5. LACK OF PREDICTIVE PROJECT BEHAVIOR limits risk assessment to current and past project activities.
   ■ A picture only portrays current activity when capturing quantitative data. We all know that projects behave in mysterious ways, and a green project can turn into a red project overnight. We've all experienced this.
   ■ Using current and historical data to predict project risk greatly improves the governance capability and, more importantly, helps project managers improve their skills in project management by developing risk mitigation strategies.

6. LACK OF AN ADEQUATE ISSUE MANAGEMENT capability prevents proper mitigation of project risk.
   ■ The current system is cumbersome to use in capturing project issues
   ■ Inability to easily record and assign tasks to mitigate issues increases project risk

7. PROJECT REQUESTS FROM AGENCIES do not capture pertinent data to rationalize investments decisions.
   ■ The current process for capturing project request data is manual and doesn't provide adequate information to assess risk, business alignment, and the overall opportunity.
   ■ Lack of business case and associated data didn't allow for proper analysis and comparison of multiple projects.

Reinventing the Governance Process and Selecting a Supporting Tool

Fruman identified a two-step process for a new innovative governance solution. The first step was to design a governance process where Reilly's Enterprise Portfolio Management Office (EPMO) could more efficiently provide oversight for state agency projects. The second step would be to identify a supporting tool for the new governance process.

1. Reinventing the governance process
   One of the cardinal rules in management is *no surprises*. Reilly's Enterprise Governance and Planning Team (EGAP) always ran surprises from Agency project teams, which impacted project scope, quality, and cost. Reilly needed to find a way for these *surprises* to stop. Her idea was to create a Critical Project

Review Panel (CPRP) that meets regularly to review critical projects where the dollar value is greater than $1 million or significantly impacts State's citizens. An example of a project with a significant impact on citizens is a driver's license renewal application project. Her organization attended project status meetings at the state agency, where projects exceeded $10 million. Figure 15.2 is an overview of the Critical Project Review Panel.

The Critical Project Panel Review (CPPR) reinvented the governance oversight process of state agency projects. Not only did the process improve the efficiency and quality of completed projects. It also created a more collaborative environment among the state agency project and leadership personnel with the GTA Enterprise Governance and Planning Organization. Following are key highlights of the reinvented Critical Project Review Panel.

i. Monthly meetings include projects greater than $1 million or having a significant business impact.
ii. Participants will include all key stakeholders as well as Agency management.
iii. Pre-meetings will occur to prepare for the formal monthly meeting. This prepares the team for the formal meeting by reviewing the data, identifying any pertinent issues, and developing appropriate mitigation plans for identified issues.
iv. The Critical Project Review Panel provides a collaborative environment for all key stakeholders to participate and contribute to the project. Integrating a formal review process for critical projects into the governance process reduces project risk and enables a higher degree of project success metrics (delivering key deliverables on time and within budget).

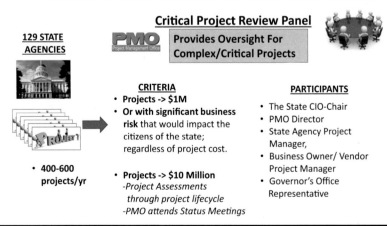

STATE OF GA NEW PROJECT GOVERNANCE PROCESS

Figure 15.2   State of Georgia new project governance process.

2. Selecting a Winning Tool.

After a few failed PPM implementations, Fruman and his team were determined to find a solution that would work for the State of Georgia. Fruman decided to "keep it simple." The team identified the following major requirements for the portfolio governance solution:

■ An easy-to-use web-enabled solution
■ Capture data in an automated way from the various state agency project management systems used to manage projects
■ Hard data capture from the Project Manager as well as soft data from key stakeholders to provide a 360-degree view of the project

Fruman's team initiated an RFP which was responded to by several different solution providers. Each selected vendor presented a demonstration of their software. When Fruman saw the demo of the CAI TrueProject Suite, the light bulb went off. "This is exactly what we need to provide adequate project assurance and governance for the state agency projects."[Ibid]

One of the key differentiators that Fruman saw in the TrueProject suite was the ability to import project data (Schedule, Financials, Risk) into the tool and to assess the potential risk of projects. The way these feature works is as follows.

i.   GEMS provides a 360-degree view of state projects using a combination of traditional, quantitative operational data and qualitative assessment data.

ii. Agency leaders can now objectively analyze projects based on business value and the probability of success.

iii. Because GEMS is a hosted, web-based application, agency leaders can access it anytime, anywhere. Stakeholders, including project managers, team members, and others, can offer input and review a project, program, or portfolio status.

iv. It analyzes the entire range of project indicators. It also provides easy standard monthly reporting, so leaders have improved visibility into the performance of projects, programs, and portfolios throughout their entire lifecycle.

"The Assessment feature coupled with other GEMS features represent the project status very well. We haven't found a green project that is really red," says Hank Oelze, Program Manager Enterprise portfolio Management Office.[6]

Implementation and Value of the CAI TrueProject Suite

Fruman selected the CAI TrueProject suite as the tool to support the governance process. It's common to use an acronym to name a vendor software solution, and the State of Georgia is no exception. The acronym chosen was GEMS (Georgia Enterprise Management Suite).

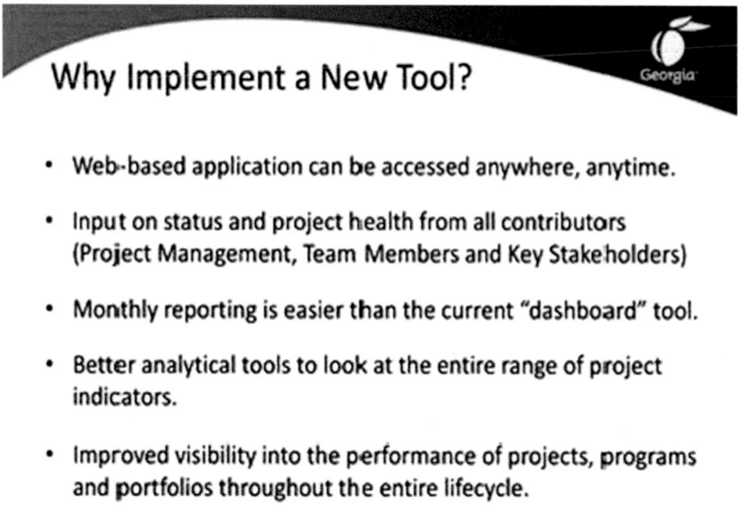

Why Implement a New Tool?

Georgia

- Web-based application can be accessed anywhere, anytime.

- Input on status and project health from all contributors (Project Management, Team Members and Key Stakeholders)

- Monthly reporting is easier than the current "dashboard" tool.

- Better analytical tools to look at the entire range of project indicators.

- Improved visibility into the performance of projects, programs and portfolios throughout the entire lifecycle.

Figure 15.3 Why implement a new tool.

Hank Oelze, Program manager for the EPMO, was responsible for implementing the GEMS solution. After the award, Oelze and colleagues prepared a presentation for the state Project & Portfolio Management Conference for state agency personnel. The meeting was part of the communication plan to orient the project managers in the new governance process. The goal was to set expectations and help the teams understand the new process's value to the state agencies, GTA, Georgia citizens, and, most importantly, the project managers. Included in the presentation is Figure 15.3 that identified why a new tool was required.[6]

During any implementation, there are always concerns about the vendor relationship, training, and consulting. Following is a summary of the GTA experience working with CAI on these three key areas.

Vendor Relationship

One major concern of organizations contracting with a solution vendor is the working relationship. Theresa Reilly said, "CAI has been a great vendor and easy to work with. They bend over backward to help us."[5]

Training

CAI prepared training videos that GTA used during the implementation. Reilly said that after an initial training session with the core implementation team, "we took over the training using our experienced project management personnel and videos."[Ibid]

Implementation Consulting

The skill and experience of implementation consultants are always a concern. "The CAI implementation team was experienced and easy to work with," says Reilly.[Ibid]

Value of CAI's TrueProject Suite

The value derived by the State of Georgia from implementing the CAI TrueProject Suite provided value for the State of Georgia in the following six ways.

Please note that a compiled set of ten capabilities every governance tool should have appears at the end of this chapter. These should be helpful to those of you looking for a governance tool for your organization.

1. Overall Value

   The value of the CAI solution provides the State of Georgia with strategic and operational value for managing the portfolio of projects executed by state agency personnel. The tool dramatically enhances communication since the PM receives and assesses input from several roles, and Stage-Gate questionnaires improve process compliance. Hank Oelze, program manager at EPMO, describes the overall value as follows:

   - The monthly update process is easier than the previous Excel-based scorecard.
   - Projects are evaluated through the proposal stage.
   - Projects evaluated from several project roles versus just the project manager.
   - Qualitative and quantitative data drive dashboard KPI dials.
   - Issue tracking automates the reporting, resolving, and closing of Issues.
   - The tool dramatically enhances communication since the PM receives and assesses input from several roles.
   - Stage-Gate questionnaires enhance process compliance.

2. Data Gathering of Project Data for Governance Analysis

   One of the significant challenges faced by Reilly's team was the time to capture data, prepare project dashboards, and properly display project status. The CAI solution overcame those challenges. For example, the 80 person-hour manual process of collecting project data from the project managers and consolidating it into a presentation package for the Critical Panel Review now takes about 4 hours.

3. Project Dashboards

   The project dashboard (left) provides a visual representation of the quantitative and qualitative data that drives the key project indicator gauges to reflect ranges within red, yellow, or green, a benefit they never had before. "Visually displaying the range within each key indicator helps the project managers and Critical Review Panel interpret the degree of risk more effectively than the previous process," says Reilly.[Ibid]

4. Predictive Analysis

The CAI solution uses algorithms based upon completed assessments to predict the project's potential risk for each key project indicator. This single capability makes the solution proactive by anticipating risk and identifying mitigating actions.

5. Improving Project Manager Skills

Governance is more than just oversight. It should involve improving the skills and capabilities of project managers. People genuinely learn from experience. The assessment questionnaires, which focus on risk categories, are completed by key project stakeholders to provide a 360-degree view of the project. Over time, project managers intuitively behave in a manner that addresses these potential risk areas proactively.

6. Quantitatively Analyzing Project Requests

One of the significant benefits is the process of reviewing and analyzing the business value for project requests. "A Collection Health Pipeline Report saves time from the previously manually prepared report that was very time consuming," says Reilly (see Figure 15.4 and Figure 15.5).[Ibid]

The CAI solution automated the preparation process and provided dashboard data for these requested projects and an analysis grid to display the business alignment and risk score for the portfolio of requested projects.

Governance Tool Capabilities

There are many Project Portfolio Management (PPM) solutions on the market. Most require lengthy implementations and training and sometimes are overkill for what a PMO organization is trying to accomplish. The CAI solution chosen by the State of Georgia hit their sweet spot of need. It is easy to implement and use, regardless of the project management tools used by the state agencies.

If your organization is looking at project governance solutions, make sure it includes the following ten critical capabilities needed to minimize project risk: These are written for State Government agencies and apply to private sector companies.

PROVIDE GOVERNANCE for the portfolio of projects regardless of the project management tools used by the state agencies.

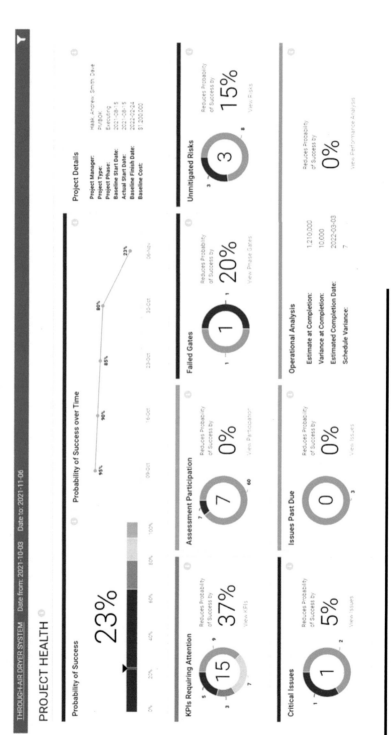

Figure 15.4   Single project health record.

Figure 15.5   Collection health report – example.

Each agency selects the tool they use for managing projects. To maintain the federated model used in the State, the GTA needed to find a tool that would quickly provide governance for the state agency projects by easily capturing, analyzing, and displaying data in a dashboard.

1. PROVIDE A SOLUTION THAT ISN'T OVERKILL for the governance team and project management personnel.
   - The initial implementation was accomplished in approximately 30 days, with configuration occurring in the following 30–60 days.
   - The solution is intuitive and easy to use.
   - Training is not complicated and can be accomplished by company personnel.
2. WEB-BASED SOLUTION that provides data to anyone, anywhere, and at any time.
   - All personnel should have access to project and governance data from any desktop at any time and from anywhere.
3. CAPTURES QUALITATIVE DATA from key stakeholders to provide a 360-degree project perspective.
   - The ability to capture quantitative data from project management tools supplemented with soft data capture from key stakeholders provides a more realistic view of the project and potential risks.
4. EASILY IMPORT PROJECT DATA into the governance solution.
   - Automated data import from state agency project management tools eliminates manual and cumbersome effort.
5. PROVIDE FOR EFFECTIVE ISSUE MANAGEMENT Capability.
   - Allows users to capture issues in an automated environment, assign issues to owners, and provide issue status updates for all stakeholders to review.
6. IDENTIFIES KEY RISK INDICATORS and provides predictive risk scores based upon quantitative and qualitative data.
   - Provide summary metrics for key project indicators.
   - Provide a predictive metric regarding future risk-based upon quantitative and qualitative data.
7. IMPROVE THE PROJECT MANAGERS' SKILLS through self-learning and 360-degree feedback.
   - Project assessments – which measure the key project indicators through a set of questions with a group of answer choices – provide insight to the project managers and implementation teams of potential risk areas.
   - Over time these assessment questions become intuitive and part of the daily activities performed by project managers in the execution of projects.
   - Provide predictive metrics regarding future risk-based upon quantitative and qualitative data.

8. DISPLAYS DASHBOARD METRICS of key project indicators and automated reporting.
   - Display key project indicators in the dashboard.
   - Provide qualitative comments for each key indicator.
   - Provide flexible reporting on key project data.
9. CAPTURES KEY DATA for project requests and analyzes data based upon business needs and potential risks.
   - Easily captures project request data in an automated environment to properly analyze investment opportunities for risk and value.

Business Value of Reinvented Governance Process

The Critical Panel Review process coupled with the GEMS tool provided significant value to the State of Georgia. The best way to share the business value is through three examples of projects and savings resulting from the new CPPR Panel and the enabling GEMS tool.

Figure 15.6 Three Project Savings Examples represent three projects in-process when the CPPR process and GEMS tool were not finalized and available for use on the project. The Finance Project's (the first project) savings estimate is real. The next two projects' (Case Management and Health Management) savings results from estimates if the CPPR and GEMS tool were used from the beginning of the project.

Finance Project

The project manager for a Banking and Finance project was reporting the project on track. Reilly said, "when the new CPPR process and GEMS tool was available for use and integrated into the project, critical vendor issues were identified. The resulting three-to four-month delay cost the project an additional \$300-\$400k.[5]

Three Project Savings Examples

Project Type	$ Value	Project Issue
Finance Project	$300k	Vendor Issue
Case Management	$700k	PM Issue
Health Management	$400k	Poor Requirements

Figure 15.6   Three project savings examples.

Case Management

The Georgia Vocational Rehabilitation Agency implemented a two-year $6 million project. When the CPPR process and GEMS tool were integrated into the project, stakeholders were asked to provide their input via assessments sent electronically as part of the GEM tool. The results of the electronic assessment showed that stakeholders had real concerns about the project. Unfortunately, the project manager was not polling stakeholders on their view of the project status. Reilly said,

> the stakeholders were not included in the project review. When we integrated the GEMS tool, the automated assessments were sent to stakeholders, and they identified this issue. As a result, we reassigned the project managers and worked diligently to get the project on track. The project extended three months at the cost of $700k.[Ibid]

Medicaid Eligibility Upgrade Project

This project was a front-end for Medicaid eligibility, allowing citizens to access one application instead of numerous applications for processing Medicaid applications. When the CPPR process and GEM tool was integrated into the in-process project, Reilly said,

> We found out that the requirements were poorly written and not adequately reviewed. So, we moved the project to another agency, monitored the project using the CPPR process and GEM tool. This allowed us to have better insight and keep closer tabs on the project. I also made sure that I sat on the Change Board to make sure I could monitor the requirements adequately. All the work upfront that resulted in poor requirements had to be scrapped. This effort cost $400k.[Ibid]

Summary

Citizens for Georgia and the state agencies reap the benefits of the governance process improvements implemented by Teresa Reilly and her team due to the reinvented Critical Project Review Panel (CPPR) and the GEMS tool. Following are some key benefits.

1. Key stakeholders meet prior to the formal CPPR to collaborate on critical projects and address any potential schedule, financial, or technology risk areas. The electronically automated project assessments enable all project team members, including key stakeholders, to address any project issues elevating them quickly for resolution.
2. Project data, dashboard data, and detailed information are imported into the GEMS tool for all to view in real time.
3. Key project indicator analysis is available to the Critical Panel for review for all the complex and critical projects.
4. The GEMS tool uses algorithms to predict the degree of potential risk for each key indicator. This feature makes the solution a more proactive solution.
5. The GEMS project dashboard provides a visual representation of the quantitative and qualitative data to drive the key project indicator gauges to reflect ranges within red, yellow, or green – a benefit they never had before. Knowing the range within each color helps the project managers and Critical Project Review Panel members interpret the degree of risk more effectively than the previous process.
6. According to CAI's who developed the TrueProject suite, "GTA saves more than $280 million a year due to using the GEMS tool.[7]

Following are quotes from Calvin Rhodes and Teresa Reilly summarizing the overall benefits of the reinvented Critical Project Panel Review process and GEMS tool:

> The new process and tool enable us to address the increased challenges of our growing portfolio of projects as we work to address project risk, schedule timelines, and budget goals. The CPPR process and GEMS tool enable us to uncover opportunities to mitigate risk, schedule, and budget challenges with proactive solutions that identify key predictors for project success and incorporate stakeholder communication and training. (Calvin Rhodes, State of Georgia CIO[2])

Agency leaders are more engaged than ever before. The CPPR process and GEMS tool enable us to make informed business decisions because we now have objective data. We now have the processes and tools to identify potential risks and make appropriate business decisions to mitigate project risk. (Teresa Reilly[5])

With an average of $400–900 million of projects to govern each year, the State can now look at ways to improve project success. They now have a solution that can minimize risk, improve governance, and improve project success.

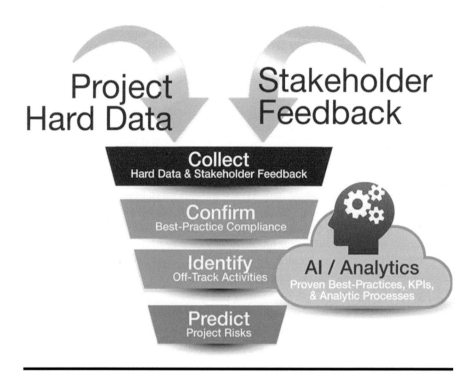

Figure 15.7 CAI's TrueProject™ framework.

So, if your organization is experiencing project assurance and portfolio governance challenges and is unwilling to accept a 25–35% project failure rate as an acceptable norm, heed the lessons learned from the State of Georgia Technology Authority. Learn how they applied an innovative process and enabling tool to minimize risk, improve project management skills, achieve project success, and, most importantly, provide value to the citizens of Georgia.

Following is additional information on CAI TrueProject Suite™ (Figures 15.7–15.11)[3].

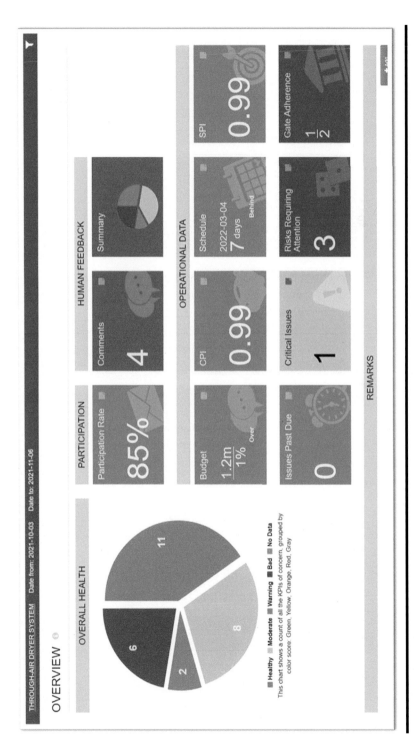

Figure 15.8   Interactive dashboard and reports.

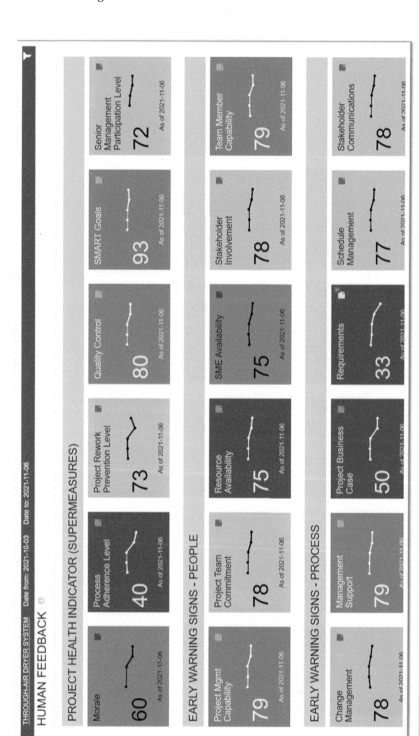

Figure 15.9 Human feedback.

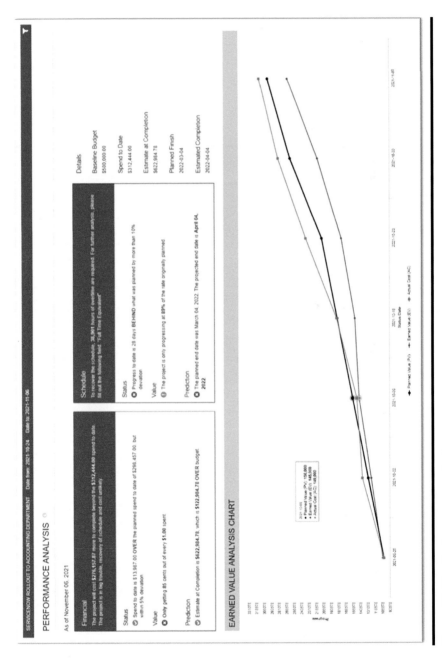

Figure 15.10 Performance analysis.

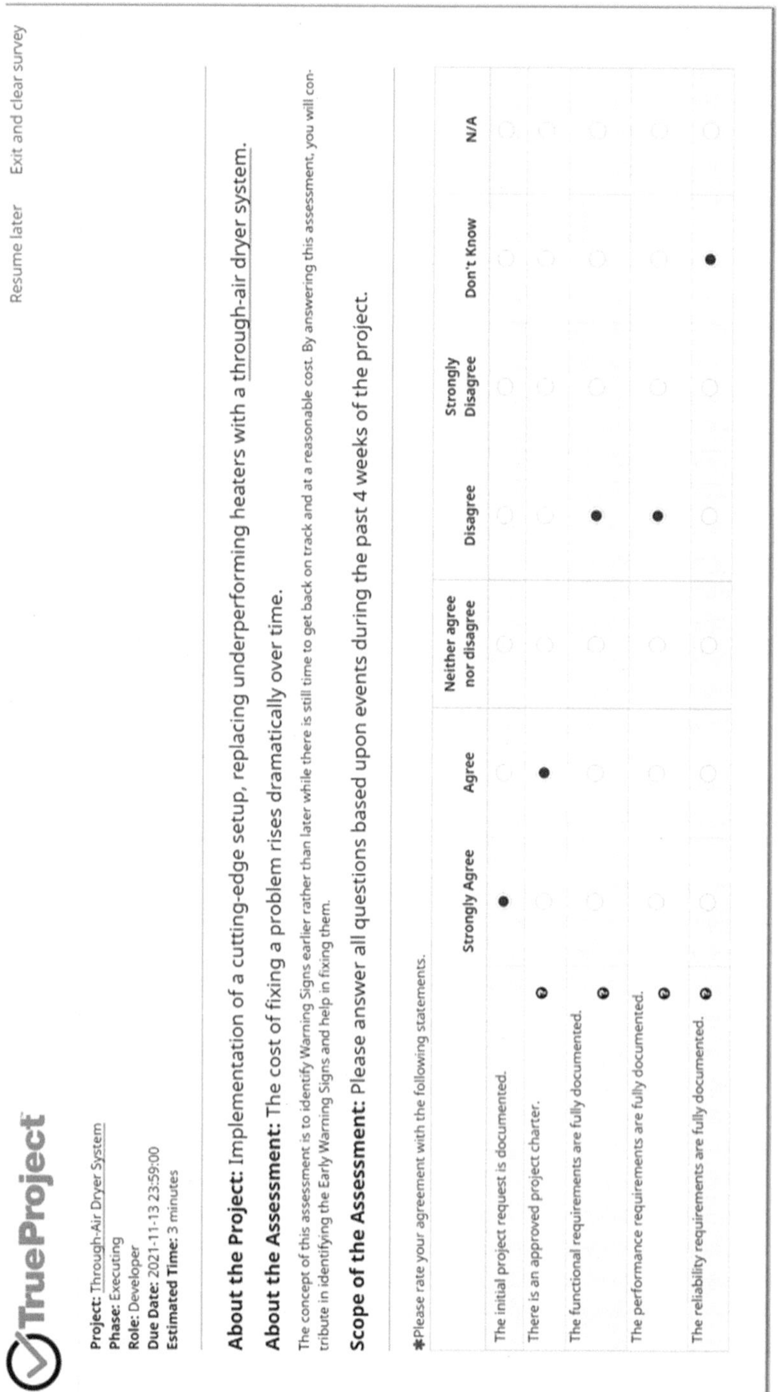

Resume later   Exit and clear survey

TrueProject

Project: Through-Air Dryer System
Phase: Executing
Role: Developer
Due Date: 2021-11-13 23:59:00
Estimated Time: 3 minutes

About the Project: Implementation of a cutting-edge setup, replacing underperforming heaters with a through-air dryer system.

About the Assessment: The cost of fixing a problem rises dramatically over time.

The concept of this assessment is to identify Warning Signs earlier rather than later while there is still time to get back on track and at a reasonable cost. By answering this assessment, you will contribute in identifying the Early Warning Signs and help in fixing them.

Scope of the Assessment: Please answer all questions based upon events during the past 4 weeks of the project.

*Please rate your agreement with the following statements.

	Strongly Agree	Agree	Neither agree nor disagree	Disagree	Strongly Disagree	Don't Know	N/A
The initial project request is documented.	●						
There is an approved project charter.		●					
The functional requirements are fully documented.				●			
The performance requirements are fully documented.				●			
The reliability requirements are fully documented.						●	

Figure 15.11 Stakeholder feedback.

Citings

1. https://gta.georgia.gov/epmo-main-page-0/reporting-applications/georgia-enterprise-management-suite-gems
2. Calvin Rhodes/Phil Weinzimer interview June 18, 2017.
3. Tom Fruman/Phil Weinzimer interviews, January 5,9,15, 2017.
4. https://trueprojectinsight.com/
5. Teresa Reilly/Phil Weinzimer interviews December 4, 2018, June 17, 2019, January 22, 2020.
6. Hank Oelze/Phil Weinzimer interview November 5, 2019.
7. https://trueprojectinsight.com/media/2226/georgia-technology-authority-success-story-two-pager.pdf

Chapter 16

How the Rochester, NY, CIO Improved Citizen Services with an Innovative Strategic Governance Process

Anyone involved in city government understands the immense challenges in providing services to its citizens. There are numerous budgetary constraints, infrastructure issues, and economic redevelopment challenges to improve the quality of life for its citizens.

Lisa Bobo was CIO for the City of Rochester in Upstate New from 2012 to 2019. During her tenure, she took on a multi-year initiative to improve the services for Rochester citizens by developing a governance process on how city agencies could leverage technology in new and innovative ways. Many of the changes involved improving or innovating business processes on how agencies communicate and work together. Bobo sums up the value of the governance process she and her team developed for the City of Rochester.

> This model helped us lay the foundation for an Organizational Enterprise Architecture, leading to a city focused on services rather than an internal structure. It helped to optimize the project selection process

DOI: 10.1201/9781003317531-16

on an enterprise level, and overall made significant progress in improving services to Rochester citizens.[1]

Read on to find out more about Bobo and the governance model developed for the transformation initiative.

Bobo is a seasoned executive with over 30 years of experience in various technology and business processing roles from the City of Rochester, including serving as the Chief Information Officer for seven years. Bobo is Chief Executive Officer and founder of Bolder IT Strategies, LLC, a Senior Advisory Services firm that provides consulting services to government and private industry. Bobo serves on the boards for the Foodlink Organization, Western NY Chapter of the Society for Information Management (SIM), and the NYS Local Government Records Archive Committee. Lisa also has served as the Vice-President of the Metropolitan Information Exchange, a national government organization, and now serves as the Event Director for their yearly conference. She was chosen as the recipient of the 2018 Nien-Ling Wacker Visionary Award and was a finalist for the Rochester Great Awards. In 2019, Lisa received the Key to the City of Rochester for distinguished service.

I had the opportunity to interview Bobo and published the interview in CIO. com.[1] I thought it would be valuable to share the interview as an example of how a CIO for a medium-size city developed a governance process that aligns with several components from The Strategic IT Governance 2.0 model. Following is the interview with some added information. I believe you will find it valuable.

Every one of us interacts digitally today with our banks, grocery stores, department stores, and even restaurants. In fact, when driving home from work, your smartphone, when connected to your home security system, turns on your home's interior lights. It's in our daily culture. And this is how citizens want to interact with municipal services. And city governments are beginning to recognize that citizen services need a more strategic focus, significantly since technology has evolved to enable new and more efficient ways to provide these services. Lisa Bobo, CIO for the City of Rochester, NY, is a visionary who has embarked on improving citizen services. Bobo has proven herself to be a visionary, strategic thinker and leads a great team of IT professionals who are reinventing how IT leverages technology to improve services for the citizens of Rochester. Rochester was selected as one of the top 21 cities in *The Smart 21 Communities of 2019* initiative. And in early 2019, the top winner will be announced. I had the opportunity to speak with Bobo, and the following is a portion of our conversation.

Phil Weinzimer: Lisa, let's start with a broad question on the value of the transformation initiative you undertook to improve Citizen services.

Lisa Bobo: How did this add value? Transformation is not a process that happens overnight, but initial stages begin when internal departments recognize themselves as service providers and see the interconnectivity of work among government agencies. When do you know this work is making an impact? Businesses within the Organization start to use the terminology, budgeting is based on enterprise solutions, and external documents show service-related activity, rather than a bureaucratic structure. In days before utilizing the Enterprise Architecture, it was common to read the yearly published budget book to discover new projects listed by a department (rather than a service) but requiring employee resources and process reengineering from various other areas within government. We transformed to ensure most programs and projects started with an initial discovery and affirmation of the enterprise architecture. Overall, this is the first stage of eliminating redundancy in government.

Phil Weinzimer: Lisa, you have a successful career in Rochester within the IT organization. Prior to being promoted to CIO, you had many different roles but you always had a focus on improving citizen services. What were some of the actions you took early on to improve citizen services.

Lisa Bobo: A major objective in improving citizen services in the public sector is setting priorities amongst the various initiatives city departments want to pursue. This becomes more difficult with budget and resource constraints faced by many municipal governments. I've had many conversations with municipal CIOs about setting priorities. It's a real challenge. Let me explain why.

Early on in our journey to improve citizen services for Rochester citizens, we focused on a few city departments that needed help. Agency leaders identified initiatives where technology solutions would help. We had some challenges in appropriately responding to their needs, especially in prioritizing projects. You can imagine the complexity of processing IT requests from the 14 city departments on an individual basis. About ten years ago, to help minimize the complexity, we created three Relationship Management positions within the IT organization to support similar Departments (Public Service, Back Office, and Public Safety). This provided us a voice within the Department to better understand their needs. This is a role I had before my CIO role. We thought this would help us to set priorities and enhance customer service. When these 3 areas were created, we focused on developing priorities within each area. Although this was an overall improvement, we still lacked the overall focus on City priorities. But this was an excellent first step that helped us focus and manage our interactions with the various city departments much more efficiently. This was the beginning of an ongoing process to improve citizen services by leveraging technology through an improved organizational model.

PW: When you became CIO there was a lot of buzz about establishing an IT Governance process. And IT Governance ties into citizen services. Would you please explain the connection in and how you addressed this need?

LB: Well, this is a very interesting question. When you ask people to define IT Governance, you receive many different responses. I see it because one of the significant IT governance objectives is to establish a process that helps us ensure that the right projects are executed efficiently. Let's leave the execution discussion for another time. What I want to focus on here is the selection process. My focus was to look at priorities from a city-wide perspective. It's almost like an aerial view of the city services looking from the top down. This led our IT Team to develop a City-Wide Enterprise Architecture model that reflects the services provided by the various city departments. We used existing documents, such as the budget book prior project documentation, and reviewed the Federal Government model to build this model. Many of the services touch several departments in the City that cross all three relationship management areas. With this approach, you quickly begin to see the various supporting technology that enables these services.

When you look at a City-wide enterprise model, you begin to view services from the "outside in" or from a Citizen perspective. You are not viewing our services from an internal departmental view, but rather the outcome they produce. Let me elaborate.

Over eight city departments process some permits or licenses. These licenses and permits cross over all three relationship management areas. Before we consider replacing technology for one permit, issued by one Department, we should consider a higher strategic organizational view that aligns similar services. Why would IT drive this type of initiative? I think there are two reasons why IT has an integral role in driving the City's organizational structure. IT tends to have a birds-eye view of the Organization. We can often see the alignment and frequently the inefficiency. There is no coincidence that we continually see CIO's taking on a Chief Operating Officer role. Also, the way we address these services are ultimately tied to streamlined technology, infrastructure and data.

PW: Lisa, now that you have a more strategic view of the services provided by city departments, have you reorganized IT to serve departments' needs better?

LB: We continue to have three relationship management areas, but overall there is more alignment than previous. It is very common for an enterprise project to touch all three areas. Four years ago, we also developed an Enterprise Process and Systems Team (EA). This group supports the development of the EA, all process work, technology selection, and support. When a new need surfaces, they work closely with the Relationship Manager and the affected departments to perform an EA discovery assessment. This allows us to validate our organizational blueprint and update where needed.

This doesn't come without challenges and resistance. As you can imagine, changing organizational structure is not always the answer, and this approach is not always a quick and dirty solution. This is a strategic approach that can take time but will replace antiquated technology solutions, ensure funding is allocated to the highest demands, and provide for more seamless business processes, where the Citizens will continue to see improved services.

We continually reevaluate the alignment of Relationship Managers to the areas they support. We want to ensure we are evolving as the Community changes. The new energy around cities is the discussion of Smart Cities and the Internet of Things. We are assessing whether our current internal structure and Governance will support the changes needed to move us forward.

This model helps us provide a much-improved response to the needs of the city departments and enables us to strategically improve services with a strategic governance process that optimizes the project selection process on an enterprise level. We still have a lot of work to do, but I believe the IT team is on the right track and making significant progress in improving services to Rochester citizens.

Citing

1. https://www.cio.com/article/3323395/rochester-ny-cio-improves-citizen-services-with-a-strategic-governance-process.html

Chapter 17

A State CIO Shares Insights on the Importance of Strategic IT Governance

State government IT organizations are beginning to understand the importance of governance. A perfect example of this is Dr. Alex Pettit, Chief Technology Officer for Colorado. Pettit served as CIO for Oregon and Oklahoma and Chief Architect for the Oregon Secretary of State. Pettit is a very thoughtful and focused IT executive, and I had the opportunity to interview Pettit and published the interview in CIO.com.[1] I thought it would be valuable to share the interview as an example of how a CIO appointed into a new role for a state views governance and how he implemented governance processes to improve communications between state agencies and improve citizen services. Pettit also addresses many of the Strategic IT Governance 2.0 model components. Following is the interview with some added information. I believe you will find it valuable.

Interview Preface

Innovating citizen services is moving to the top of every state CIOs agenda. Why? Because citizens want to engage with state agencies' services as easily as they navigate purchases on their Amazon Prime account. The challenge is how to improve citizen engagement, the supporting processes, and the value of these services. Ensuring these strategic projects are successfully implemented depends on the governance process that minimizes risk, reduces cost, manages resources, and monitors schedules. A strategic IT governance process can achieve these key metrics. CIOs who understand the importance of Governance will succeed as these strategic projects are developed and implemented. Alex Pettit is one of these CIOs who served in this capacity for Oregon and Oklahoma. Alex has received the Best of Texas Award for IT Leadership, the Public Technology Institute IT Leadership Award, and the Society for Information Management IT Executive of the Year Award for his leadership. Alex was named in the 2012 Top 25 Information Managers list at Information-Management.com for being a successful and engaging role model and example of leadership. I heard about Pettit from a colleague, and we connected via phone for an interview on governance. Following is an excerpt from that interview.

Phil Weinzimer: The need for an IT governance model is essential as more states ramp up initiatives to improve citizen services by leveraging technology. How important is the role of IT Governance to ensure that these strategic projects are successfully implemented?

Alex Pettit: The goal of Governance is to reduce project risk. The role of Governance cannot be understated, particularly in State government. The struggle with Governance is always how to keep them on the policy and out of the day to day management of IT projects. In the end, the projects are not what needs the attention of governance groups, and it is the policies and supporting processes that need their participation.

Governance at the highest level must focus on the definition and adherence to IT investment prioritization (return on investment, the total cost of ownership, what benefits will be realized for which people at who's cost), project reporting, metrics or key performance indicators, and fidelity to those metrics. Governance is hard work, and often not what interests people in participating in

Phil Weinzimer: Could you provide an example of what you mean by that?

Alex Pettit: I'm reminded of a story from my days as CIO for the City of Denton, Texas. The city manager worked diligently with the city council to focus on overall Governance and policy and not upon the specific actions of city staff in the fulfillment of city policy. The council then undertook the task of re-writing the building codes for the city in a very engaging and community-oriented manner. There were Multiple town hall meetings, small interest group meetings, one-on-one sessions with staff and citizens and property owners and builders. After nearly a year, a revised building code was published.

One aspect of the code was that home and business owners needed to keep grass in their front yard lower than 4 feet in height. The policy was that the owner would receive a verbal warning from a code officer, and then a second warning, then a police officer would write a ticket, and then the parks department would mow the grass, and they would get a bill for the mowing. The entire process would take between 3 to 4 weeks.

A month after the adoption of the new code, an elderly resident of the city came to ask the council to forgive her ticket and the parks fee for cutting her lawn. The resident said, "she had been in the hospital, her mower was stolen, her sons were away, and she had no one to help her." The manager kept the council meeting at the policy level, asking them if it should be five feet of grass instead of four or four warnings instead of two. But the council just wanted to have her ticket and fees forgiven, regardless of the policy.

This trap exists today in private and public sectors, with governance members not wanting to talk about policies or technology reference models or enterprise architecture or IT investment criteria. They want to use a new application they had demonstrated to perform some business functions better.

PW: You talk about the role of process in Governance. Can you elaborate on the importance of process as part of an effective IT governance model?

AP: Process is an essential part of an effective IT governance model, and not just for defining what is measured or discussed but also what is not to be measured nor debated. This is most apparent when a project is in difficulty. Everyone has an opinion on what to do to fix a broken project: bring in consultants, pay the staff more over time, reduce the scope, extend the schedule or start over. The problem is that this is not the domain of IT Governance. IT Governance should be involved in the go-no-go decisions to continue to fund a project or to kill it and to ensure the investments made are responsible and reasonable, not to exercise control over the management of the projects.

For over 30 years, the Society of Information Management has found that alignment of IT and the business is the number one concern for both CEO's and CIO's. This alignment begins with IT Governance, which without a process will devolve into the IT budget, funding models, or department management discussions. A well-defined governance process, beginning with the governance committee charter, defines the boundaries of responsibility. A good governance process should ensure the time spent on Governance is time well spent assuring alignment between what the business is trying to achieve and what the IT team needs to deliver.

PW: Where do metrics come into play in measuring a successful IT governance process?

AP: Well-structured IT governance success factors vary depending on how the organization functions and greatly valued. A governance structure that runs counter to the business culture will struggle to succeed regardless of the quality of the governance model. I want to share three different organization models that function differently and require different types of metrics.

1. Organizations that value consensus focuses on achieving and maintaining consensus metrics defined, measured, and reported. Consensus is not a goal once achieved and then never revisited. It is a continuous process of defining and refining the outcome sought for a project, which will change over time with technology, environmental, and personnel changes. Metrics for consensus-driven organizations will include perceived input into project charters, business cases, articulation and open discussions on issues, changes, and the agreed-upon adjustments to continue working on a project.

2. For organizations that are more consultative (where different executives are responsible for other aspects of the defined outcome), measures focus on how well governance members feel they understand issues and challenges, how well-justified changes to projects are perceived to have been made, how well they feel they have an understanding of the impacts of these changes to the project will make upon them or their departments, and how well they feel they and their peers make the necessary changes within their individual areas of responsibility to accommodate the changes are all metrics in this model of Governance.

3. In an advisory model of Governance (also referred to as a federated model of Governance, which state governments commonly use for inter-agency IT projects), measures around project progress, issues tracking, assignment, and resolution, measuring how confident they feel in their assessment of the project impact upon their own agency or business unit, and how well they feel informed on the project for them to report back to their own agency leadership on the decisions and changes to the project as it progresses are relevant and will provide meaningful measurements and early warnings of trouble.

The easiest way to measure these is with a survey at the end of each governance board meeting. The relevant questions were asked and answered and, if possible, reported at the time of collection for all members to see and compared with previous responses. This provides the governance chair the insight into what is or is not working and where future meetings should focus.

PW: Implementing IT Governance models is not an easy task, and I'm sure in your experience, you've seen some pitfalls. What are some of the key mistakes that IT organizations make in developing an IT Governance model?

I've seen many stumbles in my career, but I'd like to focus on three key areas. The first key mistake is in misreading what kind of organizational structure they are working. In-State government, it is often said that we are collaborative in our pursuit of citizen outcomes, which is not applicable in IT governance modeling. A consensus-based approach to an inter-agency IT project produces a "committee of no" that can never assist an IT project in peril as it does not map how the organization works. Discussions break down into disagreements over the definition of the assignment of responsibility and progress made (or not made). In a collaborative environment, the governance players get into a mode where a tiebreaking vote is necessary to proceed, which can fall to the IT organization itself, making it unpopular with its own IT governing group. So "know thyself" is applicable advice when setting up IT governance.

The second key mistake is in not defining and staying faithful to measurements and metrics. Fidelity in the routine measurement and reporting of perceptions is sometimes not accomplished early enough to launch a governance process, deemed unnecessary when projects are all on time and budget, and avoided when there are projects in trouble. This is particularly true when consensus governance models are employed, as the underlying assumption is that we would stop the process if we did not have consensus. Nothing could be farther from the truth. Regardless of what governance model is adopted, measurement and reporting against metrics must address risks before they become issues.

The third common mistake is allowing the governance board's discussions to devolve into project management activities and resolutions. Governance discussion topics are predicated by which model of Governance is applicable (advisory, consultative or collaborative) and what the key performance indicator measurements show a need for attention. Boundaries need to be established and revisited routinely, and rules for the governance body need to align with the model adopted. For example, suppose a collaborative model is adopted. In that case, meeting attendance will be essential and may require the identification of alternate members with the ability to commit their primary members to the path previously agreed.

PW: What advice would you provide to State CIOs who need to develop/improve their IT Governance model to ensure successful execution of projects?

AP: I would advise any state CIO to ensure that they do not neglect IT Governance to pursue excellence in project execution. IT Governance needs to be on top of every CIOs agenda. A successful IT governance model will reduce risk, lower costs, and improve project outcomes. Critical to the success of any IT governance model is establishing success metrics and measuring and report on these immediately and routinely. This provides the early warning indicator necessary to identify risks before they become issues. I'd like to share an experience that reflects strategic project governance

Shortly after I came to Oregon, I was appointed interim CIO for developing Cover Oregon, the health insurance enrollment system. I quickly realized that there was no IT governance process nor any discipline for application development. Both of these need to be addressed simultaneously. I formed a governance board of internal and external stakeholders who adopted a 100-day plan with defined milestones, each with a "go/no-go" vote requirement. Internally, adopting an agile development methodology with a comprehensive clean-up of our issues and requirements was established, with the supporting metrics necessary to measure progress. This brought more rigger to the requirements documents and the application updates. It also was reflected in the reduction of fixes that failed, issues needing rework, rollouts incompletely tested before moving to production, and improved end-user support for our efforts and satisfaction with our tools. It was the governance process. However, that determined that we needed to end funding of the project and migrate to the federal government website Healthcare.gov.

Citing

1. https://www.cio.com/article/3287100/state-cio-shares-insights-on-the-importance-of-strategic-it-governance.html; July 20, 2018.

Chapter 18

How to Assess the Maturity of Your Company's Strategic IT Governance Competencies

I hope that I have provided you with adequate knowledge of how companies like State Farm, Armstrong Ceilings, Anderson, State of Ga, and others implemented many of the Strategic IT Governance 2.0 components at this point in the book. You might now be asking yourself: *Maybe it's time for my company to determine if we should be implementing elements of the Strategic IT Governance 2.0 model in our company? If we do this, will we improve our ability to implement strategic projects more successfully?* If so, this is the chapter that will help you develop a plan to do so. Read on to understand how to improve the maturity of your company's Strategic IT Governance competency.

This chapter provides you the guidance to help you implement the Strategic IT Governance 2.0 competencies within your company. The following topics are covered in this chapter to help you navigate the process.

- The Strategic IT Governance Implementation Roadmap – Framework
- Strategic IT Governance 2.0 Maturity Grid and Maturity Matrix
- The Strategic IT Governance 2.0 Maturity Assessment – Who Should Take the Assessment

DOI: 10.1201/9781003317531-18

- How to Assess Strategic IT Governance 2.0 Maturity Level for Your Company
- How to Analyze The Strategic IT Governance 2.0 Assessment
- How to Implement The Strategic IT Governance 2.0 Competencies

The Strategic IT Governance Implementation Roadmap – Framework

The following four-step process will enable you to implement a Strategic IT Governance 2.0 methodology within your company.

- The first step is to develop an awareness of the characteristics that organizations exhibit for the four maturity levels across each of the six Strategic IT Governance 2.0 components.
- The second step is to examine a set of best practices for each of the six competencies and assess how well your organization applies these on a scale of one to ten. Additionally, you identify a maturity score goal representing how well your organization would apply these best practices within six to twelve months.
- The third step is to analyze your maturity assessment results and identify which competencies you should address in prioritized orders.
- The fourth step is to develop a maturity plan that reflects the activities, timeline, milestones, and personnel to improve the maturity of your Strategic IT Governance 2.0 competencies.
- Figure 18.1 depicts the three phases of the Strategic IT Governance Implementation Roadmap-Framework.

Now that you have a better understanding of the four-step process to develop a Strategic IT Governance 2.0 Competency within your company, let us explore each of these three steps in more detail.

Strategic IT Governance 2.0 Maturity Grid and Maturity Matrix

Many organizations have strategic IT Governance 2.0 methodology components that oversee the project identification, approval, and implementation phases. The question is, *how mature are the components in providing your organization with a robust and effective methodology?* The answer to this question is to develop an awareness and understand the characteristics of each of the four maturity paths for implementing a Strategic IT Governance 2.0 methodology within your company, as depicted in Figure 18.2 Strategic IT governance 2.0 Maturity Grid.

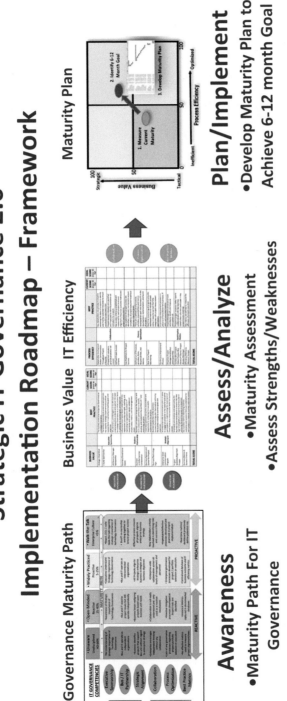

Figure 18.1 Strategic IT Governance 2.0 implementation roadmap.

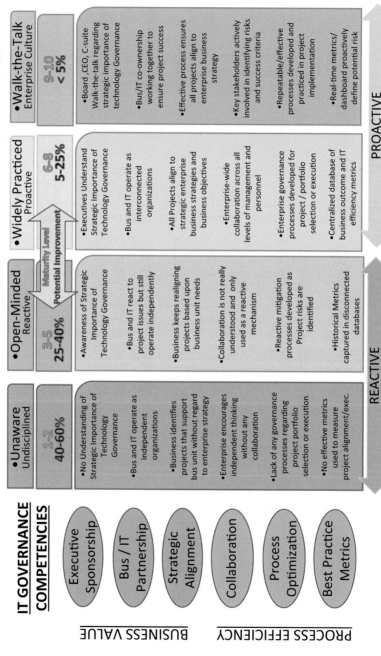

Figure 18.2 Strategic IT Governance 2.0 maturity characteristics by maturity level.

Each of the four maturity paths reflects the characteristics exhibited in the six Strategic IT Governance 2.0 competencies. You will note that I have also identified the Maturity Level (from 1 to 10) for each of the four paths. Additionally, I have identified the potential percentage improvement in project performance for each of the four levels. Let's explore some of these for each maturity level.

Unaware: This level reflects the lowest maturity level of an undisciplined organization. It reflects organizations with no understanding of the strategic importance of technology governance and the lack of business units partnering with the IT organization. Additionally, projects are selected regardless of strategic value, and there are no governance processes or metrics to manage the implementation process. Organizations that exhibit these characteristics have a maturity level of from 1 to 2 and can achieve a 40–60 percent improvement in project execution success by improving their maturity level.

Open-Minded: This is the second level of maturity and reflects an open-minded but reactive organization that has some awareness of the Strategic IT Governance 2.0 characteristics but does not exhibit them as a daily practice. These organizations may understand the strategic importance of technology governance but do not embrace it at the executive or leadership levels of the company. Additionally, these organizations do not embrace the principles of collaboration and solve problems using reactive practices. And although these organizations capture metrics, they are stored in separate databases that are difficult to access and analyze. Organizations that exhibit these characteristics have a maturity level of 2–4 and can achieve a 25–40 percent improvement in project performance success by improving their maturity level.

Widely Practiced: This is the third level of maturity and reflects an organization where Strategic IT Governance 2.0 competencies are widely practiced. In these organizations, executive level and operational managers understand the strategic importance of technology governance, and business and IT and business personnel operate in collaborative teams. All projects align to strategic goals and personnel embrace governance processes in selecting and executing projects. Organizations that exhibit these characteristics have a maturity level of 6–8 and can achieve a 5–25 percent improvement in project performance by improving their maturity level.

Walk-The-Talk: This is the fourth and highest level of maturity where the organization's culture embodies the Strategic IT Governance 2.0 competencies. The board of directors and executives at the most senior and operational level walk the talk when recognizing the strategic importance of technology governance. Business and IT teams work collaboratively to ensure project success by developing effective and efficient processes to ensure project alignment and stakeholder involvement in all project-related activities. Real-time metrics are constantly analyzed via real-time dashboards to identify potential alternative mitigation strategies to overcome preciously identify project risks.

Organizations that fall into the Walk-The-Talk maturity level can achieve up to a 5 percent improvement in project performance by improving their maturity level. Organizations that exhibit these characteristics have a maturity level of 9–10 and can achieve up to a 5 percent improvement in project performance.

The Strategic IT Governance 2.0 Maturity Matrix

Figure 18.2 included the characteristics for each of the four different paths. Figure 18.3: is a graphic representation of the Four Strategic IT Governance 2.0 Maturity Phases presented in a 2×2 matrix. The purpose of the matrix is to show that one can determine the maturity level of a company's Strategic IT Governance competencies through an Assessment process and score the results on the 2×2 Matrix. The following section discusses the Maturity Assessment.

The Strategic IT Governance 2.0 Maturity Assessment – Who Should Take the Assessment

Before I discuss the Maturity Assessment, I want to pause here to advise readers on who should be involved in the Strategic IT Governance 2.0 Maturity Assessment. In this chapter, the CIO and his leadership team took the Assessment. Every company has a different culture, especially when it comes to collaborative management.

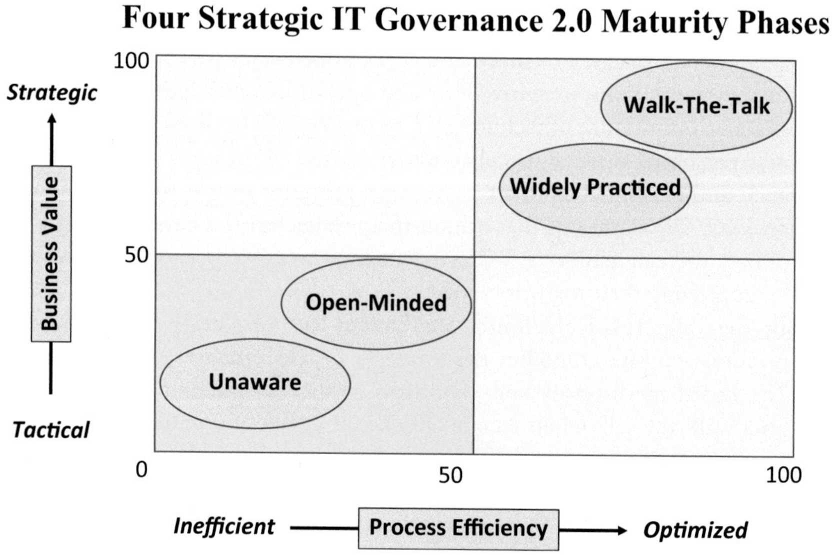

Four Strategic IT Governance 2.0 Maturity Phases

Figure 18.3   Four Strategic IT Governance 2.0 maturity phases.

So, depending on the collaborative culture within your company, you may want to perform the Strategic IT Governance 2.0 maturity Assessment initially within the IT organization, followed by including other business unit personnel in the Assessment process. For example, in a medical device company, the CIO conducted the initial Assessment with his direct reports and personnel from several IT departments. He then used the assessment results in meetings with some of his business colleagues to gain consensus that the IT Governance competency within the company needs to improve. His next step was for him and some Business Unit Executives to meet with the Executive Management team to convince them to support a Strategic IT Governance enterprise improvement initiative.

How to Assess Strategic IT Governance 2.0 Maturity Level for Your Company

Now that you better understand the four maturity levels, you are ready to assess your company's Strategic IT Governance 2.0 competencies using a maturity assessment process. But first, let me share some insights on why assessments are necessary.

Assessments are an excellent process for determining the competency level of a business process, methodology, or unique activities against a set of best practices because they help improve your organization's performance and productivity. Comparing your current state against a set of best practices provides you with a maturity level and a gap that you can improve upon through developing a maturity plan.

The Assessment enables you to identify the current maturity level of each of the Strategic IT Governance 2.0 competencies. If you examine Figure 18.4, you will see that I have identified a set of best practice categories for each of the six competencies. For example, the Executive Sponsorship competency includes three categories: Strategic Imperative, C-Suite Partnership, and VP/Director/Manager Partnership.

Let us further examine the Executive Sponsorship competency.

- Figure 18.5 is the Strategic IT Governance 2.0 Maturity Assessment for the Executive Sponsorship competency.
- I have identified three subcategories for the Executive Sponsorship competency. *(Strategic Imperative, C-Suite Partnership, and VP/Director/Manager Partnership)*
- For each Business Value Competency, I have identified a corresponding Best Practice.
- For example, the first Business Value Process is Strategic Imperative. And for this subcategory, I have identified a best practice as follows. *The business enterprise publicly recognizes Governance as a strategic imperative*
- These Best Practices are the result of input from the numerous CIOs, Business Executives I have interviewed.

Figure 18.4   Strategic IT Governance 2.0 framework.

The next step is to score your company's current maturity level on a scale of 1-low and 10-high and identify a goal score that represents your company's best guess as to what level of maturity they would desire in the next six or twelve months. If your current score is on the low end, say in the 1–4 range, you might identify a 12-month score goal since it will take your organization to achieve. If your current score is in the 5–9 range, you might choose 6 months to accomplish your score goal.

Remember the first paragraph in Chapter 1 where I shared how a recently hired CIO was preparing on Sunday evening for his first C-Suite meeting on Tuesday? Well, let me tell you the rest of the story. John is CIO of a mid-sized company that manufactures industrial metal cabinets for companies in the United States and Europe. At a virtual CIO conference, I met John, the CIO, through a mutual acquaintance who knew I was writing a book and wanted to speak to him. During our initial introductory phone call, I discussed my upcoming book and my interest in interviewing CIOs willing to share their experiences in improving their company's strategic IT governance competencies. He said to me. "Then, I'm your guy because I just started my role a few weeks ago, and I'd love to speak with you."

COMPETENCY	BUSINESS VALUE PROCESS	BEST PRACTICE	CURRENT SCORE	GOAL SCORE	GAP *(Goal)*
Executive Sponsorship EXECUTIVE SPONSORSHIP	Strategic Imperative	The business enterprise recognizes Governance as a strategic imperative			
	C-Suite Sponsorship	The entire C-Suite publicly endorses and sponsors the need for strategic Governance as a critical success factor in achieving its business goals and objectives			
	VP/Director/Mgr. Sponsorship	VPs, Directors, Managers across the business enterprise publicly endorse, sponsor, and participate in the need for strategic Governance as a critical success factor in achieving its business goals and objectives			
		COMPETENCY TOTALS			

Figure 18.5 Maturity assessment example – executive sponsorship.

John then went on to mention that he would be happy to share information for my book but that

> You only use my first name and not mention the company name as I started this role three weeks ago. My company needs help to improve its Governance processes, and I'm not sure they would want their name in a book right now. If you're ok with this, I would be pleased to continue our conversation.

I agreed with his request and said I would use the name John, which he agreed to, and he continued with his story.

> When I interviewed for the position, the CEO mentioned that he was frustrated with the constant budget overruns and vice-presidents' complaints about delays in project implementations. The CEO said that the previous CIO was very technical and not very collaborative or strategic. It was a bad hire. I told the CIO I was ready to take on the challenge to improve the performance of the IT organization. But I wanted to make sure that the CEO and the Executive Team would be open to listening about the importance of technology today and how it needs to be an integral part of your business strategy. The CEO said he and the Executive team are eager to listen and learn.[1]

John and I scheduled a Zoom call for the following week. I mentioned some of the CIOs I interviewed for the book, and I shared the graphic of my Strategic IT Governance 2.0 framework and the Maturity Assessment. John was very interested and wanted to conduct the Assessment with some of his staff and asked if I would facilitate the meeting and Assessment process. I told John that I'd be happy to do this. I then asked him who he wanted to be part of the Assessment process? He said that he had just hired a VP of PMO and Process Innovation whom he worked with in his previous job. He also mentioned that he hired a VP of Operations who worked for him a few years earlier. These two people would be instrumental in his reorganization and transformation of the IT organization and needed to be part of the Assessment process. John also wanted the CTO, Director of Application Development, and Director of Architecture to be part of the Assessment process. These five direct reports would be the core group that John wanted as part of the Assessment. Process. We then talked about the Assessment process. I mentioned that the first two meetings would have to be face-to-face to connect with your team. We can then continue subsequent sessions via Zoom.

Two weeks later, we connected by telephone to review his meetings with the Executive Leadership and next-level VPs and Directors. He identified the following three areas that needed improvement.

- Lack of understanding how technology has evolved to improve business performance
- Myriad of projects that were missing key milestones dates and over-budget
- Business Units and IT organizations operate independently with little interaction

I shared The Strategic IT Governance Maturity Grid PowerPoint slide *(see Figure 18.2)*.and the Four Strategic IT Governance 2.0 Maturity Phases (see Figure 18.3). I asked him to look at the characteristics of each of the maturity levels and identify what he thought was the maturity level for his company (see Figure 18.5). He spent a few minutes looking at the maturity path characteristics and said, "I believe our company's maturity level is very low. I would score it a 1." I then told him, "Let's see if you are correct." I shared with him the Strategic IT Governance 2.0 Maturity Assessment. I asked him to complete the Executive Sponsorship section as a test to see if his initial assessment score of 1 is correct. Figure 18.6 is the result of the CIOs Assessment. When he finished the scoring, we both examined the grid and validated the current score of 1. The CIO then targeted 12 months to achieve a level 8 goal score. I asked him why he chose a current score of 1. He replied, "that a score of 1 reflected my three main observations when he met with the company's leadership. Also, I want to be very aggressive at a future goal of 8 within 12 months. It may take longer, but we have to set a high bar." He repeated them to me.[Ibid]

- Lack of understanding how technology has evolved to improve business performance
- Myriad of projects that were missing key milestones dates and over-budget
- Business Units and IT organizations operate independently with little interaction

Over the next week, I met with the CIO and his leadership team to conduct several strategic IT governance workshops that included the group completing the Maturity Assessment.

Figures 18.7–18.13 are the results for each of the six competency assessments. Please note that each competency assessment includes a comments section that summarizes the scoring rationale.

COMPETENCY	BUSINESS VALUE PROCESS	BEST PRACTICE	CURRENT SCORE 1-LOW: 10-HIGH	GOAL SCORE 1-LOW: 10-HIGH	GAP (Goal Minus-Current)
Executive Sponsorship	Strategic Imperative	The business enterprise recognizes Governance as a strategic imperative	1	8	7
	C-Suite Sponsorship	The entire C-Suite publicly endorses and sponsors the need for strategic Governance as a critical success factor in achieving its business goals and objectives	1	8	7
	VP/Director/Mgr.	VPs, Directors, Managers across the business enterprise publicly endorse, sponsor, and participate in the need for strategic Governance as a critical success factor in achieving its business goals and objectives	1	8	7
		COMPETENCY TOTALS	3	24	21

Figure 18.6 Executive leadership maturity assessment – mid-sized manufacturing company

COMPETENCY	BUSINESS VALUE PROCESS	BEST PRACTICE	CURRENT SCORE 1-LOW: 10-HIGH	GOAL SCORE 1-LOW: 10-HIGH	GAP (Goal Minus-Current)
Executive Sponsorship	Strategic Imperative	The business enterprise recognizes Governance as a strategic imperative	1	8	7
	C-Suite Sponsorship	The entire C-Suite publicly endorses and sponsors the need for strategic Governance as a critical success factor in achieving its business goals and objectives	1	8	7
	VP/Director/Mgr. Sponsorship	VPs, Directors, Managers across the business enterprise publicly endorse, sponsor, and participate in the need for strategic Governance as a critical success factor in achieving its business goals and objectives	1	8	7
		COMPETENCY TOTALS	3	24	21
	Scoring Rational Summary	-The CIO shared with the Directors his 3 main observations from his meeting with the Executive Team. -Lack of understanding how technology has evolved to improve business performance. -Myriad of projects that were over budget and missing key milestone dates. -Business Units and IT organizations operate independently with limited interaction. -The team discussed the CIOs observations and agreed with his scoring rationale The CIO discussed his rationale for setting a high bar of "8" for a 12 month goal. He said, "we need to challenge ourselves to be very aggressive at improving our Project Governance3 capability			

Figure 18.7   CIO leadership team assessment results – executive leadership competency.

COMPETENCY	BUSINESS VALUE PROCESS	BEST PRACTICE	CURRENT SCORE 1-LOW: 10-HIGH	GOAL SCORE 1-LOW: 10-HIGH	GAP (Goal Minus-Current)
Business/IT Partnership	Business Governance Board	A Business Governance Board comprised of key stakeholders provides oversight, coaching, and mentoring to organizations involved in IT Governance and receive regular updates on project status, metrics, and risk management issues	1	6	5
	Business Unit/ Partnership & Collaboration	Business Unit Leaders recognize the need for and form collaborative partnerships to identify, develop, and implement the portfolio of IT and technology projects	1	6	5
	Business/IT Sponsor and Project Owner	Business sponsors/IT are jointly accountable and responsible for achieving the successful implementation of projects	1	6	5
		COMPETENCY TOTALS	3	18	15
	Scoring Rational Summary	-The Directors discussed the current state of the IT/Business partnership and agreed that there was none. Business units view IT as a cost center and not as a strategic partner. -The Directors also agreed that that Business Unit personnel do not feel they have any project ownership. They feel IT owns the projects. -The Directors discussed a future goal score and agreed that "6" is the appropriate number. The team agreed that changing the culture of business unit personnel was a "journey" and could achieve the goal score within 12 months.			

Figure 18.8 CIO leadership team assessment results – business/IT partnership competency.

COMPETENCY	BUSINESS VALUE PROCESS	BEST PRACTICE	CURRENT SCORE 1-LOW: 10-HIGH	GOAL SCORE 1-LOW: 10-HIGH	GAP (Goal Minus-Current)
Strategic Alignment	Business/Tech. Plan	Business Leadership jointly develop a business/technology plan that enables achieving the business enterprise business goals and objectives	1	5	4
	Enterprise-Wide Communication Program	An enterprise-wide communication plan is in place to engage all personnel in the need for and active participation in understanding the importance of Governance as a critical success factor for business success	1	6	5
	Project Selection/Alignment Process	All projects are screened and approved by the Business Governance Board to ensure that they align strategically to enterprise business plan in achieving the business goals and objectives	1	5	4
	Business Metrics & Success Criteria	Key business metrics identifying business outcomes and success criteria established for each project to measure business outcome success	1	4	3
	COMPETENCY TOTALS		4	20	16
	Scoring Rational Summary	-The CIO informed the Directors that IT has very little input to the Business Plan and -The Executive Team considers the IT Plan as a supporting document to the Business Plan. -The Directors discussed the lack of any formal process of project selection / alignment to the overall business strategy. The CIO reiterated that he has a challenge to help the Executives understand the need for this. -The Directors were frustrated at the lack of metrics defined by the business to measure real business outcomes. -The team discussed the future goal score and agreed that this would be a difficult challenge as it will change the culture of the company. A score of 4,5, or 6 would be appropriate for a 12-month goal. They did agree that they would work with the CIO and Business Unit leaders to accelerate the best practice to improve the goal score within 12 months.			

Figure 18.9   CIO leadership team assessment results –strategic alignment competency.

COMPETENCY	IT EFFICIENCY PROCESS	BEST PRACTICE	CURRENT SCORE 1-LOW: 10-HIGH	GOAL SCORE 1-LOW: 10-HIGH	GAP (Goal Minus-Current)
Collaboration	Stakeholder Involvement (Active Communication Throughout Project Lifecycle)	Key stakeholders are actively involved in assessing the status of projects to identify and monitor potential risk areas to ensure successful project execution	1	9	8
	Project Risk Indicators (*provide predictive risk scores*)	Project success indicators are identified and measured to determine predictive risk indicators for projects	1	9	8
	Defined Project Success Criteria	Key success criteria are established and measured for each project to ensure alignment of business outcome metrics and project success metrics	1	9	8
		COMPETENCY TOTALS	3	27	24
	Scoring Rational Summary	-The Directors were frustrated at the lack of collaboration between business p=and IT personnel during project status meetings as well as they rarely attend project status meetings. The Directors were equally frustrated that business unit personnel viewed IT as implementers of project requests and never participated in identifying any potential risks or project success criteria. They had more of a "just do it" attitude. -The group was very aggressive in identifying a goal score of "9". Their rationale was that this is a critical success factor for improving the project governance process and improving project performance.			

Figure 18.10 CIO leadership team assessment results –collaboration competency.

COMPETENCY	IT EFFICIENCY PROCESS	BEST PRACTICE	CURRENT SCORE 1-LOW: 10-HIGH	GOAL SCORE 1-LOW: 10-HIGH	GAP (Goal Minus-Current)
Process Optimization	Process Implementation Review Panel	Project Implementation Review Panel established to oversees project status (schedule, financials, issues, mitigation plans) to reduce project risk	1	8	7
	Defined Set of Processes, Activities, Roles, Responsibility and Metrics	There are a defined set of processes, activities, responsibilities and metrics developed for each role (business/IT) in the development, implementation, and launch of projects	1	8	7
	Real-Time Project Monitoring	Real-time monitoring of projects provides dashboard metrics to indicate project status in easy-to-use tool that fully integrates with project measurement applications	1	8	7
	Continuous Improvement Process	A continuous improvement process is in place to enhance Governance process, IT skills, and associated metrics	1	8	7
	COMPETENCY TOTALS		4	32	28
	Scoring Rational Summary	-The Directors often complained to the previous CIO that IT needed to improve its project management processes. -The previous CIO was very technically oriented and didn't have a view that process is an important element of project success. -The Directors urged the new CIO to form a team of business and IT personnel to address this issue. -The Directors agreed that improving processes is not easy and it would take time. -They agreed to a goal score of "8" and recognized that this is a continuous improvement process and would have to aggressively work to accomplish this goal.			

Figure 18.11 CIO leadership team assessment results –process optimization competency.

COMPETENCY	IT EFFICIENCY PROCESS	BEST PRACTICE	CURRENT SCORE 1-LOW: 10-HIGH	GOAL SCORE 1-LOW: 10-HIGH	GAP (Goal Minus-Current)
Best-Practice Metrics	Proactive Project Mgmt./Status (Anticipate Risk)	Project Management processes ensure activities to identify and measure anticipated risk	1	8	7
	Collaborative Project Status Process (Bus Owner/IT Owner/ Project Review Meetings)	Project manager prepares status reports collaboratively with key business stakeholders who also participate in key project review meetings	1	8	7
	Efficiency Metrics to Measure Success	Key metrics are defined to measure the efficiency of project execution	1	8	7
		COMPETENCY TOTALS	3	24	21
	Scoring Rational Summary	-The Directors agreed that business unit personnel rarely want to participate in preparing project status reports. -As discussed in the Process Optimization assessment scoring rationale, there are limited processes to manage project implementation. -Metrics are not a high priority dure to lack of project management processes and the previous CIO focus on technology and not on business process. -The Directors were very aggressive in identifying a future goal score of "8" for metrics. Their rationale was that "we can't manage what we don't measure, and if we are going to improve our project governance competency, we have to measure our progress".			

Figure 18.12 CIO Leadership team assessment results –best practice metrics competency.

BUSINESS VALUE COMPETENCIES	CURRENT SCORE 1-LOW: 10-HIGH	GOAL SCORE 1-LOW: 10-HIGH	GAP (Goal Minus-Current)
Executive Sponsorship			
Business/IT Partnership			
Strategic Alignment			
BUSINESS VALUE TOTALS			

IT EFFICIENCY COMPETENCIES	CURRENT SCORE 1-LOW: 10-HIGH	GOAL SCORE 1-LOW: 10-HIGH	GAP (Goal Minus-Current)
Collaboration			
Process Optimization			
Best Practice Metrics			
IT EFFICIENCY TOTALS			

Figure 18.13 Strategic IT Governance 2.0 maturity assessment – summary template.

Following are the result of the Maturity Assessment completed by the CIOs Leadership Team. Let's examine the scoring for each of the six competencies. In the next section of this chapter, I'll discuss how to analyze the assessment results.

How to Analyze Strategic IT Governance 2.0 Assessment

When the Directors completed the Assessment, I shared the following next steps in the process

- Summarize the Assessment Results.
- Plot the results on a 2 x 2 grid to visually show the current score and goal score.
- Identify the Business Value and Process Efficiency competencies in priority order of importance to improve the Governance process.
- Develop a Plan to implement the prioritized competency list.

Summarize the Assessment Results

To help the Directors summarize the Assessment results, I provided the group a template they could use (see Figure 18.13). I divided the Directors into two teams and provided each with the template. Team A would summarize the Business Value competencies, and Team B would summarize the Process Efficiency competencies.

BUSINESS VALUE COMPETENCIES	CURRENT SCORE 1-LOW: 10-HIGH	GOAL SCORE 1-LOW: 10-HIGH	GAP (Goal Minus-Current)
Executive Sponsorship	3	24	21
Business/IT Partnership	3	18	15
Strategic Alignment	4	20	16
BUSINESS VALUE TOTALS	10	62	52

IT EFFICIENCY COMPETENCIES	CURRENT SCORE 1-LOW: 10-HIGH	GOAL SCORE 1-LOW: 10-HIGH	GAP (Goal Minus-Current)
Collaboration	3	27	24
Process Optimization	4	32	28
Best Practice Metrics	3	24	21
IT EFFICIENCY TOTALS	10	83	73

Figure 18.14   CIO leadership team assessment summary.

When the teams completed the exercise, each team presented the summary to the entire group. Figure 18.14 shows the completed templates.

Plot the Results on a 2×2 Grid to Visually Show the Current Score and Goal Score

Earlier in this chapter, I shared Figure 18.3. I mentioned that Assessment results could be plotted on the 2x2 grid to reflect the maturity resulting from the Assessment. I shared this explanation with the Directors. I asked one team to plot the current score and the second team to plot the goal score. Figure 18.15 reflects the results. (*For reference purposes, I've included Figure 18.3's graphic to the left of the team's results.*)

Following the exercise, we had a discussion. I asked the group if the graphical representation depicts their assessment scoring? Following are some of the responses:[2]

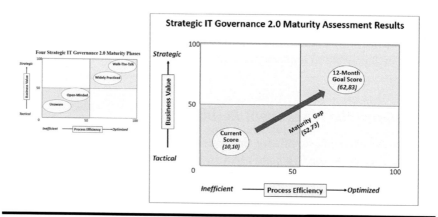

Figure 18.15   Maturity assessment high-level results.

The current scoring is in the lower-left "unaware" quadrant and supports our interactions with the Business Unit personnel.

It's been very frustrating to work in a vacuum without effectively collaborating with business unit personnel in the execution of the project, which, by the way, they define. It's not our project; it's theirs. So we need to figure out a way to get them on board. I think it's going to be a long uphill climb, but we have to do it.

We may have been too aggressive in identifying a goal score that is in the upper right-hand quadrant that reflects the 'widely-practiced maturity level. We need to get to this level of maturity, but it may take more than 12 months to achieve.

After the Directors weighed in, the CIO said the following:

Guys, I know this will not be easy to accomplish. We have a situation where projects are falling behind, dates are slipping, and costs are out of control. We have to figure out a way to do this. I'm totally on board and will work with the Executive Team and Business Unit VPs to improve the collaboration and involvement in project selection, design, and implementation. I'll support each of you as we work together to figure out a plan to improve our Strategic IT Governance competencies."[Ibid]

The Directors all nodded in approval, and I jumped into the conversation. I said,

We have completed the Maturity Assessment and are at the point where we have to analyze the results and address the best practices. I told the group that I would like to provide them with an overview of the various techniques teams can use to analyze the Assessment results.[Ibid]

Following is a summary of my presentation that outlines three main approaches.

Maturity Assessment Analysis Techniques

a. Review the Business Value Assessment Results separate from the Process Efficiency Results.
   Business Value best practices involve the Executive Team, Division VPs, Directors. In contrast, Process best practices focus on IT activities by project personnel in the execution of projects.
b. Current and Goal Scores are relatively consistent.
   If current and goal scores are relatively consistent, the team needs to discuss and determine a priority order for implementing the maturity plan for these competencies. I paused and mentioned to the Directors that their Assessment falls into this category, and we will discuss an approach for prioritizing the implementation path.

c. Assessment results where the current and goal scores vary.

If current and goal scores vary, the team can prioritize the difference between the current and goal scores based on the gap number. The result would be an initial priority list that can be discussed and adjusted based upon different factors. For example, it may be a critical best practice based on the current environment in the company and needs to move up in priority order. Another example is the gap number doesn't represent the urgency required for implementation.

When I concluded my presentation, I suggested that John and the Directors schedule some time to discuss the analysis in more detail during the following week. We could schedule another workshop the week after. I told the group that they should think about the initiatives that would help improve its Strategic IT Governance Competencies when they meet next week. The group agreed, and we concluded our session,

Summary

Using a case study example of assessing your company's Strategic IT Governance 2.0 maturity will help you better understand the assessment process (Figure 18.16)

Figure 18.16 Strategic IT Governance 2.0 framework.

reflects the Strategic IT Governance 2.0 Framework. Figure 18.17 is the Strategic IT Governance 2.0 Maturity Assessment. The next chapter will discuss how the group identified initiatives and implemented their Strategic IT Governance 2.0 Maturity Plan.

Strategic IT Governance 2.0 Maturity Assessment

Figure 18.17 Strategic IT Governance 2.0 maturity assessment. *(Continued)*

Strategic IT Governance 2.0 Maturity Assessment- Business Value

COMPETENCY	BUSINESS VALUE PROCESS	BEST PRACTICE	CURRENT SCORE *(1-Low: 10-High)*	GOAL SCORE *(1-Low: 10-High)*
Executive Sponsorship	Strategic Imperative	The business enterprise recognizes Governance as a strategic imperative		
	C-Suite Sponsorship	The entire C-Suite publicly endorses and sponsors the need for strategic Governance as a critical success factor in achieving its business goals and objectives		
	VP/Director/Mgr Sponsorship	VPs, Directors,Managers across the business enterprise publicly endorse, sponsor, and participate in the need for strategic Governance as a critical success factor in achieving its business goals and objectives		
Business Partnership	Business Governance Board	A Business Governance Board comprised of key stakeholders provides oversight, coaching, and mentoring to organizations involved in IT Governance and receive regular updates on project status, metrics, and risk management issues		
	Business Unit/Partnership-Collaboration	Business Unit Leaders recognize the need for and form collaborative partnerships to identify, develop, and implement the portfolio of IT and technology projects		
	Business/IT Sponsor and Owner for Projects	Business sponsors/IT are jointly accountable and responsible for achieving the successful implementation ofprojects		
Strategic Alignment	Business/Tech. Plan	Business Leadership jointly develop a business/technology plan that enables achieving the business enterprise business goals and objectives		
	Enterprise-Wide Communication Program	An enterprise-wide communication plan is in place to engage all personnel in the need for and active participation in understanding the importance of Governance as a critical success factor for business success		
	Project Selection/ Alignment Process	All projects are screened and approved by the Business Governance Board to ensure that they align strategically to enterprise business plan in achieving the business goals and objectives		
	Business Metrics & Success Criteria	Key business metrics identifying business outcomes and success criteria established for each project to measure business outcome success		
		TOTALS		

Figure 18.17 (Continued) **Strategic IT Governance 2.0 maturity assessment.**

(Continued)

Strategic IT Governance 2.0 Maturity Assessment – IT Efficiency

COMPETENCY	IT EFFICIENCY PROCESS	BEST PRACTICE	CURRENT SCORE (1-Low: 10-High)	GOAL SCORE (1-Low: 10-High)
Collaboration	Stakeholder Involvement (Active Communication Throughout Project Lifecycle)	Key stakeholders are actively involved in assessing the status of projects to identify and monitor potential risk areas to ensure successful project execution		
	Project Risk Indicators *(provide predictive risk scores)*	Project success indicators are identified and measured to determine predictive risk indicators for projects		
	Defined Project Success Criteria	Key success criteria are established and measured for each project to ensure alignment of business outcome metrics and project success metrics		
Process Optimization	Project Implementation Review Panel	Project Implementation Review Panel established to oversees project status (schedule, financials, issues, mitigation plans) to reduce project risk		
	Defined set of Processes, Activities, Roles,Responsibility and Metrics	There are a defined set of processes, activities, responsibilities and metrics developed for each role (business/IT) in the development, implementation, and launch of projects		
	Real-Time Project Monitoring	Real-time monitoring of projects provides dashboard metrics to indicate project status in easy-to-use tool that fully integrates with project measurement applications		
	Continuous Improvement Process	A continuous improvement process is in place to enhance Governance process, IT skills, and associated metrics		
Best Practice Metrics	Proactive Project Mgmnt/Status *(Anticipate Risk)*	Project Management processes ensure activities to identify and measure anticipated risk		
	Collaborative Project Status Process *(Bus Owner/IT Owner/Project Review Meetings)*	Project manager prepares status reports collaboratively with key business stakeholders who also participate in key project review meetings		
	Efficiency Metrics to Measure Success	Key metrics are defined to measure the efficiency of project execution		
		TOTALS		

Figure 18.17 (Continued)   Strategic IT Governance 2.0 maturity assessment.

Citings

1. CIO/Phil Weinimer interviews; April 16, 20, 2020, June 10, 15, 23, 2020.
2. Quotes from Assessment Workshop with CIO and his Direct Reports August 15, 2020, August 22, 2020, September 7, 2020, September 14, 2020.

Chapter 19

How to Analyze, Plan, and Implement Strategic IT Governance 2.0 Competencies in Your Company

In the previous chapter, I shared a case study of conducting a Strategic IT Governance 2.0 Maturity Assessment process using a case study of a CIO and his Directors. In this chapter, I will continue the same case study but share how the CIO and his team reviewed the Assessment and developed a Strategic IT Governance 2.0 maturity plan.

Developing a plan to improve the maturity of your Strategic IT Governance 2.0 competencies is a four-step process.

1. Create an Awareness within your organization of the maturity path to improve your company's strategic IT governance competencies.
2. Assess the current state of your company's Strategic IT Governance 2.0 competencies and identify a maturity goal for a future period.
3. Analyze the Assessment results and identify the competencies that need implementation in a prioritized order.

4. Review the prioritized order and make necessary adjustments due to company, regulatory, or other factors that would change the prioritization order.
5. Develop a plan to include deliverables, timelines, milestones, roles/responsibilities, continuous improvement process, etc.

In the previous chapter, we discussed the first three steps of the process using a real example of a mid-sized manufacturer of industrial cabinetry. Here's a quick review of the first three steps.

- I reviewed the maturity path for Strategic IT Governance 2.0 competencies with John, the new CIO, and his Directors.
- We then examined the maturity assessment components, the associated best practices, and the scoring instructions.
- The Directors then conducted and summarized the Assessment for the Business Value and Process Efficiency competencies.
- The final exercise of the session consisted of the Directors and John sharing their observations, and we agreed to further discuss the Analysis and Implementation Plan at our next session.

In this chapter, we will explore steps four and five.

4. Review the prioritized order and make necessary adjustments due to company, regulatory, or other factors that would change the prioritization order.
5. Develop a plan to include deliverables, timelines, milestones, roles/responsibilities, continuous improvement process, etc.

Planning for implementing a project that improves the maturity of the Strategic IT Governance 2.0 competencies requires thought and focus. Every company has a different culture that impacts the processes, activities, roles, and responsibilities of personnel.

The Strategic IT Governance 2.0 Maturity Assessment focuses on the two distinct areas that impact project success. The first is what I call Business Value, which identifies the set of best practices for Sponsorship at the Executive and Management Levels of the company and their ability to identify, select, and align projects with its strategic goals. The second is Process Efficiency, which focuses on the best practices for collaboration, processes, and metrics that enable successful implementation of projects.

So when you are developing your implementation plan, be sure to address each area separately. For example, your company may have relatively mature process efficiency competencies that result in projects executed on time and within budget. However, the projects do not necessarily support its strategic goals, and business unit personnel don't actively support or involve themselves in project execution activities. The assessment scoring should support these findings. If so, the implementation plan needs to address how to mature the Business Value competencies to improve the support and collaborative involvement of the business executives and managers.

To explore this further, let's return to sessions I facilitated with John, the CIO, and his Directors and find out how they developed an implementation plan to improve the maturity of the Business Value and Process Efficiency competencies.

After a one-week break from the previous session, we scheduled an initial face-to-face session with John and his Directors to develop a Strategic IT Governance 2.0 Maturity Improvement Plan. John and I spoke the day before the session to review my recommended agenda. He agreed and updated me on the team's excellent work in identifying the maturity initiatives for each of the six IT Governance 2.0 competencies. I traveled to the corporate office in Chicago that evening to be ready for a productive workshop.

At 9 am the following day, the group met for our implementation initiative workshop. I opened up the session with a feedback session where the CIO and Directors provided their comments on the previous sessions and if they felt we were on the right path. Following are a few of their comments:[1]

CIO: We're definitely on the right track and need to be focused and diligent in our efforts to improve project performance.

Director A: I agree with John, but I'm still nervous that we can't rush this. We have to set high targets but be realistic about what we can accomplish.

Director B: I've worked in this company for eight years, and the relationship we in IT have with the business community is poor. They don't understand the need for them to be involved.

Director C: I interact with business unit managers daily. There are some that I believe will see the light, but we need to have executive management actively support this initiative.

After the feedback session, I reviewed where we are in our process. I presented three slides that we used in our previous sessions that summarize our accomplishments to date (Figures 19.1–19.3). We reviewed our accomplishments to date.

After our review, I walked up to the whiteboard and wrote the following three steps we needed to accomplish during this session.

1. Review draft initiatives recommendations
2. Prioritize Initiatives
3. Identify Critical Success Factors
4. Work Streams/Parallel Activities.

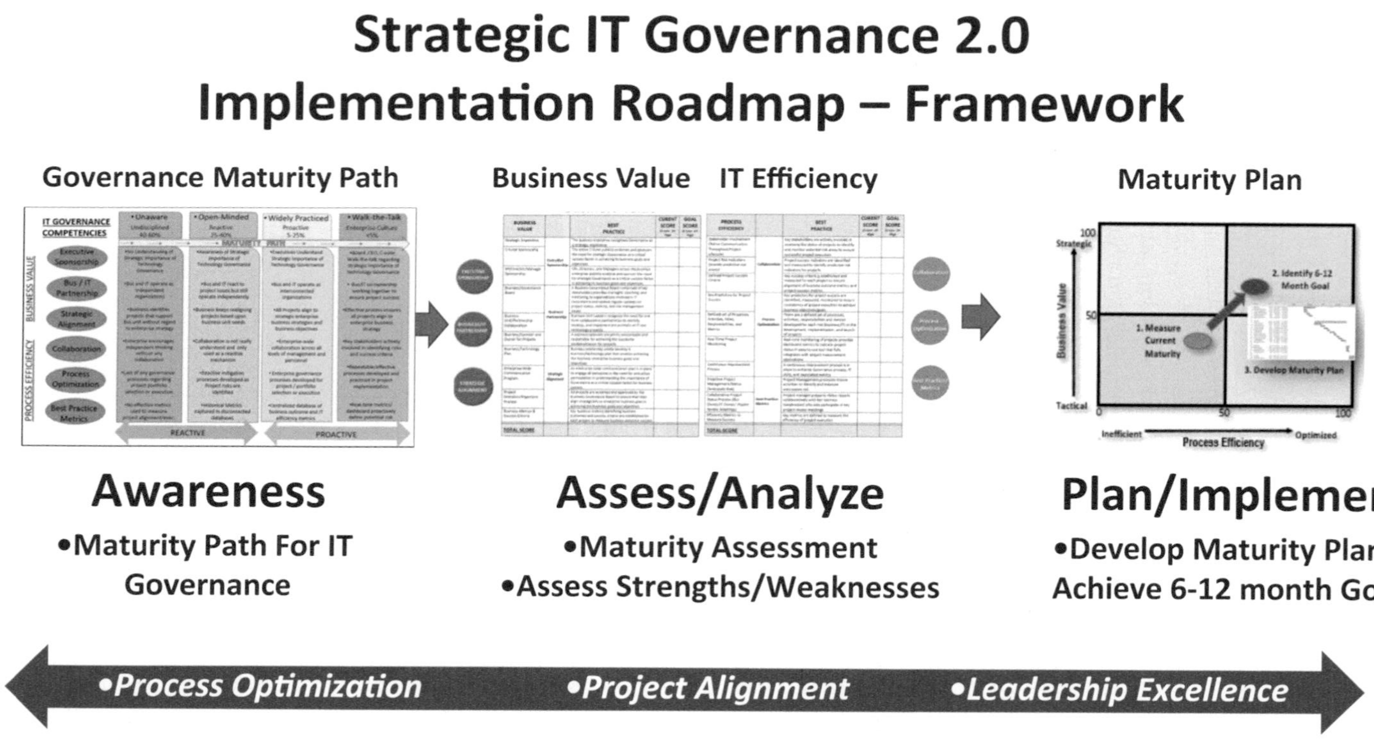

Figure 19.1   Strategic IT Governance 2.0 implementation roadmap.

BUSINESS VALUE COMPETENCIES	CURRENT SCORE 1-LOW: 10-HIGH	GOAL SCORE 1-LOW: 10-HIGH	GAP (Goal Minus-Current)
Executive Sponsorship	3	24	21
Business/IT Partnership	3	18	15
Strategic Alignment	4	20	16
BUSINESS VALUE TOTALS	**10**	**62**	**52**

IT EFFICIENCY COMPETENCIES	CURRENT SCORE 1-LOW: 10-HIGH	GOAL SCORE 1-LOW: 10-HIGH	GAP (Goal Minus-Current)
Collaboration	3	27	24
Process Optimization	4	32	28
Best Practice Metrics	3	24	21
IT EFFICIENCY TOTALS	**10**	**83**	**73**

Figure 19.2   CIO leadership team assessment summary.

Review Draft Initiatives Recommendations

I asked the teams to share with me the process they used to develop the initiative recommendations. Following are quotes from the VP-PMO and VP Operations that represent the group's responses.

> We decided to identify an initiative for each of the subcategories for the Business Value and Process Efficiency competencies.
>
> (Sally – VP PMO)

> We would then discuss in today's workshop how we would prioritize the implementation for these initiatives and develop a straw model timeline.
>
> (Curt – VP Operations)

I provided the following instructions for the exercise.

1. Break into two teams for 15 minutes to review the competency initiatives.
2. Select a spokesperson to present the teams' rationale for developing the initiatives.

Following are the spokesperson quotes, including a graphic of the recommended initiatives and the Assessment results.

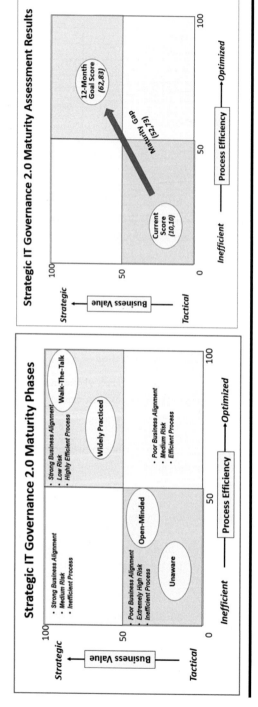

Figure 19.3   Strategic IT Governance 2.0 maturity assessment graphical results.

Executive Sponsorship

We need to begin the Strategic IT Governance initiative with Executive Sponsorship that sets the direction for the transformation. Creating 'Awareness Sessions using outside thought leaders will seed a thought change across the Executive team. Coupled\ with the formation of a Governance working group, sharing results of IT Governance Assessments and expanding Assessments to business units will help form a better understanding of why a Strategic IT Governance transformation is a necessity for our company.

(John – CIO)

Executive Sponsorship	IMPLEMENTATION PLANNING - DRAFT LIST OF GOVERNANCE MATURITY INITIATIVES	OWNER
	a) Create "Awareness" sessions for Executive Team (C-Suite) to educate on the value of developing a enterprise governance strategy that leverages technology to improve company performance. Utilize "outside in thinking" by Inviting Strategic Thought Leaders, Business Leaders, CIOs, even CEO's to address Executive Team to share their experiences and insights, helping Executive Team rethink the value of Governance.	CIO
	b) Create a bi-weekly Governance working group that includes IT personnel and business unit VP, Directors on value of Strategic IT Governance to continue educating them on value of Strategic IT Governance.	CIO / VP PMO/ Business Exec
	c) Share Strategic IT Governance Maturity Assessment with Bi-Weekly Governance Group attendees to help them understand the best practices and associated business value of developing a Enterprise Governance strategy to improve business outcomes and financial performance	CIO / VP PMO
	d) Seed the idea of Executive Team and Business Unit Executives and their Direct Reports to take Assessment to ascertain their perspective of the maturity scores for the company's Strategic Governance competencies.	CIO

COMPETENCY	BUSINESS VALUE PROCESS	BEST PRACTICE	CURRENT SCORE 1-LOW: 10-HIGH	GOAL SCORE 1-LOW: 10-HIGH	GAP (Goal Minus-Current)
Executive Sponsorship	Strategic Imperative	The business enterprise recognizes Governance as a strategic imperative	1	8	7
	C-Suite Sponsorship	The entire C-Suite publicly endorses and sponsors the need for strategic Governance as a critical success factor in achieving its business goals and objectives	1	8	7
	VP/Director/Mgr. Sponsorship	VPs, Directors, Managers across the business enterprise publicly endorse, sponsor, and participate in the need for strategic Governance as a critical success factor in achieving its business goals and objectives	1	8	7
		COMPETENCY TOTALS	3	24	21
	Scoring Rational Summary	-The CIO shared with the Directors his 3 main observations from his meeting with the Executive Team. -Lack of understanding how technology has evolved to improve business performance. -Myriad of projects that were over budget and missing key milestone dates. -Business Units and IT organizations operate independently with limited interaction. -The team discussed the CIOs observations and agreed with his scoring rationale The CIO discussed his rationale for setting a high bar of "8" for a 12 month goal. He said, "we need to challenge ourselves to be very aggressive at improving our Project Governance3 capability			

Figure 19.4 Strategic IT Governance 2.0 executive sponsorship maturity initiatives.

Business/IT Partnership

A Business/IT Partnership requires a complete understanding of the need to collaborate in business and IT teams. We need to educate our business peers on the value of Governance. A second initiative would entail creating a Business Governance Board to act as a steering committee for this transformation initiative. A third initiative would entail workshops with business and IT personnel working as a team to develop solution scenarios for mock enterprise strategic projects.

(Curt – VP Operations)

Business/IT Partnership	IMPLEMENTATION PLANNING – DRAFT LIST OF GOVERNANCE MATURITY INITIATIVES	OWNER
	a) Create a groundswell of educating value of Business/IT Partnership that will improve Governance of Enterprise Strategic Projects and begin to change culture from "isolationist" into "collaborative partnership"	CIO/ VP PMO/VP Ops Bus Unit Exec
	b) Seed the idea of a Business Governance Board that oversees the Strategic IT Governance Transformation Initiative	CIO
	c) Identify Business Unit Executive(s) who can champion Business/IT Partnership initiative	CIO
	c) Develop Business/IT Partnership Workshops for Business Unit VPs, Directors, and Management Personnel on the value of Governance and active participation and co-ownership of projects	VP PMO/VP Ops/ Bus Unit Exec

COMPETENCY	BUSINESS VALUE PROCESS	BEST PRACTICE	CURRENT SCORE 1-LOW: 10-HIGH	GOAL SCORE 1-LOW: 10-HIGH	GAP (Goal Minus-Current)
Business/IT Partnership	Business Governance Board	A Business Governance Board comprised of key stakeholders provides oversight, coaching, and mentoring to organizations involved in IT Governance and receive regular updates on project status, metrics, and risk management issues	1	6	5
	Business Unit/ Partnership & Collaboration	Business Unit Leaders recognize the need for and form collaborative partnerships to identify, develop, and implement the portfolio of IT and technology projects	1	6	5
	Business/IT Sponsor and Project Owner	Business sponsors/IT are jointly accountable and responsible for achieving the successful implementation of projects	1	6	5
		COMPETENCY TOTALS	3	18	15
	Scoring Rational Summary	-The Directors discussed the current state of the IT/Business partnership and agreed that there was none. Business units view IT as a cost center and not as a strategic partner. -The Directors also agreed that that Business Unit personnel do not feel they have any project ownership. They feel IT owns the projects. -The Directors discussed a future goal score and agreed that "6" is the appropriate number. The team agreed that changing the culture of business unit personnel was a "journey" and could achieve the goal score within 12 months.			

Figure 19.5 Strategic IT Governance 2.0 business/IT Partnership maturity initiatives

Strategic Alignment

We need to share past examples of projects recommended by business units that did not support the goals and objectives of the company. Doing this will help to reinforce the need to identify projects that optimize investment dollars by aligning the project outcomes with our company's strategic goals and objectives. A Second initiative would include business and IT personnel working together to develop a more mature strategic alignment project selection, development and execution process and present recommendations to the executive steering committee.

(Sally – VP PMO)

COMPETENCY	IMPLEMENTATION PLANNING - DRAFT LIST OF GOVERNANCE MATURITY INITIATIVES	OWNER
Strategic Alignment	a) Create a Communication Working Group to establish an ongoing enterprise-wide program to inform all company personnel of the Governance initiative with frequent updates using various communication strategies (emails, group town hall meetings, website, etc.	VP Ops
	b) Analyze past projects to develop analysis supporting that projects misalign with business goals and objectives that will be used to support need to develop a more robust strategic alignment process	VP PMO Director
	c) Create a working group of IT and Business personnel to develop a more mature process for identifying, selecting, and prioritizing projects to ensure alignment with business goals and objectives	CIO/ VP PMO / VP Ops Business Exec.
	d) Develop and present recommended strategic alignment process to Executive Team for approval, support, and implementation	CIO/ VP PMO /VP Ops Business Exec.

COMPETENCY	BUSINESS VALUE PROCESS	BEST PRACTICE	CURRENT SCORE 1-LOW: 10-HIGH	GOAL SCORE 1-LOW: 10-HIGH	GAP (Goal Minus-Current)
Strategic Alignment	Business/Tech. Plan	Business Leadership jointly develop a business/technology plan that enables achieving the business enterprise business goals and objectives	1	5	4
	Enterprise-Wide Communication Program	An enterprise-wide communication plan is in place to engage all personnel in the need for and active participation in understanding the importance of Governance as a critical success factor for business success	1	6	5
	Project Selection/Alignment Process	All projects are screened and approved by the Business Governance Board to ensure that they align strategically to enterprise business plan in achieving the business goals and objectives	1	5	4
	Business Metrics & Success Criteria	Key business metrics identifying business outcomes and success criteria established for each project to measure business outcome success	1	4	3
	COMPETENCY TOTALS		4	20	16
	Scoring Rational Summary	-The CIO informed the Directors that IT has very little input to the Business Plan and -The Executive Team considers the IT Plan as a supporting document to the Business Plan. -The Directors discussed the lack of any formal process of project selection / alignment to the overall business strategy. The CIO reiterated that the has a challenge to help the Executives understand the need for this. -The Directors were frustrated at the lack of metrics defined by the business to measure real business outcomes. -The team discussed the future goal score and agreed that this would be a difficult challenge as it will change the culture of the company. A score of 4,5, or 6 would be appropriate for a 12-month goal. They did agree that they would work with the CIO and Business Unit leaders to accelerate the best practice to improve the goal score within 12 months.			

Figure 19.6 Strategic IT Governance 2.0 strategic alignment maturity initiatives.

Collaboration

Collaboration is one of the critical success factors that will enable a successful Governance transformation initiative. To accomplish this requires us to develop a business case to support how collaboration improves project performance. In addition, we need to include business personnel as part of every project team in reviewing projects, identifying potential project risks, and taking ownership of projects by actively participating as key stakeholders. We can integrate these initiative recommendations in workshops attended by business and IT personnel.

(Gail-CTO)

Collaboration	IMPLEMENTATION PLANNING - DRAFT LIST OF GOVERNANCE MATURITY INITIATIVES	OWNER
	a) Create business case that supports improved success of projects through active participation of business personnel in the development and implementation of projects	CIO / VP PMO
	b) Develop a "collaborative workshop" that includes business and IT personnel working in teams in mock project planning and implementation projects	CIO/ VP PMO/ Business Exec.
	c) Work with Business Unit Management to collaborate with IT Project Management Office to define potential project risks in project planning phase to promote collaborative project co-ownership	CIO/ VP PMO/ Business Exec.
	d) Work with Business Unit Management to support the role of Business Project Owner that defines the roles, responsibilities, and accountabilities in the active participation of project definition, development, and implementation	CIO/ VP PMO/ VP Ops / Business Exec.
	e) Improve project requirement documentation to include business outcome metrics separate from IT efficiency metrics.	CIO/ VP PMO/ Business Exec.

COMPETENCY	IT PROCESS EFFICIENCY	BEST PRACTICE	CURRENT SCORE 1-LOW: 10-HIGH	GOAL SCORE 1-LOW: 10-HIGH	GAP (Goal Minus-Current)
Collaboration	Stakeholder Involvement (Active Communication Throughout Project Lifecycle)	Key stakeholders are actively involved in assessing the status of projects to identify and monitor potential risk areas to ensure successful project execution	1	9	8
	Project Risk Indicators (provide predictive risk scores)	Project success indicators are identified and measured to determine predictive risk indicators for projects	1	9	8
	Defined Project Success Criteria	Key success criteria are established and measured for each project to ensure alignment of business outcome metrics and project success metrics	1	9	8
		COMPETENCY TOTALS	3	27	24
	Scoring Rational Summary	-The Directors were frustrated at the lack of collaboration between business p-and IT personnel during project status meetings as well as they rarely attend project status meetings. The Directors were equally frustrated that business unit personnel viewed IT as implementers of project requests and never participated in identifying any potential risks or project success criteria. They had more of a "Just do it" attitude. -The group was very aggressive in identifying a goal score of "9". Their rationale was that this is a critical success factor for improving the project governance process and improving project performance.			

Figure 19.7 Strategic IT Governance 2.0 collaboration maturity initiatives.

Process Optimization

An effective Governance competency requires a set of processes to guide personnel in executing the Governance processes. We need to form a core working group comprised of business and IT personnel to develop the supporting documentation for our Strategic IT Governance processes.

(Paul – Director of Application Development)

Process Optimization	IMPLEMENTATION PLANNING - DRAFT LIST OF GOVERNANCE MATURITY INITIATIVES	OWNER
	a) Create a Business / IT Core Working Group and supporting sub-groups to identify and develop processes, roles, accountabilities, and success metrics required to improve the Project definition, development, and implementation activities that will improve project success	PMO Director
	d) Work with Business Unit Management to support the role of Business Project Owner that defines the roles, responsibilities, and accountabilities in the active participation of project definition, development, and implementation	CIO/ PMO Director/ Business Exec.
	c) Identify potential SaaS tools in marketplace that provide real-time dashboard metrics to help project teams collaborate in real time regarding project status, issues, challenges, potential risks, etc. and integrate with Project Management tools	CIO /PMO Director
	d) Develop a continuous improvement process that captures project success, challenges, risks, and mitigation strategies that can be applied on future projects to minimize risks and optimize project success	CIO/ PMO Director/ Business Exec.

COMPETENCY	IT EFFICIENCY PROCESS	BEST PRACTICE	CURRENT SCORE 1-LOW: 10-HIGH	GOAL SCORE 1-LOW: 10-HIGH	GAP (Goal Minus-Current)
Process Optimization	Process Implementation Review Panel	Project Implementation Review Panel established to oversees project status (schedule, financials, issues, mitigation plans) to reduce project risk	1	8	7
	Defined Set of Processes, Activities, Roles, Responsibility and Metrics	There are a defined set of processes, activities, responsibilities and metrics developed for each role (business/IT) in the development, implementation, and launch of projects	1	8	7
	Real-Time Project Monitoring	Real-time monitoring of projects provides dashboard metrics to indicate project status in easy-to-use tool that fully integrates with project measurement applications	1	8	7
	Continuous Improvement Process	A continuous improvement process is in place to enhance Governance process, IT skills, and associated metrics	1	8	7
	COMPETENCY TOTALS		4	32	28
	Scoring Rational Summary	-The Directors often complained to the previous CIO that IT needed to improve its project management processes. -The previous CIO was very technically oriented and didn't have a view that process is an important element of project success. -The Directors urged the new CIO to form a team of business and IT personnel to address this issue. -The Directors agreed that improving processes is not easy and it would take time. -They agreed to a goal score of "8" and recognized that this is a continuous improvement process and would have to aggressively work to accomplish this goal.			

Figure 19.8 Strategic IT Governance 2.0 process optimization maturity initiatives.

Best Practice Metrics

Metrics help you measure your path to success. Failing to capture and utilize metrics, especially real-time metrics, can result in unnecessary risks, quality failures, financial costs, and schedule delays. We need to benchmark other companies to identify the key metrics and associated tools that will help us improve our project success. Additionally, we need our business partners to understand the importance of business outcome metrics and process efficiency metrics and actively participate in the preparation of project status reports.

(Sally – VP-PMO)

Best-Practice Metrics	IMPLEMENTATION PLANNING – DRAFT LIST OF GOVERNANCE MATURITY INITIATIVES	OWNER
	a) Establish Best Practices Working Group to benchmark best practice metrics used by companies in the management of projects to proactively manage potential project risk and determine applicability for use in our company	CIO / Business Unit Exec
	b) Work with Business stakeholders to actively co-own preparation and presentation of project status reports that include key project metrics	CIO/ VP-PMO / VP Ops Business Exec.
	c) Identify key project efficiency metrics that measure project success that are in addition to traditional cost and schedule metrics	VP-PMO / VP Ops Business Exec.

COMPETENCY	IT EFFICIENCY PROCESS	BEST PRACTICE	CURRENT SCORE 1-LOW: 10-HIGH	GOAL SCORE 1-LOW: 10-HIGH	GAP (Goal Minus-Current)
Best-Practice Metrics	Proactive Project Mgmt./Status (Anticipate Risk)	Project Management processes ensure activities to identify and measure anticipated risk	1	8	7
	Collaborative Project Status Process (Bus Owner/IT Owner/ Project Review Meetings)	Project manager prepares status reports collaboratively with key business stakeholders who also participate in key project review meetings	1	8	7
	Efficiency Metrics to Measure Success	Key metrics are defined to measure the efficiency of project execution	1	8	7
	COMPETENCY TOTALS		3	24	21
	Scoring Rational Summary	-The Directors agreed that business unit personnel rarely want to participate in preparing project status reports. -As discussed in the Process Optimization assessment scoring rationale, there are limited processes to manage project implementation. -Metrics are not a high priority dure to lack of project management processes and the previous CIO focus on technology and not on business process. -The Directors were very aggressive in identifying a future goal score of "8" for metrics. Their rationale was that "we can't manage what we don't measure, and if we are going to improve our project governance competency, we have to measure our progress".			

Figure 19.9   Strategic IT Governance 2.0 best practices/metrics maturity initiatives.

I recommended we take a 45-minute break for lunch and then proceed to the next exercise. I asked the group to spend 45 minutes discussing the launch timeline for each competency initiative. I didn't want to participate, so I asked John, the CIO, to facilitate the discussion. To assist the group in completing the exercise, I provided a template the group could use. The template included five columns: the first column listed each of the competencies and their subcategories. The following four columns represented the next four calendar quarters. See Figure 19.10.

I walked around the meeting room, observing the group dynamics as they discussed the launch schedule. There was much debate about when specific initiatives should launch and their sequence. John, the CIO, let the dynamics play out without interruption other than some coaching tips to ensure the discussion did not get out of hand. When the group completed the exercise, the spokesperson for each initiative summarized the rationale. See Figure 19.11, which represents the completed template and the rationale from each competency.

IMPLEMENTATION PLANNING-INITIATIVE LAUNCH SCHEDULE

		Next Qtr	Q2	Q3	Q4
Executive Sponsorship	Strategic Imperative C-Suite Sponsorship VP / Director/Mgr Sponsorship				
Business/IT Partnership	Bus. Governance Board Bus. Unit Partnership & Collaboration Bus/IT Sponsor & Project Owner				
Strategic Alignment	Bus. / Tech. Plan Enterprise-Wide Comm Program Project Selection/Alignment Process Bus. Metrics & Success Criteria				
Collaboration	Stakeholder Involvement Project Risk Indicators Defined Proj. Success Criteria				
Process Optimization	Process Impl. Review Panel Defined Set of Processes Real-Time Project Monitoring Continuous Improvement Process				
Best Practice Metrics	Proactive Project Mgmnt/ Status Collaborative Project Status Process Efficiency Success Metrics				

Figure 19.10   Implementation planning template– initiative launch schedule.

IMPLEMENTATION PLANNING-INITIATIVE LAUNCH SCHEDULE

		Next Qtr	Q2	Q3	Q4
Executive Sponsorship	Strategic Imperative	X			
	C-Suite Sponsorship	X			
	VP / Director/Mgr Sponsorship	X			
Business/IT Partnership	Bus. Governance Board	X			
	Bus. Unit Partnership & Collaboration	X			
	Bus/IT Sponsor & Project Owner		X		
Strategic Alignment	Bus. / Tech. Plan		X		
	Enterprise-Wide Comm Program	X			
	Project Selection/Alignment Process		X		
	Bus. Metrics & Success Criteria		X		
Collaboration	Stakeholder Involvement		X		
	Project Risk Indicators		X		
	Defined Proj. Success Criteria		X		
Process Optimization	Process Impl. Review Panel			X	
	Defined Set of Processes			X	
	Real-Time Project Monitoring				X
	Continuous Improvement Process	X			
Best Practice Metrics	Proactive Project Mgmnt / Status			X	
	Collaborative Project Status Process			X	
	Efficiency Success Metrics			X	

Figure 19.11 Implementation planning – initiative launch schedule.

Executive Sponsorship

We reviewed the low current Assessments scores of "1" for the Business Value and Process Efficiency competencies and discussed the prioritization process for each of the competencies. We decided that the Executive team (C-Suite) recognize that Governance is a strategic imperative and support this transformation initiative. Therefore, we need to launch the Executive Sponsorship initiatives as a critical first step. We could then launch the initiative to gain support from the next management level, including the VPs, Directors, and Managers, before addressing the other competencies.

(John – CIO)

Business/IT Partnership

The group discussed the timeline to begin the launch of the Business/ IT Partnership. We felt that we could commence the launch about eight weeks following the Executive Sponsorship launch. The group also recognized that establishing a Business Governance Board and changing the culture of the business unit personnel to partner and collaborate with IT on project initiation, design, and implementation would be an ongoing process and could be very slow-moving.

(Curt – VP Operations)

Strategic Alignment

The group discussed the importance of establishing an enterprise-wide communication program for the Governance initiative and decided that the launch for this initiative should commence in parallel with the Executive Sponsorship initiative launch. Communicating this initiative is an integral part of the culture change required for all personnel to recognize Governance as a strategic initiative. The associated activities will involve everyone in some shape or manner. The launch for the remaining Strategic Alignment initiatives needed to lag by a quarter as these activities required proper planning and coordination.

(Sally – VP-PMO)

Collaboration

The group decided that the launch of the collaboration initiatives should commence at the end of Q2 since Q1 activity involves numerous initiatives. It's essential that business unit personnel actively involve themselves as part of the project execution process. The group felt it would be beneficial to prepare a business case to reflect project execution success when business personnel are actively involved. We also discussed the need to conduct collaborative workshops where business and IT personnel work on mock projects. The teams identify project risk indicators and define project success criteria. The more we can integrate business and IT personnel, the more successful we will be.

(Gail – CTO)

Process Optimization

The group decided that we need to commence a continuous improvement initiative initially to capture lessons learned and integrate these learnings in all the initiatives. Every transformation initiative requires supporting processes that define the activities, roles, responsibilities for personnel. Reinventing or reengineering processes is a change management challenge for any organization. To succeed requires forming a working group to develop the supporting processes, and personnel who these changes will impact should be part of the working group. We scheduled this activity for Q3. We must also investigate tools that support these processes to ensure that project execution can leverage technology to improve process efficiency, and we estimated the launch for this effort in Q4.

(John – CIO)

Best Practice Metrics

We thought that best practice initiatives should commence in parallel with the process development initiatives in Q3. We could then conduct benchmarking exercises to investigate best practices we can integrate into our processes. One of the best practices the group was interested in benchmarking is how other companies succeed at business owners actively in project execution activities. Benchmarking would go a long way to improve collaboration and project success.

(Sally-VP PMO)

After the presentations, we took a 15-minute break. John said he wanted to talk to me about accelerating the business/IT collaboration. John added:

Changing the culture within our company to be more collaborative and recognize that we need a much more mature Governance process will not be easy. I remember you mentioning something about a workshop you run that helps business and IT personnel understand the importance of Governance and exercises where they work in teams to build collaborative partnerships. Am I correct 19.[1]

I told John he was correct and opened up my laptop and shared the workshop framework (see Figures 19.12 and 19.13).

I walked John through the framework and shared a one-pager with more detail (see Figure 19.25). John thought that this type of workshop could help. I told John that I would recommend the workshop but only if we could implement it using a

Strategic IT Governance-Day of Learning

The Strategic IT Organization *The Changing Role of PM's*	*Strategic IT Governance* *Case Study*	Strategic IT Governance *A Business Imperative*	Closing Workshop *Tying it all Together*
PRESENTATION Why Companies Leverage Technology for Competitive Advantage and It's Impact on Increased the Role and Skills Required By Project Managers	**PRESENTATION** Sanitized Case Study Overview of Multi-Division Business with Project Portfolio History of Excessive Risk/ Cost Overruns	**PRESENTATION** Market Drivers Requiring Strategic IT Governance Process/ Critical Success Factors/ Framework to Measure Maturity/APO Demo	Work in Teams to Identify Value of Today's Learning Experience. -Helping Your *Business*
WORKSHOP Assess the Maturity of Your Business Competencies/ Skills and Develop a Maturity Plan	**WORKSHOP** Attendees Work in Teams to Analyze Case Study Material and Develop and Share Recommendations	**WORKSHOP** Assess Maturity of Your Strategic IT Governance Competency/Develop Target Goal and Improvement Plan	-Enhancing Your *Career* -Improving Your *Skills* -Identify Your *Next Steps Action Plan to Provide Value to Your*
DELIVERABLE Business Competency/ Skills Improvement Plan	**DELIVERABLE** IT Governance Improvement Plan-Major Components	**DELIVERABLE** Strategic IT Governance Maturity Plan	*Company, IT Organization, and Your Career*

Figure 19.12   Strategic IT Governance 2.0 workshop.

train-the-trainer model that included both IT and business personnel conducting the workshop. I suggested the following five-step process.[1]

1. *Conduct a Walk-through of the workshop for John and his IT leaders and designated IT Trainers (you would need to identify some business unit personnel as trainers as well, although this might not occur until you get the business community on board).*
2. *Attendees for the second workshop should include IT personnel. I would conduct the second workshop with IT trainers.*
3. *Trainers would conduct the third workshop for IT personnel, and I would observe and coach as necessary.*
4. *Your role during this Train-The-Trainer program would be to leverage your relationships with your business unit peers and get them on board with the program. Invite them to one of the sessions (second or third workshop) to observe.*
5. *If you wanted, I could observe a few of the subsequent workshops via Zoom to observe and offer some additional coaching.*

After the break, the group reconvened; John presented conducting the Strategic IT Governance 2.0 workshops to improve collaboration using my five-step process. There was some discussion and questions, so I did a quick walkthrough of the

Strategic IT Governance Workshop Series

A Strategic Imperative for Business Success

As your company leverages technology in new and innovative ways, it is imperative to excel in your strategic governance competency to prevent unnecessary risk, ensure the selection and execution of projects and technology investment decisions align with company strategy, and enables your enterprise to achieve its strategic objectives and goals.

This workshop series will help your organization to develop and/or mature a strategic IT governance initiative that will drive business success.

Strategere Consulting

Strategic IT Governance 2.0

The Strategic IT Governance Workshops include the following 7 modules that can be delivered as individual sessions or coordinated to a full day workshop, and customized based upon your organization's specific needs.

1. **Changing Market Forces**: Overview of the market dynamics transforming IT organizations from a cost center to a strategic asset and the changing role of project managers into effective collaborative partners (1 hour)
2. **Assessment Workshop**: Assess the strategic maturity of your IT organization (1 hour)
3. **Strategic IT Governance Challenges**: The key issues and challenges faced by a real company that experienced lack of governance process/tool and how it impacted business success.
4. **IT Governance Case Study Workshop**: Work in teams to analyze case study, develop and share recommendations and opportunity to experience Governance tool (1 hour)
5. **Strategic IT Governance–A Business Imperative**: The market drivers requiring strategic IT Governance process, critical Success factors, framework, implementation methodology (1 hour)
6. **Strategic IT Governance Assessment Workshop**: Assess strategic maturity of your IT governance competency, develop target goals, and high-level improvement plan (1 hour)
7. **Closing Workshop**: Work in teams to identify value of Strategic IT Governance competency and how it will help improve the competitiveness of your company, your skills, and enhance your career (1 hour)

MIT/Capgemini Study

"1500 executives worldwide identified *governance* as a major obstacle to business success. 40% of respondents have governance processes."

McKinsey

"Many executives expect IT will play a growing *role* in driving business results, ...the key challenge for CIOs to solve is inefficient governance."

Architecture and Governance Magazine

"IT governance is the responsibility of executives and the board of directors, and consists of leadership, organizational structures, and processes that ensure the enterprise's IT sustains and extends the organization's strategies and objectives."

Phil Weinzimer

Strategic IT Governance Workshop Series

The Strategic IT Organization The Changing Role of PM's	Strategic IT Governance Case Study	Strategic IT Governance A Business Imperative	CLOSING WORKSHOP
PRESENTATION What is Causing the Dramatic Increase in Technology Projects/ /It's Impact on the Changing Role of PMs / Business Skills Required to Succeed	**PRESENTATION** Sanitized Case Study Overview of Multi-Division Business with Project Portfolio History of Excessive Risk/ Cost Overruns	**PRESENTATION** Market Drivers Requiring Strategic IT Governance Process/Critical Success Factors/Framework to Measure Maturity	Work in Teams to Identify Value of Today's Learning Experience.
WORKSHOP Assess the Maturity of Your Business Competencies/ Skills and Develop a Maturity Plan	**WORKSHOP** Attendees Work in Teams to Analyze Case Study Material and Develop and Share Recommendations	**WORKSHOP** Assess Strategic Maturity of Your Strategic IT Governance Competency/Develop Target Goal and Improvement Plan	-Helping Your Business? -Improving Your Skills? -Enhancing Your Career? -What is Your Next Steps Action Plan to provide value to your company, your role, and your brand?
DELIVERABLE Business Competency/ Skills Improvement Plan	**DELIVERABLE** IT Governance Improvement Plan-Major Components	**DELIVERABLE** Strategic IT Governance Maturity Plan	

Figure 19.13 Strategic IT Governance 2.0 workshop.

materials for the group. After my walkthrough, the group agreed that this was a good idea and supported the concept.

John closed the workshop with the following thoughts.

> During the past number of weeks, we have learned new ways to improve our project governance maturity, and I thank each of you for your active

participation. I also want to thank Phil for coaching us through this process. Now the real work begins as we flush out all the details to implement these initiatives. I've asked Phil to be on call so we can checkpoint with him every few weeks. I've arranged for a group dinner this evening for us to celebrate the success we've had during the past number of weeks.[1]

Six-Month Checkpoint

During the next few months, John updated me on the progress of the Governance initiatives. The team was making progress. In March 2021, John asked me to return for a six-month checkpoint session with the team.

The checkpoint started with John providing a quick overview of the initiative activities using the initial Launch Schedule. Q3 and Q4 columns were grayed out so we could concentrate on Q1 and Q2 activities. A "Y" indicated a launch date rescheduled (see Figure 19.14).

IMPLEMENTATION LAUNCH SCHEDULE-Six Month Checkpoint

		Next Qtr	Q2	Q3	Q4
Executive Sponsorship	Strategic Imperative C-Suite Sponsorship VP / Director/Mgr Sponsorship	X X X->Y			
Business/IT Partnership	Bus. Governance Board Bus. Unit Partnership & Collaboration Bus/IT Sponsor & Project Owner		X--->Y X->Y X		
Strategic Alignment	Bus. / Tech. Plan Enterprise-Wide Comm Program Project Selection/Alignment Process Bus. Metrics & Success Criteria	X---Y	X X→ Y X		
Collaboration	Stakeholder Involvement Project Risk Indicators Defined Proj. Success Criteria		X X X		
Process Optimization	Process Impl. Review Panel Defined Set of Processes Real-Time Project Monitoring Continuous Improvement Process	X		X X	X
Best Practice Metrics	Proactive Project Mgmnt/ Status Collaborative Project Status Process Efficiency Success Metrics			X X X	

Figure 19.14 Implementation planning – initiative launch schedule: six-month checkpoint.

John provided an overall summary before turning the floor over to the initiative spokespersons to present their status updates. Following are his main points.

- *We are making good progress. There have been some delays, but we're generally on track with our plan.*
- *Our Executive Team is on board; This was an essential first step in supporting our Strategic Governance initiative.*
- *We are experiencing a more inclusive and collaborative environment within our company.*
- *There is more of a focus on ensuring that projects align with our strategic goals.*
- *Business personnel begin to participate in project development and implementation activities actively.*
- *We have a long way to go, but we are making progress, and I see it in our project status reports.*
- *Our Executive Team support for this transformation initiative is paying off as project performance improves, and we see a positive trend in future project execution.*

To my surprise, John invited Martin, the VP of Marketing, to the checkpoint. He arrived in the middle of John's update. When John concluded his remarks, he introduced Martin to me and invited Martin to say a few words to the group.

> I want to thank John for inviting me to this checkpoint update meeting. When John approached me many months ago, I was a bit skeptical about this initiative. I knew that our company faced many challenges in executing projects, but I thought the issue was with the IT organization because we did not have a governance process. When John invited some thought leaders to present to the Executive Committee, the light bulb went on. And I'm glad I finally saw the light and was an early champion on the business side to support this Strategic IT Governance 2.0 transformation initiative.[Ibid]

As Martin concluded his last sentence, he applauded, and everyone in the room applauded as well. John then segued into the next section of the checkpoint, where each spokesperson provided updates for each of the competency initiatives.

Executive Sponsorship: John – CIO[Ibid]

- *The Executive Team agreed that IT Project Governance is a strategic imperative.*
- *We succeeded at creating "Awareness Sessions" with the Executive Team. Bringing in outside thought leaders was very helpful in convincing the executives that Governance was an essential strategic imperative.*

- *The Executive Team agreed to support creating a bi-weekly Governance working group of IT and business personnel.*
- *We shared the Governance Assessment results with the Executive Team and informed them we would conduct these assessments across the business enterprise.*
- *We had some interesting discussions, and we experienced some challenges.*

Business/IT Partnership: Curt – VP-Ops[Ibid]

- *Due to company priorities, we had a two-week delay launching the VPs, Directors, and Managers Sponsorship initiative. We had some interesting discussions, and we experienced some challenges.*
- *We identified the VP of Marketing and Manufacturing as champions who supported the Governance initiative and spread the word across their respective business units.*
- *We conducted a series of Governance workshops that included business personnel as facilitators. The workshops were very helpful in getting business personnel on board with our Governance transformation initiative.*
- *We finally got an agreement to establish a Business Governance Board.*

Strategic Alignment: Sally – VP-PMO[Ibid]

- *We organized a small group of IT and business personnel to begin analyzing past projects to support the notion that misaligned projects are not the best use of enterprise resources and can impact company performance. The group successfully found several misaligned projects that impacted the start of some strategic marketing and manufacturing projects. This helped to support strategic alignment as a core concept in project selection, approval, and execution.*
- *We organized a project alignment team of business and IT personnel to develop a more robust process for selecting, developing, and implementing projects. The team is making good progress, and personnel across the company are following the new procedures. We recognize that this will take some time.*

Collaboration: Gail – CTO[Ibid]

- *We utilized the Strategic Alignment team to create a business case reflecting that past projects that included business personnel actively involved in project development and execution were more successful than projects where business personnel were not involved.*

- *We conducted several workshops with business and IT personnel working together on mock projects. The workshops helped seed a collaborative working environment. We also found that we would include some outside "fun" activities to help personnel improve their collaborative relationships during these workshops.*
- *We finally were successful as part of the new strategic alignment process to institute the role of business owner for every project. In this role, the person would actively participate in project development and execution activities.*

Process Optimization/Best Practice Metrics: Paul – Director Application Development and Sally – VP PMO[Ibid]

- *These two initiative categories are just at the beginning planning stages.*
- *We have organized a group of Business and IT personnel to act as a continuous process improvement group overseeing recommendations to improve our processes supporting our Strategic IT Governance activities.*
- *We are at the beginning of creating a working group of Business and IT personnel to develop the supporting processes, roles, accountabilities supporting Strategic IT Governance. We found that we had to replace some team members due to their lack of process skills as this delayed some progress, but we're making headway, and personnel are following the new processes.*
- *We will shortly begin planning our benchmarking activities to determine how other companies utilize real-time metrics to support their project implementations.*

Chapter Summary

My objective in this chapter is to provide you with a framework to assess and implement a more mature Strategic IT Governance 2.0 competency within your business. Following is Figure 19.15 that I presented at the beginning of this chapter. I repeat it here as a single graphic to help you remember the framework for your governance transformation effort.

I used the mid-sized manufacturer of industrial cabinet case to share some real-life examples of how a CIO leads an initiative to implement a Strategic IT Governance 2.0 in an organization with many challenges in project alignment and execution.

I followed up with John in June of 2021 to catch up with the progress he made. I found out from John that he and his team made significant progress during the 12-months following the initial Maturity Assessment. They didn't quite meet their 12-month goal scores, but project performance improved dramatically. Here are some examples of how they accomplished enhanced business performance.

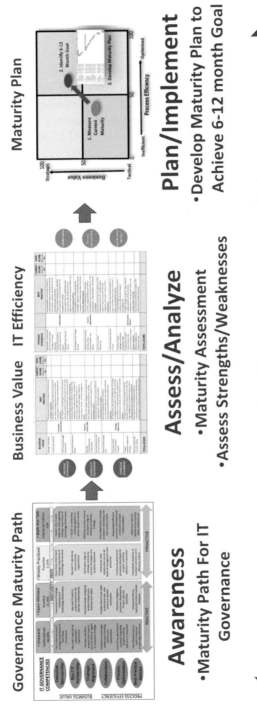

Figure 19.15   Strategic IT Governance 2.0 implementation roadmap.

- **Business Value:**
  - Executive Sponsorship was a critical success factor, and John was instrumental in helping the Executive team *see the light.*
  - Sales improved by 15 percent despite the challenges of the COVID-19 Epidemic. The Marketing VP championed John's Strategic IT Governance initiative, and he and his team worked closely with IT personnel to identify and implement focused customer initiatives to improve sales.
  - Development and implementation of Strategic Alignment processes dramatically reduced the number of NON-ALIGNED projects from over 85 to just 15 in the final stages of implementation.

- **Process Efficiency**
  - On-Time Delivery (plus or minus 10 percent) improved 45 percent.
  - Rework decreased 47 percent.
  - Scope Changes reduced by 70 percent
  - Collaboration improved dramatically as Business personnel took ownership of projects and actively participated in project implementations.
  - Implemented IT Business Relationship Managers assigned to specific business units as Relationship Managers who were embedded amongst business teams to improve the collaboration of business with IT personnel.
  - IT is now considered a Strategic Partner and is actively involved in strategic business discussions on how technology can leverage improved business value.

You can see from the data above that John and his team of IT and Business personnel accomplished a lot in 12 months. Most importantly, the Executive Team and Division VPs and Managers actively supported the Strategic IT Governance transformation initiative.

Those of you considering embarking on a similar journey to improve the maturity of your company's Governance competencies may want to reread this chapter as well as the previous one. You may find some golden nuggets to help your company improve its revenue and create new and innovative services that increase shareholder value.

Citing

1. Quotes from Assessment Workshop with CIO and his Direct Reports September 20-21-22, 2020.

Chapter 20

Final Thoughts

My goal throughout this book was to make the case that companies need to review, assess, and embrace the Strategic IT Governance 2.0 model for successfully planning and implementing digital transformation initiatives. I hope I have accomplished this goal. I realize that there is a lot of information to digest. I've provided you with a methodology, processes, and tools, as well as case studies of how companies in different industries have implemented components of The Strategic IT Governance 2.0 model.

To help you focus on the essential concepts, I am providing you with some of the key messages to help you in your journey of reassessing your project governance competencies. So, review the key messages below and revisit the appropriate chapters to determine how you can mature your Strategic IT Governance 2.0 competencies through project alignment, process reinvention, and leadership excellence.

- ■ **Chapter 2: The Changing Landscape - The Case for Change**
- ■ This chapter discusses the root causes of continuous project failure companies experience year after year. Also provided are project failure statistics that support the reasons for continuous project failures (Figure 20.1). I also discussed how companies are moving from a reactive governance 1.0 model to a proactive 2.0 model to reduce project risk and improve project success by implementing the Strategic IT Governance 2.0 framework discussed in more detail in Chapter 3.

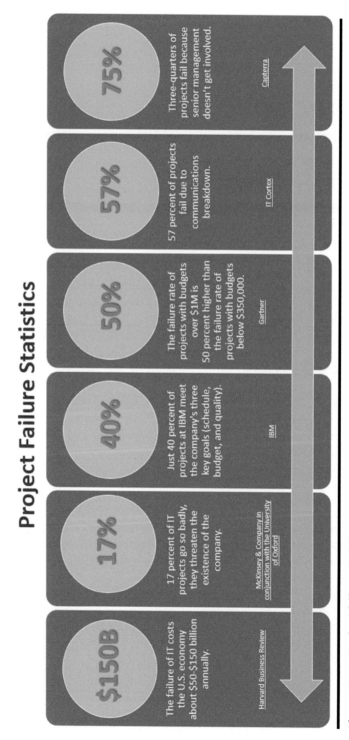

Figure 20.1   Project failure statistics.

- **Chapter 3: Strategic IT Governance 2.0 – An Introduction**
  This chapter provides you with an overview of the Strategic IT Governance 2.0 framework that includes the following:
  – The six competencies of Strategic IT Governance 2.0
  – The six characteristics of a business-driven Governance competency
  – Best-in-class practices for each of the six competencies
  – Implementation framework that consists of Awareness (four phases of governance maturity path), Assessment (best-in-class tool to assess strengths and weaknesses of your current governance competency), and Plan and Implement (develop a maturity plan to improve your organization's strategic IT governance competency)

This introduction provides a basic understanding of the methodology. To support the model's validity, subsequent chapters provide case studies of companies in different industries that embraced and implemented components of the methodology (Figure 20.2).

- **Chapters 5–17: Case Studies**
  These chapters provide ten case studies of companies in different industries with different levels of organizational maturity that improved their project governance competencies by implementing components of the Strategic IT Governance model. Each company experienced project failure rates and recognized the need to improve its Strategic IT Governance 2.0 competency.

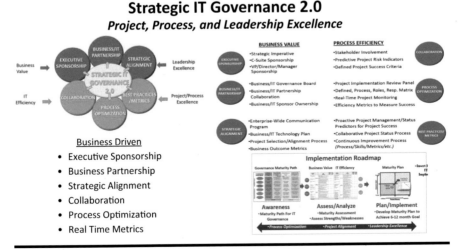

Figure 20.2   Strategic IT Governance 2.0 framework.

Each case takes the reader through how each company implemented components of the six Strategic IT Governance 2.0 model

■ **Chapter 18: How to Assess the Maturity of Your Company's Strategic IT Governance Competencies**

This chapter uses a case study of a CIO and Directors who attended a series of workshops to assess the maturity of their organization's Strategic IT Governance 2.0 competencies. This case study will help you to learn how to utilize a best-in-class Assessment Process and gain an understanding of the four phases of maturity for evolving to your organization's strategic IT Governance 2.0 model.

The Assessment tool includes value areas that align to a best-in-class organizational characteristic for each of the six Strategic IT Governance 2.0 competencies. The assessment enables one to determine on a scale of 1–10 (10 reflecting the best alignment) how well the organization exhibits the best-in-class characteristic and assign a goal score for the following 6- or 12-month period (Figure 20.3).

■ **Chapter 19: How to Analyze, Plan, and Implement Strategic IT Governance 2.0 Competencies in Your Company**

This chapter uses a case study for an organization that utilized a series of workshops to develop a three-step Implementation Path to improve its Strategic IT Governance 2.0 maturity (Figures 20.4 and 20.5).

 - Create awareness in their organization of the four-phase maturity path for improving its governance competency.
 - An Assessment to measure the current maturity of their organization's Strategic IT Governance 2.0 competency.
 - A plan to achieve their Strategic IT Governance 2.0 maturity goal.

CATEGORY	BUSINESS VALUE	BEST PRACTICE	CURRENT SCORE (1-Low; 10-High)	GOAL SCORE (1-Low; 10-High)
Executive Sponsorship	Strategic Imperative	The business enterprise recognizes Governance as a strategic imperative.		
	C-Suite Sponsorship	The entire C-Suite publicly endorses and sponsors the need for strategic Governance as a critical success factor in achieving its business goals and objectives		
	VP/Director/Mgr Sponsorship	VPs, Directors, Managers across the business enterprise publicly endorse, sponsor, and participate in the need for strategic Governance as a critical success factor in achieving its business goals and objectives		
Business Partnership	Business Governance Board	A Business Governance Board comprised of key stakeholders provides oversight, coaching, and mentoring to organizations involved in IT Governance and receive regular updates on project status, metrics, and risk management issues		
	Business Unit/Partnership-Collaboration	Business Unit Leaders recognize the need for and form collaborative partnerships to identify, develop, and implement the portfolio of IT and technology projects		
	Business/IT Sponsor and Owner for Projects	Business sponsor/IT are jointly accountable and responsible for achieving the successful implementation of projects		
Strategic Alignment	Business/Tech Plan	Business Leadership jointly develop a business/technology plan that enables achieving the business enterprise business goals and objectives		
	Enterprise-Wide Communication Program	An enterprise-wide communication plan is in place to engage all personnel in the need for and active participation in understanding the importance of Governance as a critical success factor for business success		
	Project Selection/Alignment Process	All projects are screened and approved by the Business Governance Board to ensure that they align strategically to enterprise business plan in achieving the business goals and objectives		
	Business Metrics & Success Criteria	Key business metrics identifying business outcomes and success criteria established for each project to measure business outcome success		
		TOTALS		

CATEGORY	BUSINESS VALUE	BEST PRACTICE	CURRENT SCORE (1-Low; 10-High)	GOAL SCORE (1-Low; 10-High)
Collaboration	Stakeholder Involvement (Active Communication Throughout Project Lifecycle)	Key stakeholders are actively involved in assessing the status of projects to identify and monitor potential risk areas to ensure successful project execution		
	Project Risk Indicators (provide predictive score)	Project success indicators are identified and measured to identify predictive risk indicators for projects		
	Defined Project Success Criteria	Key success criteria is established and measured for each project to ensure alignment of business outcome metrics and project success metrics		
Process Optimization	Key Predictors for Project Success	Key predictors for project success are identified, measured, monitored to ensure consistency of project execution to achieve business objectives/goals		
	Defined Set of Processes, Activities, Roles, Responsibility, and Metrics	There are a defined set of processes, activities, responsibilities, and metrics developed for each role (business/IT) in the development, implementation, and launch of projects		
	Real-Time Project Monitoring	Real-time monitoring of projects provides dashboard metrics to indicate project status in an easy-to-use tool that fully integrates with project measurement applications		
Best Practice Metrics	Continuous Improvement Process	A continuous improvement process is in place to enhance the Governance process, IT skills, and associated metrics		
	Proactive Project Mgmt/Status (Anticipate Risk)	Project Management processes ensure activities to identify and measure anticipated risk		
	Collaborative Project Status Process (Bus Owner/IT Owner/Project Review Meetings)	Project manager prepares status reports collaboratively with key business stakeholders who also participate in key project review meetings		
	Efficiency Metrics to Measure Success	Key metrics are defined to measure the efficiency of project execution		
		TOTALS		

Figure 20.3 Strategic IT Governance 2.0 maturity assessment.

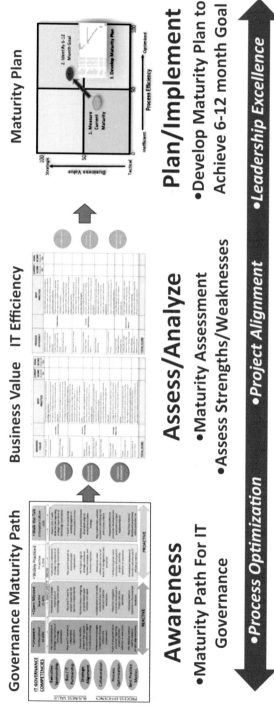

Figure 20.4 Strategic IT Governance 2.0 implementation roadmap.

Strategic IT Governance 2.0

The Strategic IT Governance Workshops include the following 7 modules that can be delivered as individual sessions or coordinated to a full day workshop, and customized based upon your organization's specific needs.

1. **Changing Market Forces:** Overview of the market dynamics transforming IT organizations from a cost center to a strategic asset and the changing role of project managers into effective collaborative partners (1 hour)

2. **Assessment Workshop:** Assess the strategic maturity of your IT organization (1 hour)

3. **Strategic IT Governance Challenges:** The key issues and challenges faced by a real company that experienced lack of governance process/tool and how it impacted business success.

4. **IT Governance Case Study Workshop:** Work in teams to analyze case study, develop and share recommendations and opportunity to experience Governance tool (1 hour)

5. **Strategic IT Governance–A Business Imperative:** The market drivers requiring strategic IT Governance process, critical Success factors, framework, implementation methodology (1 hour)

6. **Strategic IT Governance Assessment Workshop:** Assess strategic maturity of your IT governance competency, develop target goals, and high-level improvement plan (1 hour)

7. **Closing Workshop:** Work in teams to identify value of Strategic IT Governance competency and how it will help improve the competitiveness of your company, your skills, and enhance your career (1 hour)

Strategic IT Governance Workshop Series

The Strategic IT Organization The Changing Role of PM's	Strategic IT Governance Case Study	Strategic IT Governance A Business Imperative	CLOSING WORKSHOP
PRESENTATION What is Causing the Dramatic Increase in Technology Projects/ /It's Impact on the Changing Role of PMs / Business Skills Required to Succeed	**PRESENTATION** Sanitized Case Study Overview of Multi-Division Business with Project Portfolio History of Excessive Risk/ Cost Overruns	**PRESENTATION** Market Drivers Requiring Strategic IT Governance Process/Critical Success Factors/Framework to Measure Maturity	Work in Teams to Identify Value of Today's Learning Experience.
WORKSHOP Assess the Maturity of Your Business Competencies/ Skills and Develop a Maturity Plan	**WORKSHOP** Attendees Work in Teams to Analyze Case Study Material and Develop and Share Recommendations	**WORKSHOP** Assess Strategic Maturity of Your Strategic IT Governance Competency/Develop Target Goal and Improvement Plan	-Helping Your Business? -Improving Your Skills? -Enhancing Your Career? -What is Your Next Steps Action Plan to provide value to your company, your role, and your brand?
DELIVERABLE Business Competency/ Skills Improvement Plan	**DELIVERABLE** IT Governance Improvement Plan-Major Components	**DELIVERABLE** Strategic IT Governance Maturity Plan	

Figure 20.5 Strategic IT Governance 2.0 implementation workshop.

Index

Page numbers in **bold** indicate tables, pages in *Italics* refer figures.